Shattered Tablets

ALSO BY DAVID KLINGHOFFER

The Lord Will Gather Me In

The Discovery of God: Abraham and the Birth of Monotheism

Why the Jews Rejected Jesus: The Turning Point in Western History

SHATTERED TABLETS

*Why We Ignore the
Ten Commandments at Our Peril*

DAVID KLINGHOFFER

DOUBLEDAY
*New York London Toronto
Sydney Auckland*

PUBLISHED BY DOUBLEDAY

Published in the United States by Doubleday,
an imprint of The Doubleday Broadway Publishing Group,
a division of Random House, Inc., New York.
www.doubleday.com

DOUBLEDAY and the portrayal of an anchor with a dolphin
are registered trademarks of Random House, Inc.

Library of Congress Cataloging-in-Publication Data
Klinghoffer, David, 1965–
Shattered tablets : why we ignore the Ten commandments
at our peril / David Klinghoffer.
— 1st ed.
p. cm.
Includes index.
1. Ten commandments. 2. United States—Moral conditions. I. Title.
BV4655.K64 2007
222'.1606—dc22
2007000153

ISBN 978-0-385-51567-2

PRINTED IN THE UNITED STATES OF AMERICA

1   3   5   7   9   10   8   6   4   2

First Edition

FOR HANNAH

CONTENTS

SHATTERED TABLETS

SHATTERED
IN SEATTLE

I n 1995, an Alabama circuit court judge set off what has now become a national controversy, exposing the profoundest rift in
American society. Into a pair of rosewood tablets, the judge, Roy
Moore, burned the Ten Commandments. He proceeded to hang the
homemade ornament on his courtroom wall. "Not only do the Ten
Commandments not belong in public courthouses or classrooms," Harvard legal scholar Alan Dershowitz would later comment, "they do not
even belong—at least without some amendments and explanatory foot-
notes—in the hearts and minds of contemporary Americans." The the-
ologian and former Episcopal bishop John Shelby Spong calls them
"immoral." In his best-selling atheist screed *The God Delusion*, Darwinian advocate Richard Dawkins dismisses them as "obnoxious," explaining, "To be fair, much of the Bible is not systematically evil but just
plain weird." He proposes his own secular Ten Commandments, includ-

ing the directive "Do not indoctrinate your children. Teach them how to think for themselves, how to evaluate evidence, and how to disagree with you." But teaching your children the truth is the sine qua non of biblical religion.

In 2001, having been elevated to the office of chief justice of the state's supreme court, Moore installed a 5,280-pound granite monument of the Ten Commandments in the Alabama Supreme Court building—a monument that was finally removed in 2003, when the will of the U.S. Supreme Court prevailed over the truculent and defiant Judge Moore's.

An October 13, 2004, Associated Press story bore the striking headline TEN COMMANDMENTS REPLACING ABORTION AS KEY CHRISTIAN ISSUE, SCHOLAR SAYS. A couple of ambiguous 2005 Supreme Court rulings, dealing with the display of the Ten Commandments on public property, seemingly calculated to keep the issue in litigation for decades to come, are only the most recent illustration of the power of the Decalogue to reveal philosophical, religious, and cultural fault lines.

In the Bible, the children of Israel fall into disastrous behavior patterns whenever they abandon the majestic authority of God revealed to them through Moses at Mount Sinai. In fact, they commenced rebelling and kicking at the Lord almost immediately after the Sinai revelation was completed. While still on their forty-year extended camping trip in the desert, the Jews vexed Him by whoring after the women of neighboring Midian, joining an outright revolution against Moses under the radical reformer Korach, sending spies to reconnoiter the Holy Land and then declaring that they would rather return to pagan Egypt to be slaves again, and, of course, by fashioning the idolatrous Golden Calf.

So what happens in modern America when moral authority is disconnected from traditional ideas about religion, as is increasingly the case in our country? You get a place like Seattle, my home.

Ah, Seattle, beautiful and gentle in so many ways. The prophet Daniel saw the writing on the wall of King Belshazzar's palace and pre-

dicted the overthrow of the wicked Babylonian empire. I see the feces
on the wall of the seventh-floor men's room in the Seattle Central
Library, where I often do research. The place is an education all right.
Designed by celebrity architect Rem Koolhaas and finished in 2004 for
$165 million, it is regarded as an artistic triumph in metal and glass. It
has also been overrun by the homeless, who make the elevators stink of
unwashed flesh. At their most harmless, they merely stole my lunch on
one occasion, but at their most repulsive, someone actually festooned
the bathroom wall with his own waste.

One of the local newspapers, the *Seattle Post-Intelligencer*, carried a
story praising the library for its tolerance, with a comment from a security officer: "I think this is one of the places in Seattle where people can
come and everybody is the same." How sweet.

It's all good and everyone is the same no matter how grotesque their
behavior. A deadly underlying disease is often indicated by a seemingly
superficial symptom. So it is with the vagrant-infested library. Of the
two tablets of the Ten Commandments, the second is devoted to laws
governing respect for other people. Even at the price of befouling a
prized architectual and cultural landmark, Seattle refuses to insist on
such respect being given to its own citizens, who pay the taxes that
built that grand edifice. Can such a city possibly have the internal for-
titude to demand the observance of other, more sweeping moral standards?

A few blocks away, the view from my office window downtown provides a panoramic lesson in the relevance of the Ten Commandments
to understanding what's gone horribly wrong in American life. While
this city is famous for Microsoft and Starbucks, even tourists and con-
ventioneers get a different perspective when they merely stroll the six
blocks between downtown's main visitor attractions, quaint Pike Place
Market by the waterfront and the core shopping area around the Convention Center. To get from one to the other, you walk up Pike Street.
For three blocks, this thoroughfare and the intersecting avenues become a parade of derelicts, criminals, and punks.

When I walk out the front door of our office building, I see ready evidence of the crumbling of traditional authority epitomized by the Decalogue. These ten great statements about reality reveal the gravest threat America faces—not from terrorism, global warming, or pandemic influenza, but from our own vapid ideas about God, morality, and the meaning of life.

As we often forget, Moses was a prophet, and the two tablets of the law he brought down from Mount Sinai were prophecy. To be a prophet means that you speak for God, offering guidance and censure to the people, advice meant to help avert future calamity. I'm no prophet, nor a moral exemplar, nor a visionary to whom God speaks. I'm a journalist, one whose observations are informed by the universally relevant insights of traditional Judaism. I offer for your consideration a neglected and critically important instance of prophecy, the Ten Commandments, today more pertinent to the future than it has been in the 3,319 years since it was revealed.

The Bible's prophetic books typically begin by noting the place where the prophet lived when he began to prophesy, rebuking the citizens of ancient Israel for their backslidings toward paganism. Jeremiah, the most splendidly furious of them all, was among "the priests who were in Anathoth, in the land of Benjamin," when "the word of the Lord came" to him. Ezekiel was "in the land of Chaldeans, by the River Chebar; and the hand of the Lord came upon him there." There's a reason for this. Often the microcosm of your city turns out to reflect the macrocosm of your region, state, or country. This is what I find. For a moral accounting of America, Seattle is the perfect microcosm.

Everyone knows the cliché about San Francisco—that it's the Sodom and Gomorrah of the Left Coast and all that. Forget it. While San Francisco is a sick place, the degree to which its bent character is determined by a disproportionate representation of a rare sexual orientation makes that city irrelevant to any attempt to chart the ethical future of the rest of America. The City by the Bay is too odd to be representative of anything but itself.

Not so Seattle, the city by Puget Sound, which, to those who don't live here, presents a much more normal profile. We're at the distant edge of the country, geographically and morally. But it is also the leading edge. What happens here could happen anywhere in the United States. And it looks like it soon will.

The neighborhood where I work isn't a skid row, but, rather, the first destination of almost all tourists, who must weave their way through a colorful array of locals while taking in the grungy storefronts. The latter include Seattle's seediest restaurant, the Turf (COCKTAILS, SCRATCH TICKETS, NO PUBLIC RESTROOM), and the city's leading retailer of apparel for pimps, Leroy's Menswear. Imagine if visitors to Manhattan, choosing to walk the thirty-plus blocks up Fifth Avenue from St. Patrick's Cathedral to the Metropolitan Museum, had to pass through a gauntlet of the city's most crime-ridden and anarchic blocks. Our city's downtown commercial area is by far Seattle's highest-crime area. It boasts, for example, a theft rate twice that of any other U.S. census tract in the city, and ten times or more that of many other Seattle neighborhoods.

At the epicenter, Third and Pike, some of the denizens have the tooth-rotted appearance of meth addicts. Others are traditional drunks. But many are fourteen- to seventeen-year-old "gangstas," the "youths" who come from surrounding communities like Kent, Auburn, or around the SeaTac airport, many belonging to one of Seattle's thirty to sixty street gangs. They may come here to fight, shoplift, or sell crack. Sometimes the substance is sold discreetly—around the back of the building that houses my office, in a urine-reeking, Dumpster-lined "Crack Alley." Other street dwellers are older, grown-up "youths" known as "Original Gangsters," who have spent time in prison but now are back at Third and Pike. There are several bus-stop shelters, and they gather there as if waiting for a bus. Maybe that's what they really are doing. Or they pass up and down the blocks, walking "large"—a few individuals taking up the whole breadth of the sidewalk, so you have to walk in the gutter to get around them.

My colleagues on the eighth floor trade stories of encounters with the street denizens. Youths have been observed pummeling a homeless man in Crack Alley. There have been knifings observed in broad daylight on Third Avenue. There were the two women who got into a punching and kicking fight outside the Starbucks. One, a mother with a baby in a carriage, lost the fight, and her opponent kicked the carriage over, screaming baby and all. A report comes that an employee of the Walgreens drugstore, trying to stop a shoplifter, was pulled out into the street and beaten. When there's no observable violence, there's the verbal harassment—insults to passing women, insults to those who refuse to donate to the aggressive panhandlers. And there's the noise. The street dwellers shout to one another or call out to no one in particular in an eerie cry that carries up to the eighth floor: "Hoooo-oooot! Hoooo-oooot!"

Do you wonder where the cops are? That interesting question bears directly on the subject of this book. If you want to gauge the moral health of a society, look at its policemen. Sometimes, two or three Seattle cops watch over the carnival at Third and Pike. I have even seen four officers standing together for mutual protection. Like UN peacekeepers and almost as effective, the cops mainly observe. They are meticulous about ticketing jaywalkers.

The city says it would like to clean up the district, but it clearly lacks the moral confidence to do so. What it would really take to clean up this area—the police intimidating the street people, rather than the other way around—is not on the table in Seattle.

It's not a new situation. In 1999, the Seattle police were overwhelmed by forty thousand protesters against the World Trade Organization's meeting. The police lost control of the streets around the Sheraton Hotel, where the WTO delegates were staying. With a price tag of $2.5 million in property damage, the "Battle in Seattle" riots that followed were a celebration of anarchy.

The police chief at the time, Norm Stamper, was the nicest and most emotionally sensitive person ever to head up a major U.S. city's law-enforcement operation. He had instituted "community policing" and "community problem solving," which meant casting the police as friends and neighbors, rather than as traditional authority figures. After losing his job, he grew a beard, spoke of the enlightenment he had received through therapy and a men's retreat, and wrote a book in which he advocated that cops learn the samurai art of flower arranging.

When a society loses confidence in its laws, unable any longer to explain why it is right to insist on their observance, we naturally wonder what kind of cultural shift resulted in this tragic breakdown. Here in Seattle, from the corner of Third and Pike, you only have to look up a bit and to the east, a mile away, toward the Capitol Hill neighborhood. There, quaint bohemian Seattle Box–style homes give way to imposing Victorian mansions.

One of the city's two alternative papers, the *Seattle Weekly*, does a clever parody in each issue of the typical Seattle resident whom you'd meet if you climbed up Capitol Hill from downtown. The column is called "Ask an Uptight Seattleite." It is so dead-on accurate that when my wife first came across it in the paper, she didn't realize it was a parody. In an illustration, the Uptight Seattleite wears tiny spectacles over his nose, sports a goatee and a ponytail, carries a coffee cup marked ORGANIC, and has an NPR bag slung over a shoulder, with a copy of the *Utne Reader* peeking out. In each issue, he answers queries from readers in the classic, fussy, moralizing Seattle manner.

Actually, *moralizing* may be the wrong word. *Moralesque*, a burlesque of morality, would be closer to the mark. When a reader asks about the etiquette of requesting an environmentally insensitive plastic bag at Capitol Hill's Rainbow Natural Grocery, the Uptight Seattleite gives a "friendly little reminder" about the virtue of "putting my groceries into my burlap sacks." Asked about the "tattered Tibetan prayer flags," called *lungtas*, on certain Seattle porches, he lectures, "I'm hanging colored fabric on my porch; what are *you* doing for the Tibetan people?" On another occasion, a "Closet Christian" asks, "I accept that Seattle is more of a yoga town than a church town, but why are people so anti-religion here?"

Seattle truly is more a yoga than a church town. The whole Pacific Northwest ranks as the country's most secular, unchurched region. How it got to be that way may have something to do with the quirks of its pioneer past, which only goes back a century and a half. (European Americans settled Seattle in 1851.) Some say it's because the city's pioneers were disproportionately single men—loggers, fishermen, dock workers, merchants supplying goods to Alaska-bound gold prospectors—without family or religious ties. Others say it has to do with the wilderness that still predominates in the landscape of the Pacific Northwest, a backdrop more appropriate to pagan musings than Christian or Jewish ones. "In Seattle, Earth Day is a kind of public holiday," writes a columnist in the *Seattle Times* with admiration. Still others explain that the pioneer mind-set itself, emphasizing individualism and a resistance to authority, is the key to understanding Northwest secularism.

Put it all together and you arrive at the conclusion that this green, dank, and chilly corner of the country represents the steadily advancing prow of a resurgent pagan moral perspective in American culture. By "pagan," I don't mean that the silly modern-day pseudoreligion of Wicca, or witchcraft, with its laughable invocation of the "Goddess," is threatening to take hold in a serious way in the Northwest or anywhere else. (Though it's no coincidence that when Wiccans and other pagans from across the country gathered to decide whether to form a united Pagan Church in America, they chose Redmond, home of Microsoft, for their venue.) Instead, I'm saying that secularism itself is the real modern and resurgent paganism.

As we'll see in the following chapters, in the biblical perspective, there really are only two spiritual choices: to adhere to God, the God of Israel, who speaks directly to us in the first commandment ("I am the Lord your God"), or instead to opt for the imaginings of false religion—paganism, idolatry, call it what you will. Bible translations that have God and his prophets warning us against worshiping "other gods" are really a mistranslation. The Hebrew word conventionally rendered as "gods" (*elohim*) is actually a generic designation meaning something more like "sources of moral authority."

We fool ourselves into imagining that there are many spiritual paths, all legitimate. In fact, there are just these two, God and "other gods"—one true, the other the most terrible but seductive lie. My fellow citizens in the Pacific Northwest are devoted, more than almost anywhere else in the nation, to the lie.

Yet human beings seem unable to live without a behavioral code of some kind. So when they stop going to church and shrug off the biblical code, they naturally embrace another, one that bears little relationship to the Ten Commandments, on which our Judeo-Christian civilization has been based for thousands of years.

The code of the moralesque is no less particular about its commandments being observed than is the traditional moral system about its directives. In Seattle, for example, they take great offense at cigarettes. Here we have the country's strictest state-level ban on smoking. You can't smoke in any business establishment or within twenty-five feet of the entrance to any publicly accessible building. Outside the Rainbow Natural Grocery, a pair of soberly lettered signs warn against the crime, so that if you want to smoke, you'll have to stand in the middle of Fifteenth Avenue and risk getting run over by a Prius.

Here are some other points of reference if you want to understand Seattleites. They make a fetish of fitness. A 2005 survey by *Men's Fitness* magazine ranked us as the country's fittest city. The ranking was based on factors like the number of fast-food restaurants per capita and hours spent watching TV. Seattle is the sort of place where people have dogs instead of children. We are second only to San Francisco as the most childless city in America.

When you look at Seattle as a microcosm of what happens when biblical religion falls away, this is what you discover. You find traditional ideas about behavior replaced by a parallel but entirely different moralesque code that makes primary obligations out of things the traditional code makes secondary (fitness), looks down on other things the traditional code strongly encourages (having kids), strictly forbids things the old code leaves to personal discretion (smoking), and feels conflicted and uneasy about still other things that the traditional code feels entirely comfortable with and that are crucial to maintaining public order (policing).

The moralesque presents itself as an upside-down system of moral imagining. Consider the sixth commandment, forbidding murder. In Seattle, we entertain some peculiar ideas about how to respond morally to murder.

Not that we are unfamiliar with it. On the contrary, the Pacific Northwest is famous as the ground zero of serial killers. We scorn other regions with higher murder rates, where most killers score only a victim or two apiece before being apprehended. Our murderers, if fewer in number per capita, are incomparably more prolific. Gary Ridgway of Auburn, Washington, may have slaughtered as many as seventy-four women, later allowing that he "killed so many women I have a hard time keeping them straight." Robert Lee Yates of Spokane dispatched up to thirty. Don't forget Ted Bundy, a University of Washington grad who stalked the sorority houses there, with his fifty or so victims. Other celebrity Northwest killers include Kenneth Bianchi, Westley Alan Dodd, and Clifford Olson. We live in "America's killing fields," according to a well-known FBI profiler, John Douglas.

Some say serial killers favor our region because it provides ample wilderness well suited for dumping bodies. I think it has more to do with the moralesque code that doesn't know how to respond even to a sin as grave as murder with the proper gravity.

One thinks of the heartbreaking 2001 murder of a twenty-year-old Good Samaritan, Kristopher Kime, during the Mardi Gras festivities in Seattle's Pioneer Square. He was punched by seventeen-year-old thug Jerell Thomas "over and over again, until he had literally driven his head into the pavement," as the prosecutor put it. Thomas then did a little dance, "like a victorious boxer."

The killer's attorney admitted that his client "did some things that were offensive."

Yes, in Seattle we find vicious, brutal murder "offensive," kind of like smoking.

In 2006, a Muslim man walked into the Jewish Federation office a few blocks from my office and opened fire on six defenseless women, killing one. A local Jewish group, the American Jewish Congress, in a gesture of extraordinary moral ineptitude, responded with a call to study Islam under the tutelage of leaders of the Seattle Muslim community. The event was titled "Understanding the Quran."

Among some Seattleites, much greater "offense" is taken not at actual murderers but, instead, at U.S. soldiers sworn to defend the lives of all Americans. In a throwback to the insanity of the Vietnam era, servicemen here are derided as "baby killers." That was the experience of a veteran of the Iraq war, Jason Gilson, when he marched in an Independence Day parade on liberal Bainbridge Island, across Puget Sound from Seattle. On a still more shameful occasion, again in the context of the debate about the Iraq conflict, a National Guardsman in uniform was kicked and punched just for walking down the street in Parkland, Washington. The assailants called him a "baby killer" and drove off in their SUV, leaving him crumpled on the sidewalk.

Vapid ideas about religion produce vapid—indeed, evil—ideas about morality. This principle encapsulates the main lesson of the Ten Commandments, which collides head-on with one of the great lies of our time, a central lie associated with our culture of "tolerance." If the main point I hope to leave you with in this book can be crystallized in one sentence, it is this: How people think about God, which is the general topic of the first five commandments, determines a society's moral health, which is the subject of the second five.

Notice that I speak here of *society's* moral health, not necessarily the individual's. This is how the Hebrew Bible analyzes the effects of religious backsliding on the culture as a whole. Do not be misled by the facile objection that many of the most outspoken atheists are clearly upstanding citizens, so therefore nobody needs religion. As Sam Harris, a best-selling atheist author (*Letter to a Christian Nation*), has commented, "If religion were the only durable foundation for morality you would suspect atheists to be really badly behaved. You would go to a group like the National Academy of Sciences. These are the most elite scientists, 93 percent of whom reject the idea of God. You would expect these guys to be raping and killing and stealing with abandon." No, obviously you wouldn't expect that at all, because the members of the National Academy of Sciences could only have achieved such a level of professional distinction by reining in personal anarchic impulses. Sam Harris, a successful writer and doctoral student in neuroscience, is by definition a functional individual. I worry not about elite scientists and best-selling authors but about the rest of us, ordinary Americans, upon whom the atmosphere of secularism rains down like nuclear fallout, spreading contamination.

For our morally sick culture, the Ten Commandments is a desperately needed diagnostic tool. Any reader who finds this idea outrageous or offensive certainly isn't alone. For two thousand years, the Ten Commandments have served as a potent symbol of the clash between moral cultures. Ancient Christians and Jews, twentieth-century fascists, and twenty-first-century political liberals and conservatives have all understood the stakes in the tug-of-war over the Decalogue.

The Bible's Book of Exodus relates how the Jews were freed by their God from Egyptian slavery and, at the foot of Mount Sinai, heard the Lord's voice speaking the ten statements that would become the heart of the Jewish faith, as well as of the Christian religion. God inscribed the Decalogue on two tablets. When Moses came down from the mountain, he discovered the Jews cavorting around an idolatrous depiction of a golden calf: "It happened as he drew near the camp and saw the calf and the dances, that Moses' anger flared up. He threw down the Tablets from his hands and shattered them" (32:19). According to tradition, the Israelites had gone so far as to violate every single one of the Ten Commandments, a scene depicted pretty effectively in Cecil B. De-Mille's schmaltzy 1956 epic. Moses later climbed back up Sinai and brought down another set of tablets, carved by his own hand.

After the Hebrew tribes had spent forty years in the wilderness, immediately before entering the promised land of Israel, Moses reviewed for them the whole Teaching—in Hebrew, *Torah*—that God had revealed at Sinai. This was the Pentateuch, or Five Books of Moses. As given in the written text of the Torah, this Teaching actually comprises 613 commandments—including rules for everything from distinguishing between kosher and forbidden foods to circumcising baby boys—of which the Ten Commandments add up to less than one-sixtieth.

However, the ancient rabbis granted a certain elevated status, a symbolic significance, to the Decalogue. That was as a sort of a table of contents for the rest of the commandments. The ten items of the Decalogue are like chapter headings to a book, with the other commandments each falling under one of these ten headings. Which is why, when the great Jerusalem Temple still stood, before its destruction by Roman forces in 70 c.e., the reading of the Ten Commandments was a central fixture of the Temple liturgy. When Jesus attended worship services in the Temple, he undoubtedly witnessed this liturgy.

After Jesus died, the status of Jewish law became a point of contention among his followers. Saint Paul seemed to take a dim view of "the Law" (his term for the Torah) altogether, calling it a "captor" and a "curse" (Romans 7:6, Galatians 3:13). Had the Torah indeed been rendered "obsolete," as the New Testament's Letter to the Hebrews frankly put it (8:13)? Not entirely. The Roman Catholic Church taught that the Ten Commandments summarized natural law evident to all peoples even before Moses met God at Sinai. Among Protestants, Martin Luther argued that when Jesus declared the eternality of the law, he had in mind the Ten Commandments. John Calvin, by contrast, took

a much more "Jewish" view of the Hebrew Bible, granting high regard
to the legal observance of Old Testament precepts even apart from the
Ten Commandments.

It was Calvinist Protestants, the Puritans, who gave the initial religious inspiration to what became the founding of the United States,
the most philo-Semitic country the world has ever known. This rap-
prochement of Judaism and Christianity found its most remarkable
expression in American law, which from the seventeenth century on
drew inspiration not only from the Ten Commandments but from the
entire Hebrew Bible. The earliest legal codes of colonial Massachusetts
and Connecticut were based explicitly on the Pentateuch's legislative
system.

With the flowering of the American legal system, the Ten Commandments as a symbol of Jewish-Christian culture clash had largely
faded—that is, outside Europe. On the bloody old continent, however,
there arose in the 1930s a new and demonic culture. Nazism, as Rabbi
Abraham Joshua Heschel observed, "in its very roots was a rebellion
against the Bible, against the God of Abraham. Realizing it was Christianity that implanted attachment to the God of Abraham and in-
volvement with the Hebrew Bible in the hearts of Western man,
Nazism resolved that it must both exterminate the Jews and eliminate
Christianity, and bring about instead a revival of Teutonic paganism."
To a fellow Nazi, Hitler confided his thoughts that the "life-denying
Ten Commandments" symbolized the "tyrannical God" of the Jews.
The Nazi regime must, consequently, make war on the Decalogue.

Though Hitler was thwarted, his hostility to the Bible survived af-
ter him. So Heschel, a political liberal who marched with Martin
Luther King, Jr., plainly recognized: "Nazism has suffered a defeat, but
the process of eliminating the Bible from the consciousness of the
Western world goes on. It is on the issue of saving the radiance of the
Hebrew Bible in the minds of man that Jews and Christians are called
upon to work together." Those prophetic words were published in 1966.
Scant decades later, the current culture war pits traditionally minded

Christians and Jews against those secularists who also would wish to diminish public respect for God and the Bible.

Richard Dawkins, the celebrity Darwinist and God hater, spoke for the more aggressive secularists when he declared recently, "The God of the Old Testament is arguably the most unpleasant character in all fiction—a petty, unjust, unforgiving control freak; a vindictive, bloodthirsty ethnic cleanser; a misogynistic, homophobic, racist, malevolent bully."

In the twenty-first century, the secular challenge may indeed be the ultimate dilemma facing our culture. Once deadly rivals when the epicenter of Western religious culture was not the United States, but Europe, Jews and Christians today are cast in a new and surprising alliance, based on the observation that there is such a thing as moral truth in the first place, and that it comes from God. In the sense that American law similarly assumes that right and wrong are a matter of objective reality, the Ten Commandments are at the foundation of our moral and legal culture. It's for this good reason that Moses carrying the two tablets of the Decalogue is carved on the wall of the U.S. Supreme Court.

The United States has long regarded itself as the continuation of the history of ancient Israel—an "extension of the Jewish church," as the Pilgrims put it in 1620. Thomas Jefferson authored the majestic statement of the Declaration of Independence: "We hold these truths to be self-evident, that all men are created equal, that they are endowed by their Creator with certain unalienable Rights, that among these are Life, Liberty, and the pursuit of Happiness." Of these words, Jonathan Sacks, the chief rabbi of the United Kingdom, has written that "Jefferson's 'truths' were self-evident only to a culture steeped in the Hebrew Bible, from its opening declaration that the human individual is 'the image of God,' to its enactment in history in the Exodus and the covenant at Mount Sinai."

Therefore, when we compare our national life to the standard set up at Sinai in the form of the Ten Commandments, we are doing more than merely judging the current moral stature of our culture. We are also making an estimate of the future viability of American democracy. How do we measure up?

The question is vital, urgent, and not only for religious believers.

I n the ten chapters that follow, we'll take a tour of the United States' increasingly degraded culture, considering the collapse of traditional moral authority through the lens of the Ten Commandments.

I begin each chapter with a vignette of Seattle, this community I care about and am committed to, seen through my eyes—the eyes of a biblical believer—then widen the focus to include the rest of the country. That's partly because this city has become my own, close to my heart. More important, it's because the unchurched Northwest represents a close-up picture of what secularism has in store for the rest of the country if we don't reconsider our ideas of right and wrong and where they come from. Secularism, which is to say modern paganism, draws its moral conceptions from the thin air. This nation's traditional culture drew its morality from the Ten Commandments. We'll see the difference, in practical terms, that that difference makes.

So let's get down to it. If the United States were graded on the ultimate scale of one to ten, the scale of Moses and of the Hebrew prophets who followed him, how would we fare?

GOD-CONSCIOUSNESS

I am the Lord your God,
who has taken you out of the land of Egypt,
from the house of slavery.
(Exodus 20:2)

On a damp winter night in Seattle, I attended a protest rally against the first commandment. The Oxford biologist and best-selling author Richard Dawkins had come to address a crowd at Town Hall, a cavernous defunct church now used for cultural events. The suave Brit, a type for which Americans swoon, roused and delighted his listeners. Ostensibly, Dawkins's subject was Darwinian evolution, of which he is the English-speaking world's boldest and most charming advocate. But the mostly middle-aged, flannel-bundled Seattlites, packed tightly in the curving wooden pews of the old vaulted sanctuary, seemed less fired up by scientific details than by what the author had to say about modern life and values.

Dawkins set the evening's tone by declaring himself "hostile to all forms of religion." Over and over, he stuck his thumb in the eye of religionists by referring to the Darwinist belief that, far from being God's children, humans are no more than animals. "We are all glorified lung-fish," he said with relish, exhaling contempt for any contrary opinion, "cousins of kangaroos and bacteria," "fellow apes."

He warned that with an evangelical Christian like George W. Bush in the White House, "People need to understand what they are up against in a society which is ruled by religious bigotry." The audience clapped and guffawed. When Dawkins reflected on the fact that "My publishers are no fools and planned the best places to go" to promote his book, wild applause interrupted him. He continued: "Of eight states we're visiting, all eight are blue states. Presumably these are states where they read books." More wild clapping and giddy laughter ensued as Dawkins's listeners applauded themselves for not being religious bigots, for living in a blue state, and for reading books. At one point, a member of the audience, standing up to ask a question, put her finger on the very central point, speaking passionately of how she "finds the naturalistic worldview immensely liberating compared to the alternative."

I have set before you the fans of Richard Dawkins only as an initial illustration of a much wider-spread attachment to naturalism, also known as materialism, the viewpoint in which everything that ever happened in cosmic history, from the big bang to today, did so for purely natural, material reasons, never due to supernatural causes. It's not atheism exactly, but it makes God beside the point. Darwinism is a prime example. Secularism, whose effects on our country's national life I intend to measure in this book, is the ideological view that would enshrine materialism as the official quasi-religion of American culture and government.

A goodly number of us assume that anyone who's not an idiot will of course take the purely naturalistic view. This question, which may sound abstract, is tearing America apart.

The Town Hall event occurred as America was heading for a crisis in the war over "intelligent design," the minority scientific viewpoint that finds evidence of a designer's hand at work in life's history over hundreds of millions of years. Darwinism and religious faith begin from mutually exclusive assumptions about reality. In *The Origin of Species*, Darwin's working premise is that God has no role in the unfolding of the story of life. In view of this belief, which he never states or defends, but simply assumes, he goes on to detail his theory about natural selection operating on random variation. It is only in the absence of a supreme being working out his will in history that we would even undertake Darwin's search for a purely materialistic explanation of how complex organisms arise. As Darwin himself clarified in his correspondence, "I would give absolutely nothing for the theory of natural selection if it requires miraculous additions at any one stage of descent." Religion, by contrast, does not assume that material reality is all there is. In the struggle between Darwin and intelligent design, a naïve literal interpretation of the Bible's creation story is not what is at issue. Rather, the point being debated, ultimately, is whether the universe ever had a need for a designer, whether God or otherwise.

It just so happens that, centuries before Darwin, medieval Jewish scholars understood that the distinction between the "naturalistic worldview" and its "alternative" was exactly the key to understanding the first commandment. Recall the exact wording: "I am the Lord your God, who has taken you out of the land of Egypt, from the house of slavery." The Jewish sages asked why, in defining Himself, God had harked back to the exodus of the Jews from Egyptian slavery, recounted in the Bible's Book of Exodus shortly before the giving of the Ten Commandments, rather than to a still more dramatic event: the creation of the world, which He accomplishes in the Bible's opening chapter. It's as if a parent, wanting to impress her child with the awesomeness of the parent-child bond, were to say, "I'm your mother, who picks you up from school every day," rather than, "I'm your mother, who gave birth to you."

Rabbi Ovadiah Sforno, an Italian sage born about 1470, taught that God saw it as a matter of highest priority to warn against what we today call a naturalistic worldview. If He had defined Himself here as the creator, that would not draw the line sharply enough. After all, there

are ways to explain certain aspects of creation within the limits of naturalistic terms. But the Exodus is different. Accompanied by ten bizarre
plagues that God inflicted on the Jews' Egyptian oppressors, and cli-
maxing with His splitting of the Sea of Reeds to drown the Egyptian
army as it pursued the escaped slaves, the Exodus can only be compre-
hended as a miracle, a blatant violation of nature's laws.

The point is, God does what He wants. He interferes. He gets involved in our lives and the lives of all creatures past and present, if often from inscrutable motives, reserving the right to direct the whole
world down to the smallest details. He runs the show. And He doesn't
let nature stand in His way. This is the claim made by the first commandment, and it is one at which many Americans bridle.

Can it be true that such modern-sounding questions are what
Moses had in mind in 1312 B.C.E., when, according to tradition,
he led two million escaped Egyptian slaves to freedom and gave them
the Ten Commandments? Did Moses somehow foresee our contemporary lives of more than three thousand years later? I don't know what
Moses thought, but the words attributed to him make an explosive and
timely prediction. They predict the way a society's ideas about God will
influence the way its members interact with one another. You don't
have to be a religious believer to wonder if that prediction accurately
reflects the way human cultures work. The United States today—whose
culture, high and low, we're about to embark on a tour of—will be our
test case.

But the first nation to be confronted with the Ten Commandments
and the incisive cultural critique they imply was, of course, that of the
Jews. The first generation of the Jewish people, on their way to freedom
in the land of Canaan, encamped in the wilderness at the foot of a low
mountain, Sinai. There was thunder and lightning and a fire descending on the mountaintop. God instructed the people's leader, Moses, to
climb the mountain to receive an indication of what God wanted them

to do now that they were no longer slaves. As the Bible's Book of Exodus recounts, the Jews heard God's own voice.

The entire Jewish people, as they would tell their children down through the millennia, heard God pronounce the first two of the Ten Commandments. But the sound of the divine voice was too much for them. They pleaded with God henceforth to communicate directly only with Moses. God agreed. Forty days later, Moses came down from Mount Sinai with a full record of what God had to say. This was the Torah, the Bible's first five books, along with an explanatory tradition, conveyed orally. There is a Written Torah, and an Oral Torah. When I refer to "Torah" without qualification or definite article, I mean the combined tradition, or written and oral together.

This vast Torah, in turn, was summarized in just ten statements, the ultimate CliffsNotes. In the Bible itself, the Ten Commandments aren't numbered. Different religious traditions, Jewish and Christian, number the verses of the scriptural text in slightly different ways, but everyone agrees there are ten separate statements. In this book, I will rely on the oldest tradition, that of Judaism—not only for numbering but for illuminating the meaning of the commandments altogether—because Jewish sages for three thousand years have been reflecting on the Hebrew Bible's text in remarkable detail, basing their interpretations on the ancient oral tradition, or Oral Torah, later written down in the Talmud and the Midrash, for which other religions have no precise parallel. Following in the same spiritual and intellectual vein as the Hebrew prophets, some of the sages I will be introducing in this book lived in Talmudic times (roughly the first through the fourth centuries of the Common Era), others in the Middle Ages. Their unfamiliar names will become familiar as we go along.

I have called the commandments "statements" because the verses in Hebrew aren't literally phrased as commandments, but as affirmations in the future tense. "You will not recognize the gods of others," "You will not take the name of the Lord in vain," "You will not kill," "You will not commit adultery," et cetera.

This is a curious feature of the so-called commandments. So, too, is the fact that God had Moses write them down on *two* tablets. Why not one? Did Moses lack a font size small enough to fit these relatively few words on a single tablet?

The use of two tablets was not due to an inadequacy in the available word-processing software. It was deliberate, and thus obviously crucial to understanding what the statements mean. As far back as the second century of the Common Era, in the rabbinic book Mechilta, Jewish tradition has taught that the mirror symmetry—five commandments on one tablet, five on the other—show how values influence a society's success in every field of endeavor. The idea is alluded to in a cryptic form, according to the medieval commentator Rashi, in a verse from the Bible's Song of Songs: "Your two breasts are like two young roes that are twins, which feed among the lilies" (4:5). The two "breasts," mirroring each other, are the two tablets.

The first five statements deal with man's relationship with God. The second five concern our relationships with other people, thus with how humane and civilized a way of life we enjoy. The nation that gets one through five right will stand a better chance of getting six through ten right also.

We can be more specific. Moses inscribed the commandments in descending rows on each tablet—the first commandment at the top of the column, with the second directly under that, the third under that, and so forth. On the second tablet, the sixth commandment comes first, followed by the seventh under it, and so on. The first lines up horizontally with the sixth, the second with the seventh, et cetera. The commandments can therefore be read not only from top to bottom but also *across*. So if you picture the first tablet as positioned next to the second, the first commandment may be read as if it were followed not by the second commandment but, rather, moving horizontally to the second tablet, by the *sixth* commandment. The paired commandments form a series of if/then statements: *If* a culture understands and reveres the first commandment (whose meaning we are investigating in this chapter), *then* it will also fulfill the sixth (against murder); if that culture lives by the second commandment (against idolatry), then it will fulfill the seventh (against stealing); et cetera. Since the chapters of this book are organized in the obvious fashion, one chapter per commandment, proceeding in the order the Bible gives, we'll really start to see what this means only when we reach the sixth commandment.

In short, most of us, in contemplating the familiar yet highly enigmatic biblical text, understand a lot less about what Moses was communicating than we think we do. Which brings us back to the most enigmatic of the commandments, the first.

It doesn't sound like a commandment, nor is it an affirmative statement in the future tense like the other nine on our list. It plainly concerns the belief in God—though the word *belief* doesn't quite convey the factual certainty of the statement, in the Deity's own voice: "I am the Lord your God."

Rashi, the French medieval sage (1040–1105), greatest of the rabbinic expositors of the Bible, highlights the phrase "from the house of slavery." He notes the irony that, having been released from one form of bondage, the Jews were entering another, as if God were saying, "From now on you will be slaves to the King, and not slaves to slaves." Meaning that God is the true King. In relationship to Him, even Egypt's pharaoh, who held the key to the bonds that held the Jews, is only a slave. The truth is, we are all enslaved, if not to a physical master then to a set of ideas. We all have our preset assumptions about how reality works, about how moral questions are adjudicated, about where truth is to be found. Otherwise, we could hardly get through the day. People who regard themselves as "freethinkers" are invariably enslaved to their own "transgressive" or "progressive" notions of right and wrong, notions that they received in turn from earlier self-congratulatory intellectuals or just from breathing the air of "enlightenment" and "open-mindedness" that envelops many of us so closely that, as with breathing actual air, we never realize what we are absorbing deep into ourselves at every moment.

The difference between someone who takes the first commandment
to heart and someone who doesn't is that the former accepts servitude
to the King, to God, as a conscious act, wide awake, while the latter
sleepwalks, never even guessing how enslaved he really is to other people, to the spirit of his times.

However, a more pertinent meaning of the first commandment has
to do with negating the perspective of the materialist. In the vocabu-
lary of the Talmud, a materialist is called an *apicorus*. The ancient rabbis urged believers in the Bible to know how to rebut the philosophical
claims of such a person. The hallmark of the *apicorus*, they said, is the
contempt he shows toward the teachers of biblical tradition. Obviously,
the conflict between the "naturalistic worldview" and its "alternative"
goes back a long way.

The word itself, *apicorus*, is simply an adaptation of the name of a
Greek philosopher, Epicurus, whom scholars today credit with being
the first Western thinker to spell out the implications of materialism.

Epicurus, born in 341 B.C.E., himself was an ascetic. And unlike
Richard Dawkins, who says, "Darwin made it possible to be an intellectually fulfilled atheist," Epicurus believed in gods, or said he did at least.
But he regarded those gods as practically irrelevant to men's lives. In his
view, gods lived high up on top of Mount Olympus, from which they
hardly deigned even to look upon human affairs, much less to get involved directly.

This philospher's chief priority was to show people how to avoid
spiritual and physical distress. Such distress arose from various causes,
Epicurus thought. It came from imagining that the gods watched over
you and would hold you responsible for your actions in this world and
the next—that is, in the afterlife. And it came from overindulgence in
physical pleasures. To counteract these sources of angst and discomfort,
he urged his followers to take to heart his assurance that the gods didn't
care a bit about people and thus would never punish them for their sins.
And he advocated a monkish lifestyle—not much more than bread and

water for nourishment—to alleviate any possibility of suffering from overeating or overdrinking.

For him, the only reality was that of the material world—an observation that was supposed to be calming. Using a term he borrowed from the earlier Greek philosopher Democritus, he taught that there was nothing more to humankind, or to the rest of the cosmos, than "atoms."

His writings have a curiously modern feel, as do those of the Roman philosophical poet who brought him to the attention of the larger Western world: Lucretius (died c. 55 B.C.E.). Lucretius's poem *De Rerum Natura* (*On the Nature of Things*) is an exposition of materialism at epic length, including a remarkable explanation of how different animal life-forms evolve through a process of natural selection of the fittest—Darwin's idea in a nutshell. He was, as Richard Dawkins would say, "hostile to all forms of religion." Like his hero Epicurus, he was also an ascetic. Advocating the avoidance of all possible distressing emotional entanglements, he distrusted sexual relationships and instead advocated masturbation: "it is fitting to flee images [of the beloved] and drive away fearfully from oneself the foods of love, and turn the mind elsewhere and ejaculate the liquid collected in the body and do not retain it."

In the century of Jesus' birth, educated Romans were divided between followers of Epicurus by way of Lucretius, who prioritized the avoidance of pain as the chief goal of life, on the one hand, and, on the other, followers of the Stoic philosophy, who believed the gods indeed had their eyes on humans and would see to it that, in the end, justice was done to sinners.

With the conversion of the Roman empire to Christianity, Epicureanism went into a long hibernation. It emerged only in 1417, when Poggio Bracciolini, an antiquarian and typical Renaissance man, enamored of the Greek and Roman classics, uncovered an ancient manuscript of Lucretius's *On the Nature of Things*. A modern scholar, Benjamin Wiker, has traced the course of revived Epicurean materialism through a succession of great Western philosophers and scientists. The hit parade includes Machiavelli, Spinoza, Bacon, Hobbes, and Rousseau. It culminates in Darwin, who reasoned that an explanation of how the various species developed must be found that admits no role whatsoever for a designing deity. The alternative to naturalism isn't supernaturalism, the assumption that nothing happens in the world owing to natural causes, but only because God wills it. The real alternative is simply an openness to seeing God's hand at work—as opposed to ruling out such a possibility before even considering the evidence.

Ruling out God a priori is what materialists do, and it's what they demand we do, and our children. Darwin's name has become a flash point in our own culture because believers in his doctrine—that is, our day's most prominent opponents of the first commandment—are not content to find intellectual fulfillment in their personal commitment to naturalism, but insist that the negation of the first commandment be taught to all American public school students, as well. They have been remarkably successful in their insistence.

Consider the frank admission of one Darwinist—a remarkable statement that appeared on January 9, 1997, in *The New York Review of Books*, a publication that evidently it was assumed no one but committed believers in Darwinism ever reads, hence the fierce honesty of the sentiments sometimes expressed therein. On the occasion of the death of Carl Sagan, the most popularly celebrated advocate of naturalism in recent decades, Harvard geneticist Richard Lewontin wrote of how the commitment to materialism precedes all else:

> We take the side of science in spite of the patent absurdity of
> some of its constructs, in spite of its failure to fulfill many of its
> extravagant promises of health and life, in spite of the tolerance
> of the scientific community for unsubstantiated just-so stories,
> because we have a prior commitment, a commitment to

materialism. It is not that the methods and institutions of science somehow compel us to accept a material explanation of the phenomenal world, but, on the contrary, that we are forced by our *a priori* adherence to material causes to create an apparatus of investigation and a set of concepts that produce material explanations, no matter how counter-intuitive, no matter how mystifying to the uninitiated. Moreover, that materialism is absolute, for we cannot allow a Divine Foot in the door. . . . To appeal to an omnipotent deity is to allow that any moment the regularities of nature may be ruptured, that miracles may happen.

It is in the sclerotic, materialist habit of mind that the large majority of American tenth graders are drilled in their biology classes. The shock that self-consciously sophisticated Americans feel when Darwinism is challenged comes from the lingering orthodoxy that equates materialism with rationality, a prejudice we picked up in high school. I'm always bemused when Jewish groups like the Anti-Defamation League decry the "targeting for conversion" of Jews by Christians—but have nothing to say about the far more widespread targeting of children for conversion to naturalism, the negation of the first commandment, by their own schools.

Materialism positively permeates our culture—not only in the popular understanding of science but also in the ways we think about more frequently contemplated subjects, like sex and death.

The revered Sagan, deceased Cornell astronomer, remains the saint of naturalism. The signature phrase of his popular 1980 PBS series *Cosmos* was, "The Cosmos is all that is or ever was or ever will be"—a slogan that a colleague of mine, Nancy Pearcey, was startled to find repeated almost verbatim in an unlikely place. Her little boy was reading a science book for kids, based on the beloved family of apparently Jewish cartoon bears, the Berenstain Bears. The book, *The Bears' Nature Guide*, begins with the bears appreciating a gorgeous sunset. The caption reads "Nature . . . is all that IS, or WAS, or EVER WILL BE."

This is Darwin's, and Epicurus's, assumption. It's also the assumption behind the American media's breathless search for life on other planets. Assuming God does nothing in cosmic history, then the development of life on our planet can't have been a unique event. It must have been a snap. Since that's so, it stands to reason there must be life elsewhere. This accounts for the hysterical enthusiasm for every burp of data from NASA hinting at the possibility of water on Mars, which could mean there were or are . . . bacteria! While finding extraterrestrial life would not trouble believers in the Bible, it really is essential to believers in materialism. It must be found, or else life on Earth starts to look very special, possibly miraculous.

In tracing the descent of Epicureanism, Benjamin Wiker draws our attention to latter-day figures like Alfred Kinsey (1894–1956), the sex researcher, who accepted Epicurus's assumption that physical matter, atoms and molecules rubbing up against one another, is all that counts. What matters is our bodies, whose existence is undoubted, not our entirely hypothetical, probably mythical souls. Kinsey, for all that his research methods have been called into question while his sexual idiosyncrasies have been revealed by biographers (tastes for bisexuality, adultery, and sticking foreign objects in his penis), remains a sainted figure in the popular imagination—at least in the imagination of that part of the populace that took to heart Hollywood's reverential 2004 biopic *Kinsey*, starring the ruggedly elegant Liam Neeson. The point of the film was that when it comes to sex, it's all about matter rubbing up against matter. Certainly, no God-given rules apply when two (or more) people, whether adults or children, want to experience sexual pleasure together. Or for that matter, alone. In the film's telling, a formative experience in Kinsey's life was the boyhood clash with his foolish pietist of a father (John Lithgow), a raging Christian fundamentalist, over the issue of self-love. He rebelled, left home, and studied entomology, becoming an expert in the sex lives of gall wasps, later publishing the epoch-making *Sexual Behavior in the Human Male* (1948) and *Sexual Behavior in the Human Female* (1953). At a turning point, young Alfred is shown enjoying a tender moment with himself, making *Kinsey* the first movie ever to portray masturbation as a heroic gesture.

His books, which bequeathed the sexual attitudes we'll consider in detail when we come to the seventh commandment (forbidding adultery), convinced millions of Americans that the large majority of us indulge in sexual perversities of all kinds, and that it's all good. Without God setting the terms of our moral lives, people are simply animals. So *Kinsey*'s closing-credit images—nature films of skunks, cats, iguanas, and pigs copulating—graphically remind us.

If people are animals, it starts to become a challenge to defend the taboo on interspecies intimacy. Could this be the next frontier as the implications of the all-material, God-free universe gradually become clear?

There is a man who holds an endowed chair at Princeton University, the Ira W. DeCamp Chair of Bioethics, who minimizes the offense of bestiality. Besides justifying infanticide on the grounds that a human newborn has less self-consciousness than an adult dog, Peter Singer, in 2000, penned a cheery article on the highbrow sex Web site Nerve in which he came achingly close to endorsing sex with animals. The latter, he said, should be no "cause for shock or horror," no "offense to our status and dignity as human beings." For we *have* no such special status, being "great apes" ourselves. It's only because of "the Judeo-Christian tradition [that] we have always seen ourselves as distinct from animals, and imagined that a wide, unbridgeable gap separates us from them. Humans alone are made in the image of God. Only human beings have an immortal soul."

One might reasonably wonder how deeply such views as Singer's actually penetrate the minds of the average American. After all, polls indicate that belief in God remains widespread. A 2004 poll by Fox News indicated that 92 percent of Americans believe in God, while 85 percent believe in an afterlife including heaven, and 82 percent believe in miracles. However, articulating an opinion to a pollster

is different from feeling it in your gut. A person may continue expressing a certain conviction after it has evaporated from his heart. The
"conviction" by that point has become more like a wish.

How can we measure the depth of our beliefs about God? One way
is to find out what we think about death and what follows it. The existence of God means little of practical importance if there is no chance
of our meeting Him and being called to account for ourselves after we
die. Overwhelmingly, we *say* there is such a thing as an afterlife. A 2003
Barna Research Group poll found that 79 percent of us agree with the
statement that "every person has a soul that will live forever, either in
God's presence or absence." This poll found that 76 percent believe in
heaven, 71 percent in hell.

Yet what are we to do with countervailing evidence that Americans
are more afraid of death than ever—evidence that strongly suggests
many of us are inclined to view our end as oblivion? What other conclusion is there to draw from the country's intensifying obsession with
health and mortality?

News venues allocate coverage—how much to sports, to politics, to
religion, and so forth—based on careful market research. Recently, no
single subject has garnered more attention than health, especially the
question of how to stave off death. The newsweeklies devote about one
in five of their covers to health-related topics. In the year of the 2004
presidential election—the big story of the year, one assumes—*Time* ex-
pended ten covers on the election, and ten on health-related subjects:
"Diabetes: Are You at Risk?" "The Secret Killer: The Surprising Link Between Inflammation and Heart Attacks, Cancer, Alzheimer's, and Other
Diseases," "The Stealth Killer: America's High Blood Pressure Crisis Is
Spinning Out of Control," "How to Live to Be 100," and others. Unlike
the election stories, which contained real news, these mostly hyped and
massaged information that had long been available to the public.

We've become a nation of amateur physicians, looking up every
stray hypothetical symptom on diagnose-yourself Internet sites like
WebMD and countless others. Every study or finding touting a new or

augmented health risk is blasted across front pages and home pages, no matter how ludicrous—like the National Institutes of Health's "body mass index" (BMI), heralded by scary headlines about an "obesity crisis." The BMI standard was taken seriously until someone noticed that President George W. Bush, a slim, teetotaling fitness buff, was, according to his BMI, officially overweight and therefore "at risk."

We are scared to death—of death. Even religious folk are affected. When in the winter of 2004 the country was thrown into a panic because of a shortage of flu vaccine, churches began encouraging clergy and parishioners to refrain from touching their lips to the Communion cup and even from shaking hands. The Catholic diocese of Burlington, Vermont, made this official policy for its priests. A writer in Kansas, for the *Wichita Eagle*, asked sensibly, "If any place should be less hysterical over such matters, it is houses of worship. Have we forgotten what it means to trust in the One who created us? When did fear overcome faith?"

Because we're scared, we are also intimidated by those now overly familiar figures, the health fanatics. A fellow at the pool where I swim, a seventy-five-year-old Ironman triathlete, charming in his way but certainly a fanatic, fits the profile of the most pugnacious, aggressive evangelists, except he has no religion—unless you consider secularism a religion. He evangelizes for health—lecturing me about how I have "no excuse" for failing to compete in triathlons, or harassing a fat kid ("You really are endangering your heath. I could show you some exercises.") until the kid tells him, "Leave me alone!" in the tone you'd use in addressing a possible child molester. The other day in the locker room, he adopted an ominous tone and said to me, "I'm sure your spiritual health is very good. But how is your *physical* health?"

H ow to Live to Be 100," as *Time* magazine puts it, has become the chief *moral* priority for many of us. And while the same polls highlighting our purported faith in the next life also indicate a belief in miracles, the latter is also subject to doubt. Remember that the first commandment poses its challenge to materialism by reminding us of God's omnipotence, without which He isn't God.

Divine omnipotence is no longer taken for granted. When someone innocent dies before his time, or when a tragedy of any kind occurs, mourners and others who are left behind, or who are simply left confused about why bad things happen to good people, are likely to be given, or to purchase for themselves, a little book called *When Bad Things Happen to Good People*, by Rabbi Harold S. Kushner. I remember buying it as a college student in 1983, when my mother died of bone cancer at age fifty. For those of us who have experienced tragedy, this, unfortunately, is one of the most influential books around. Published in 1981, it argues that when bad things happen, we shouldn't blame God. Rather, we should be consoled by Him because He feels our pain, and gives us "strength." That's all He does, however. From a reading of the Book of Job, Kushner proves to his own satisfaction that God is not all-powerful at all. The world is out of His control, as it is out of ours. When we hurt badly, He passes us the Kleenex box; then we pass it back to Him because He's blubbering along with us. I was so impressed by this argument at the time I read it that, later the next year, when I heard that my Latin professor of the previous semester was gravely ill, again with cancer, I wrote her a letter. By way of comforting a dying woman, I vacuously explained that while God could do nothing to heal her, He did stand ready with the offer of compassion and empathy. Today, as cultural critic Ron Rosenbaum observes, Kushner's "cop-out has become *the* contemporary evasive answer to questions of theodicy"—how a good God could allow evil in His world—"an almost unquestioned meme."

The Epicurean worldview has touched our culture more deeply than we realize. We may *say* we believe God operates in this world and that we will be with Him in the next, but the evidence—the thinkers we admire, the news we read and watch, the fears we struggle against, the comforts we accept when troubled—all suggest that materialism has a hold on us.

That hold seems bound to strengthen. Some Americans, feeling even the current level of God-awareness is too much, seize every opportunity to correct the situation. Every week brings a news story about how the ACLU or some similar organization (often, alas, Jewish) has intimidated somebody into erasing a hint of that consciousness, "I am the Lord your God," that is urged upon us by the first commandment. Usually, it is the Christian God that offends; other times, it's any allusion to God at all. One week, the civil libertarians have successfully liberated the official seal of Los Angeles County, which contained a tiny, tiny cross, symbolizing California's mission history. The cross will now be expunged. Another week brings news that the American Jewish Committee would like to take God out of Thanksgiving, turning the holiday of thanks (to whom?) into a secular celebration of "democracy and diversity." Another week, a school in the San Francisco Bay area bans the Declaration of Independence from being studied by its fifth graders—along with George Washington's journal, John Adams's diary, and William Penn's *The Frame of Government of Pennsylvania*—because it mentions God.

The reason we should be concerned about that is—what exactly? Sociologist Rodney Stark has written about "the social implications of belief"—specifically, how "different conceptions of the supernatural have dramatically different effects on the human experience." In other words, how a culture conceives of God directly affects how we get along together.

One reason for that is that it matters where you think morals come from. There are two possibilities. Either we know what's right because God or His earthly agents inform us through objective revelation or tradition or we know because that's just what the better-informed human beings appear to have decided, through a subjective process of moral democracy.

And what is wrong with moral democracy? A conservative cultural critic, Jonah Goldberg, opines that "God doesn't need me to believe in Him or agree with Him." After all, Goldberg thinks, what matters is morality, not theology. "My motives to be a good person or a bad person are my own. If I get my morality from a can of chicken-and-stars soup, you shouldn't care until that morality drives me to commit evil. At which point we can have an argument about whether or not soup-can religion is bad for America."

I have no beef with chicken soup, but surely only a God who can enforce His will—as chicken soup cannot—stands a chance of inspiring consistent, widespread good behavior. Moral democracy has no heaven, no hell, no afterlife. It suggests, but it can't command. Are moral truths objective or subjective? That's the bottom line.

The first commandment functions as a preamble, explaining why we need to listen to the remaining nine: because "I am the Lord your God," who sanctions commandments two through ten. Some Americans affirm God's role in establishing right and wrong. They are Jews, Christians, and members of other faiths. Many nonreligious folk agree that morality has an objective basis, perhaps in nature. Others may respect the morality of the Ten Commandments especially in some of their less controversial directives: against murder and stealing, for respecting your mother and father. But they leave open the possibility of subjecting moral truth to the criterion of their own opinion.

This explains why the first is the most incendiary of the commandments. It's not a coincidence that many of the monuments bearing the Ten Commandments on public property that have been the subject of intense legal battles, culminating before the justices of the Supreme Court, turn out to give unique prominence to the first commandment. In big capital letters, in the center of the man-size granite slab, we read "I AM the LORD thy God."

Those six words, asserting that the authority of all ethical precepts depends on God, are, in fact, key to understanding why the Ten Commandments lie at the foundation of the American legal tradition. In trying to sever religion entirely from governance, secular activists threaten the very basis of that tradition—as not only religion itself but even secular viewpoints affirm.

British chief rabbi Jonathan Sacks draws a comparison between ancient Israel and modern America. He points out that there are two ways to keep a nation ordered and peaceful. The people may be restrained either by fear of the government or by respect for values underwritten by an unseen lawgiver, God. In the second model, the citizens are joined by a convenant expressing their will to abide by God's laws.

Ancient Israel was the first convenantal society. For centuries, it had no government per se at all. There were judges and courts, which issued verdicts on matters of civil dispute, but no recognizable apparatus of law enforcement—no prisons, for example. True, written in the Torah's legal code we find a death penalty for egregious crimes, including some that we wouldn't regard as criminal (like breaking the Sabbath or adultery, to cite two sins prohibited by the Ten Commandments). But the rules of evidence and procedure were so strict that getting a conviction was practically impossible and so from the time the Jews entered Israel, capital punishment was carried out rarely, if ever. So why make breaking the Sabbath a capital crime, if it was so only in theory? Because the Bible intended to create a teaching model, indicating the severity of the moral offense by attaching to it, as a matter of principle, if not of practicality, the ultimate punishment. The intent wasn't to execute people who disregarded the sacred day of rest, but, rather, to emphasize that the day was indeed very sacred. This created a shared moral code, received at Mount Sinai.

The society of ancient Israel was a deeply religious one with a very high quotient of God-consciousness—necessarily so. Religious education and a very public religious culture both constantly reinforced the message that morality isn't a preference but an objective reality handed down from heaven—without these, the convenant would have been unsustainable and the nation would have had to revert, in the manner of every other nation that had ever been on Earth, to fear of the government to keep people in line.

In world history, the United States was the second experiment in covenantal politics. Yes, there was a proper government with law enforcement and jails. But the promise of American freedom was based on a shared pledge among the citizens, a pledge of loyalty to an idea of freedom, underwritten by a very Hebrew understanding of God. As the signers of the Declaration of Independence put it in their concluding sentence, "And for the support of this Declaration, with a firm reliance on the protection of divine Providence, we mutually pledge to each other our Lives, our Fortunes and our sacred Honor." Limited government, American-style, is possible only when the people similarly pledge themselves to control their own actions out of awe for a moral power, God's, beyond the merely legal power of the state. Secularism is an attack on this most basic idea of the Founding Fathers.

Israel, writes Rabbi Sacks, was a "republic of faith under the sovereignty of God." So is America—or it was. He writes sadly that "one of the ironies of the post-modern West is that the triumph of freedom over totalitarian regimes has gone hand in hand with an erosion of the moral bases of freedom. Morality has been relativized into self-fulfillment. Responsibilities have taken second place to right. The very idea of objective standards of right and wrong has become suspect. If history teaches any lesson at all it is that this, if unchecked, is a prelude to disaster." To illustrate the peril, Sacks cites ancient Greece and Renaissance Italy, which both sunk into moral decay, and ultimately descended to anarchy, because people ceased to believe that morality had any transcendent basis.

In short, American freedom depends on a shared God-consciousness. A secularized America is "a prelude to disaster"—as we'll see in the next nine chapters.

PAGAN NATION

You shall not recognize the gods of others in My presence.
You shall not make yourself a carved image or any likeness of that which is in
the heavens above or on the earth below or in the water beneath the earth.
You shall not prostrate yourself to them nor worship them, for I am the Lord
your God—a jealous God, Who visits the sin of fathers upon children to the third
and fourth generations, for My enemies; but who shows kindness for thousands
[of generations] to those who love Me and observe My commandments.
(Exodus 20:3–6)

T he Bible's idea of paganism is surprisingly capacious. It would
probably include most of Seattle.

There could be nothing more decorous, more redolent of
the Establishment, than the squat, massive neo-Byzantine bulk of St.
Mark's Episcopal Cathedral on Tenth Avenue on Capitol Hill. The
Episcopal Church in general is one of those mainline Christian denominations that are notable today for having lost the ability to say no to
their parishioners or anyone else, to insist on moral absolutes of the
kind typified by the Ten Commandments. Instead, the liberal churches
have as their only absolute the all-encompassing value of *compassion*.

When I visited St. Mark's for the 11:00 A.M. Holy Eucharist service,
compassion was the main theme. A hand-lettered sign propped up

against a wall advised, "Compassion is a wounding of the heart which love extends to all without distinction." It's a noble-sounding ideal, but foreign to the Bible, which advises that there are occasions when pity has no place. When the Israelites encountered the native idol-worshiping and brutally immoral Canaanites, God said, "Your eye shall not pity them; you shall not worship their gods, for it is a snare to you" (Deuteronomy 7:16). God at times withholds His own compassion, as when speaking of the retribution due to be vented upon Jerusalem, "O city of bloodshed, the pot in which there is filth," promising that "I, the Lord, have spoken; it is coming, and I shall carry it out; I will not hinder, I will not pity, I will not relent" (24:6, 14).

The service at St. Mark's was, by all outward appearances, very traditional. The atmosphere was hushed and reverential. But was the reverence directed toward God, or something else? In his sermon, the dean of the cathedral, the Very Reverend Robert V. Taylor, spoke in what sounded like a muted South African accent about a number of topics all related to the theme of compassion—the lamentable fact that World AIDS Day had not received as much attention that year as it deserved, the commendable fact that a new movie about Jesus' birth, *The Nativity Story*, depicted baby Jesus as a "person of color." He spoke of an acquaintance who regularly visits sick and dying children in Seattle Children's Hospital, learning valuable lessons in love, courage, and so on.

Sensitivity and compassion, both wonderful qualities, are the watchwords at St. Mark's. The Holiday Bazaar benefits "social justice, multiculturalism, and environmental sustainability." The needs of the physically handicapped are consistently taken into account. In the explanatory handout pamphlet given to each visitor, worshipers are instructed that when it's time for everyone to get on their feet to say the Nicene Creed, "All rise as able." The needs of the allergic are taken into account at Communion: "Rice wafers for those with wheat allergies are available at the communion station."

What's wrong with any of this? In itself, nothing, except that it becomes clear in religious liberalism generally that the ancient content of the Bible's moral law has been hollowed out and that pity and sensitivity are merely what's left.

And when we turn from the moral law, we have inevitably, by definition, turned toward idolatry. The Bible recognizes only these two states of existence: You have either cast your lot with God or with the idols. The greatest codifier of biblical law, Maimonides, put the idea in stark terms: "All who affirm idolatry reject the whole of God's Teaching, all the prophets, and that which was commanded to the prophets from Adam until the end of the world. . . . And all who reject idolatry affirm the whole of God's Teaching, all the prophets, and that which was commanded to the prophets from Adam until the end of the world" (Mishneh Torah, Laws of Idolatry 2:5).

In other words, while the second commandment, forbidding idolatry, is only one of the Ten Commandments, in a sense it is the essence of the whole Decalogue. Since the Ten Commandments include a variety of sins that in biblical law would subject the violator not only to moral censure but to the death penalty, the ideal of compassion "without distinction" is by its very nature a denial of the Bible as the preeminent moral authority and therefore, automatically, a turning toward paganism.

As I stressed in the last chapter, my intention here isn't to call for capital punishment against commandment-breakers—no, I'm not a theocrat—but merely to note the seriousness that Scripture attaches to these issues. In this sense, we can put expressions of liberal religion that have only one biblically derived commandment, to be compassionate, in the same category as secularism, which has none. Since both liberal religion and secularism deny traditional norms of behavior as rooted in the Bible, both equally represent a turn toward paganism. As I noted in the introduction, barely 30 percent of the people in the region where I live are churchgoing Christians. That would make the Pacific Northwest, with its huge secular majority, a bastion of paganism.

Calling religious liberalism and secularism "pagan" may seem like a theoretical application of an abstract idea—that is, a stretch. If so, then meet some followers of pure and unambiguous paganism.

My kids' favorite baby-sitter assures me that she's not a practicing witch, "though," she says, "I do hang out with a lot of Wiccans." There was the time, for instance, out on the Kitsap Peninsula, near Seattle, when she joined a group of witches for a "sky-clad" (that is, naked) romp in the woods, a May Day ritual. Having tossed off their clothes, the pagans ran around a maypole chanting in Gaelic. "The pole is a phallic symbol," thirty-two-year-old Jenny helpfully explains. "They're white witches, not bad ones. I never really asked them about it. I just know."

"I think she takes it all with a grain of salt," my wife later assures me. Yet the next day Jenny, responding to my curiosity, brings over a stack of books from her collection. The well-thumbed volumes smell like incense and one is stained with a dark liquid. They have titles like *Embracing the Moon: A Witch's Guide to Rituals, Spellcraft and Shadow Work* and *The Witch's Familiar: Spiritual Partnerships for Successful Magic*. A thick and serious-looking book is called *The Great Cosmic Mother: Rediscovering the Religion of the Earth*.

Jenny is far from alone. One fine Sunday, I was an observer at a Wiccan worship circle in a public park in Tacoma, Washington. The setting was sylvan and beautiful, overlooking Puget Sound toward Gig Harbor. The water sparkled and the incense wafted. About thirty-five people showed up, from teenagers to the middle-aged, plus a couple of senior citizens. They could have been any church group out for a weekend picnic—well, maybe any liberal church group.

They stood around a rock in the center of their circle. Placed beside the rock were corn-husk dolls, flowers, a glass of beer, and some wheat stalks—for it was the *sabbat* or festival (from the Hebrew for Sabbath) of Lammas, which celebrates the first harvest and the death and rebirth of the god of grain. A man who wore a Scottish kilt led a group recital of Robert Burns's "John Barleycorn: A Ballad," while others in the group were fitted out in homemade robes of blue or red that would not have looked out of place on the guy behind the fish counter at your local supermarket. A teenage girl passed out wheat stalks and paper cups of apple juice. Then they all turned to the north, east, south, and west to bless the spirits of the four directions and four elements, fire, water, earth, and air. They concluded by calling out, "May the gods preserve the Craft, and may the Craft preserve the gods!" This was followed by hoots of "Yeah!" "Yay!" "Yoo hoo!" and then the pagans dispersed.

It may be hard to picture a full-scale polytheistic revival in modern America. Before Europe was Christianized, my pagan Swedish and Welsh ancestors no doubt engaged in human sacrifice—at the great festival held every nine years at the ancient Swedish holy city, Uppsala, or the yearly Celtic fire festivals, where a giant figure of a man constructed from wicker, filled with live animals and actual men, was burned to ward off—well, witches. A giant wicker man, minus the human sacrifice, is still burned at the yearly fiesta in Santa Fe, New Mexico, by the city's Kiwanis Club, of all things, the nation's oldest civic celebration; the Burning Man festival held each summer in the Nevada high desert also culminates in the torching of a fifty-foot effigy. These are not pagan rites. Modern witches, however, worshipers of a dualistic pantheon comprising a god and a goddess, say that in just the past few years they have discerned a genuine pagan revival, or what my neighbor Jeremy Allen, a self-described "Druid archpriest," called "the Awakening of the Ancients." Says Jeremy, who goes by the alternative name Gannandelff of the Boulder, "A lot of like-minded people have been drawn to the Wiccan religions and lately we always seem to find each other. It's happening all over the country—in Canada, even."

The New York Times, quoting the American Religious Identification Survey, put the number of Wiccans nationally at 134,000 in 2001. That's up from only eight thousand in 1990. J. Gordon Melton, who directs the Institute for the Study of American Religion in Santa Barbara, calls Wicca, and paganism generally, the country's fastest growing religion.

Even if only a distinct minority of Americans identify as Wiccans, the influence of paganism and witchery is evident across the culture. J.K. Rowling's Harry Potter series, with its tales of Hogwart's School of Witchcraft and Wizardry, stirs the anguish of Evangelical Christian parents every time a new Rowling book is launched by young readers to the top of the best-seller list. It's likewise impossible to take a plane, train, subway, or any other public transportation without seeing at least one or two people reading *The Da Vinci Code*. Dan Brown's admiring treatment of Goddess worship, which dominates the second half of the novel, has received some attention. Besides Jesus' previously undisclosed genetic legacy, the other secret related here has to do with how Christianity tragically displaced the wonderful ancient religion of the Goddess. In the course of the novel, Brown includes an awestruck rendition of the pagan Great Rite, the Hieros Gamos, or "sacred marriage"—namely, sexual intercourse performed before worshipers, the coupling being between a man representing the God and a woman representing the Goddess.

The Blair Witch Project was the sensational independent movie of 1999, followed by *Blair Witch 2*, whose producers hired a Wiccan consultant and included a Wiccan character in a sympathetic role. In *Eyes Wide Shut*, the character played by Tom Cruise stumbles upon a high-toned soirée that turns out to be a celebration of the Hieros Gamos. Other films, like *Practical Magic* (1998), with Nicole Kidman and Sandra Bullock, try to make witchcraft seem everyday and normal. *The Craft* (1996), in which four high schoolers picturesquely worship the made-up pagan god Manon, became a cult classic for teenage girls. Another Wiccan consultant was brought in to make sure the religion was depicted fairly—which is to say, positively.

The U.S. armed forces recognize Wicca as an official religion. There are Wiccan representatives in the military's chaplaincy, and eighteen hundred active-duty soldiers claiming Wicca as their religion, according to the Department of Defense. The number is small, but still surprising, given the traditionalism of the military as a whole. The

Military Pagan Network claims that 100,000 "military personnel or dependants" practice Wicca, though this is surely an exaggeration. A few years ago, Republican congressman Bob Barr of Georgia raised a fuss about the fact that the country's largest military base, at Fort Hood, Texas, has a Wicca group that worships the goddess Freya. A fallen serviceman, Sgt. Patrick Stewart, who died in Afghanistan, was buried in 2005. A Wiccan pentacle adorns his grave marker at the Northern Nevada Veterans Memorial Cemetery in Fernley, Nevada.

The Bible would take a dim view of these developments. The Pentateuch advises that witches be stoned to death: "You shall not permit a witch to live" (Exodus 22:17)—though pagans nowadays claim, improbably, that the Hebrew word *m'chashefah* doesn't really mean witch at all, but "poisoner," as if Moses would have been perfectly okay with offering incense and wheat stalks to John Barleycorn. In fact, two verses later, this misconception is laid to rest: "One who brings offerings to the gods shall be destroyed—only to the Lord alone!" In the sixteenth and seventeenth centuries, at witch trials and witch burnings across Europe, and at Salem, Massachusetts, these biblical verses were eagerly enforced. Obviously, that is not what I am advocating.

The scriptural injunction against witchcraft is rooted in the second commandment, which begins: "You shall not recognize the gods of others in My presence." This much is familiar to everyone. But the second commandment goes on to say, "You shall not make yourself a carved image or any likeness of that which is in the heavens above or on the earth below or in the water beneath the earth. You shall not prostrate yourself to them nor worship them for I am the Lord your God—a jealous God, Who visits the sin of fathers upon children to the third and fourth generations, for My enemies; but who shows kindness for thousands [of generations] to those who love Me and observe My commandments."

What this language makes clear is that idolatry, polytheism, and witchcraft are really just three manifestations of the same error—to which, interestingly, Hebrew gives no name. They share the mistaken

assumption that divinity can be broken down into discrete entities
(gods) and manipulated for our benefit. By contrast, the God of the
Bible, a purely spiritual being, must be the ultimate unity and perfectly
free to act as He sees fit, unaffected by our attempted manipulations or
any other circumstances.

Polytheism and witchcraft, in other words, are associated with physical representations of divinity, since both have to do with putting the
god to work for you, and we are accustomed to using *objects* for our own
purposes (penicillin, an umbrella, and an air conditioner would be non-
magical examples). Where you find polytheism and magic, you are
likely to find idols. That's how Moses, returning from his forty days on
Mount Sinai, where he received the Ten Commandments, knew at the
very moment he caught sight of the Golden Calf that the Jews who had
made it in his absence had plummeted to the spiritual depths. God had
given him the two tablets for the same purpose that a groom gives his
bride a ring at their wedding, as a token of their union. Moses quickly
perceived that the Jews had severed the union, so the tablets lost their
sanctity, which is why he smashed them to pieces on the ground.

The word *jealous*, which the Bible uses in speaking of God only
when the context is idolatry, sums it all up. Where there is no possessiveness, there is no love. What wife would be pleased if her husband
could never be moved to jealousy, no matter how forwardly she might
flirt with other men? God doesn't actually feel jealous anger—being
perfect and unchanging, He is above being moved by human actions,
but He does act in response to polytheistic provocations in a way that
reminds us of the spouse consumed with passionate possessiveness. This
is the one sin for which God has no tolerance whatsoever.

Isaiah, Jeremiah, Amos, and their company got worked up about
nothing else to quite the degree that they did about idolatry. The passion against it dominates their words, which make it evident that their
fellow Jews were highly susceptible to the pagan temptation. Things got
so bad in the sixth century before the Common Era that idols were set
up even in the heart of biblical religion itself. In a vision, God showed

Ezekiel the holy Temple, which writhed in poisonous heathen images: "So I entered and I saw, and behold, every sort of image—disgusting creeping things and animals and all the idols of the house of Israel— were carved upon the wall all around. . . . And He said to me, 'Do you see, Son of Man? Now you will see yet again even greater abominations than these.' Then He brought me to the inner courtyard of the Temple of the Lord, and behold, at the entrance of the Sanctuary of the Lord . . . were some 25 men, with their backs to the Sanctuary of the Lord, with their faces turned eastward; they were bowing eastward to the sun" (Ezekiel 8:10, 15–16). The reader of the Bible is meant to tremble at the unthinkable desecration, and anyone who reads these passages with an open mind will indeed shudder.

The context for Ezekiel's prophecy was the lead-up to a terrifying Babylonian assault on the Holy Land. Jeremiah portrays God as warning, "And I will make Jerusalem heaps, and a den of dragons; and I will make the cities of Judah desolate, without an inhabitant" (Jeremiah 9:10). What did the Jews do to deserve this? "Because your fathers have forsaken me, says the Lord, and have walked after other gods, and have served them, and have worshipped them, and have forsaken me, and have not kept my law; and you have done worse than your fathers" (16:11–12). Jeremiah depicts idolatry as a form of adultery, with Israel in the role of the cheating wife, God as the scorned husband.

A great day for such spiritual adultery was October 3, 1965. In New York City, sheltered beneath the Statue of Liberty, President Lyndon B. Johnson signed into law the Immigration and Nationality Act. The act opened America's gates wide to immigrants, whose numbers previously had been restricted, immigrants bringing with them— beside the gift of their talents and love of freedom—a variety of religions that previously had, for the most part, been unknown in the United States.

This infusion of diverse beliefs and practices is applauded today by

well-meaning advocates of tolerance and pluralism. Harvard professor
Diane L. Eck wrote a celebratory book, *A New Religious America: How
a "Christian Country" Has Become the World's Most Religiously Diverse
Nation* (2001), about the transformation of the country's spiritual landscape:

> The huge white dome of a mosque with its minarets rises from the
> cornfields just outside Toledo, Ohio. You can see it as you drive by
> on the interstate highway. A great Hindu temple with elephants
> carved in relief at the doorway stands on a hillside in the western
> suburbs of Nashville, Tennessee. A Cambodian Buddhist temple
> and monastery with a hint of a Southeast Asian roofline is set in
> the farmlands south of Minneapolis, Minnesota. In suburban
> Fremont, California, flags fly from the golden domes of a new
> Sikh gurdwara on Hillside Terrace, now renamed Gurdwara Road.

The 2001 American Religious Identification Survey gives no figure
for the precise number of faiths represented in this most religiously diverse country on Earth. We can assume that there are dozens, if not
hundreds. But what is really remarkable is the surging growth of these
once-unfamiliar religions with their once-unfamiliar gods. Between
1990, the year of the last survey, and 2001, the number of both Bud-
dhists and Muslims more than doubled in size (growing from 401,000 to
1,082,000 and from 527,000 to 1,104,000, respectively), while the
number of Hindus more than tripled (from 227,000 to 766,000). Believers in New Age spirituality tripled (from 20,000 to 68,000), while
adherents of Native American religion doubled (from 47,000 to
103,000). Other new religions weren't even counted in 1990 but registered significant numbers in 2001. Apart from the 134,000 Wiccans,
there were 140,000 generic self-identified pagans, another 33,000
Druids, and 22,000 believers in the Afro-Caribbean religion Santeria.
    When you consider these figures in the context of America's tradi-
tional majority faith, Christianity, you get a clear picture of the chang-

ing spiritual scenery. Projecting these trends into the twenty-first century, we may imagine formerly Christian America becoming increasingly *heathen*.

By "heathen," I simply mean any religion that believes in a god or gods other than that of the Bible. Most heathen Americans are perfectly pleasant individuals, but they all run afoul of the second commandment. Some of the religions more recently represented in this country, like Hinduism, are colorfully polytheistic. Buddhism is presented in the media as nontheistic, and no doubt this is how a large proportion of its many recent converts among Americans of European ancestry conceive of it. Yet the religion as actually practiced in the Dalai Lama's homeland is uninhibitedly idolatrous.

Starkly monotheist Islam presents a different problem. Historian of religion Jack Miles, for one, has exerted himself mightily to remind fellow Americans that we all—Christians, Jews, Muslims—worship the same God. True, Allah simply means God, and the Quran alludes to many of the same personalities who inhabit the Bible, telling some startling tales about them, as if they were reflected in a fun-house mirror. However, Muslims regard the Bible as a falsified or distorted version of sacred history. They say only the Quran gets the story—of man's relationship to God—right. The Quran alone bears the marks of God's authentic authorship. If somebody came along and declared that Jack Miles's books are really distortions of the author's true beliefs, and if this person then published *his own* very different books under Jack Miles's name, purporting to give the true version of the distorted texts, we would be compelled to admit that the Jack Miles of the first set of books is not the same person as the Miles of the second. By the same token, we can only conclude that Muslims believe in a different God than do Jews and Christians, who equally venerate the God of the Hebrew Bible.

This situation—our society, with its many gods and idols, all increasingly accepted as normal and mainstream—is a striking historical development of a kind not seen in many centuries. Before the rise of the first Christian emperor, Constantine, the Roman Empire presented much the same picture of bewildering religious diversity. The second-century historian Cornelius Tacitus wrote mournfully of the imperial capital, "where all things horrible or shameful in the world collect and find a vogue." The shameful things that had collected there included Asiatic gods like Mithra, the Persian sun god, and the Oriental goddess, the Great Mother of the Gods, the Babylonian Astarte.

The calculated policy of religious tolerance was premised on the hope that welcoming and assimilating the gods of the conquered peoples of the East would make foreigners easier to rule; however, the strategy misfired. The new religions spread to the West, where they undermined the common culture on which the Roman state was based. Any religion brings with it a unique set of assumptions about what is important and what is trivial, what is right and what is wrong. However, to keep order, a nation or an empire must rely either on force or assent; and as Rome discovered, assent could only be obtained if the people shared the same basic assumptions. With the coming into vogue of the "horrible" Asiatic cults, the common culture of the Romans was lost.

But the pluralism of ancient Rome was itself not without precedent. The prophet Isaiah's declamations about Israel—jammed with foreign gods before the fall of the First Temple—recall those of Tacitus: "Therefore You have forsaken your people the house of Jacob, because they were filled with [sorceries] of the East and divinations, like the Philistines" (Isaiah 2:6). Since the arrival of the Puritans, Americans have thought of themselves as a new Israel, cultivating a Promised Land whose laws were modeled in many respects on the Mosaic legislation. Might God forsake America, too?

In speaking of idolatry American-style, I should make clear that I don't have in mind the familiar charge made by secular Europeans (and the Americans who admire them) that American prosperity is the

real source of modern idolatry. Europhiles condemn Americans for worshiping our Rolexes and BMWs, our McMansions and SUVs. Certainly
the pursuit of the good life, defined in terms of luxurious comforts, can
be taken to an unhealthy extreme; however, a bracing truth from the
Bible is that God doesn't mind our enjoying wealth. On the contrary,
He promises it as a reward for keeping His commandments. The society that obeys Him will enjoy not only peace but *prosperity*, which the
Bible illustrates in terms that can easily be translated to fit our own time
and place—ample grain and wine, bustling commerce, fertile wives,
children blushing with health, secure cities and towns. Note, however,
that the promise is made not to individuals but to the collective whole.
In a good society, bad people will still prosper. In a bad society, good
people will suffer.

Our true paganism, by contrast, is crystallized in the modern buzz-
word *tolerance*, or, alternatively, *compassion*. The only civic duty an
American has today is to decline all judgment of others—except when
it comes to those who refuse to accept tolerance as the ultimate virtue.
Thus traditional Christians, Jews, and anyone else who insists on what
Edward Said called "false universals"—universally applicable standards
of behavior and judgment—are the one group to whom tolerance is not
extended.

The word *tolerance* was once used to describe a very different attitude. Before the 1960s, it meant living peaceably with Bible-believing
and other well-behaved Americans, no matter how eccentric their sec-
tarian faith. That was *Christian* tolerance. What we have now is *pagan*
tolerance, which is quite a different thing. America, no less than Rome,
has always relied on its common moral culture, supplied by broadly
agreed-on religious principles, without which a constitution counts for
little. The Soviet Union also had a very noble-sounding constitution,
apparently full of the love of freedom and democracy, which was never
put into practice. Instead, to keep order, the Soviet state relied on co-
ercion. If you had told George Washington or John Adams, William
Penn or Roger Williams, that it's an American value to deliriously

praise the Hindu temple in a Nashville suburb or a Cambodian Buddhist monastery in rural Minnesota, they would have thought you were out of your mind. Even a freethinker like Jefferson, no orthodox Christian, hailed the victory of monotheism over "heathenism." As he wrote in 1820, "The religion of Jesus is founded in the Unity of God, and this principle chiefly gave it triumph over the rabble of heathen gods then acknowledged." The American experiment has been suffused with biblical monotheism to its core. To dispense with it (which is apparently where we are headed) will mean a very different kind of experiment, one whose outcome is far from assured.

Not only are we modern folk more likely than ever before to give a respectful hearing to heathenism but the second commandment itself, with its one-God-fits-all perspective, is increasingly condemned as a formula for intolerance, hatred, and terrorism. Doesn't insisting on the worship of one God inevitably feed the impulse to persecute those who worship differently, or who worship a different God, or no God at all? *Atlantic Monthly* magazine blogger Andrew Sullivan has wondered if the horror of Islamic terror cannot be attributed to "something inherent in religious monotheism."

In a painful irony, it's often the modern descendants of the prophets themselves who take the most aggressive stand in defense of paganism. "The Holocaust did not happen in pagan Europe," Abraham Foxman, national director of the ADL, has pointed out. "It happened in Christian Europe." Jonathan Kirsch, a columnist for the *Los Angeles Times*, recently brought forth a solemnly praised book extolling the virtues of ancient paganism, *God Against the Gods: The History of the War Between Monotheism and Polytheism*. Writes Kirsch, "We make a mistake if we write off the pagan tradition as something crude and demonic. After all, the values that the Western world embraces and celebrates—cultural diversity and religious liberty—are pagan values."

———

If the Ten Commandments forbid idolatry, it can't be that only a dummy, an evil person, or someone from the distant past could fall into the trap of worshiping false gods. If they are indeed still relevant to our lives, then polytheism and idolatry must be something to which we are all tempted in some form. We'll see how deep in American life the temptation goes, and how real are the dangers.

Jewish mysticism teaches that the other gods mentioned in the Bible are not merely a fiction, having nothing whatever to do with *the* God. Not for nothing does the Bible almost invariably speak of them, these "other gods," in language that would lead you to think they were indeed real. If your wife told you to stop looking at "other women," would you assume she thought these other women were a figment of your imagination? Says Moses in Deuteronomy, "You shall not follow after gods of others, of the gods of the peoples that are around you" (6:14). The second commandment uses this formulation: "You shall not recognize the gods of others in My presence."

What could this mean? How can a religion that claims there is only one God refer to others as though they really exist?

A rabbi I admire says that polytheism sees only the *backside* of Reality. The backside of a human being or any creature is still part of the creature, but to take the back as the whole thing is a gross error. After all, it is from the back of a human and most other creatures that waste is emitted. That's why in biblical Hebrew, false gods are called *gillulim*—literally, "dung balls." According to the Talmud, one particularly nasty false god, Baal Peor, alluded to in the Book of Numbers, had as its unique form of worship a ritual defecation on the idol itself.

The nineteenth-century Italian mystic Elijah Benamozegh defined polytheism as "the worship of one or several attributes of God to the exclusion of all others." Thus "a trace of the authentic idea of God survives in the various pagan divinities, mixed with error." The God of Scripture can therefore be understood as "the synthesis of all the partial truths represented by the divinities of paganism—whence the name 'God of gods' which we find in the Bible."

From what I have just said, neopaganism doesn't sound so terrible. After all, it contains "a trace of the authentic idea of God"! To see what's awful about modern paganism, and how powerfully the pagan temptation ramifies in our moral culture, you have to understand three things. I will start with what's bad, continue with what's worse, and conclude with what is truly terrifying.

First, the bad: American polytheism is simply the religious face of the cultural relativism that has undermined our former certainties in other areas. Rabbi Benamozegh saw it coming more than a century ago: "Polytheism is but relativism in religion: a different truth for every mind, a different god for every seeker." Since in classical paganism everyone can pick his own personal god, or his own personal pantheon, that means you may also pick your own personal moral system. It follows that no culture's conception of right and wrong can be definitive. This is multiculturalism in a nutshell. What, if not relativism, is the very gospel of our time? When Wiccans worship their gods, they are only giving an explicitly religious cast to an idea that is accepted by the vast majority of those Americans who consider themselves to be sophisticated and urbane. And many others who might not personally be able to tell you what the unfamiliar word relativism means but who have simply absorbed the values implicit in mainstream American media, entertainment, and education are relativists nonetheless.

Obviously, a country like ours that doesn't regard its norms as absolutes, good and true and therefore worth defending, will lack the will to defeat those who would challenge her. This is what happened to pagan Rome. The United States is challenged by radical Muslim terrorists, whose victory would be an unmitigated curse—say in the form of a portable nuclear bomb detonated in lower Manhattan. We hear this threat discussed as if the only defense against it were not moral but purely technical—nuclear nonproliferation legislation, technology to detect radiological traces in cargo containers unloaded at our ports, that sort of thing. Jeremiah and all the other prophets, while not disdaining practical matters, saw the best defense as moral, centered on the rejection of false gods.

The problem with today's ideal of "tolerance" is that under the guise of making us better people, it robs us of the vital capacity to make moral distinctions, to discern a bad idea and call it bad. When tolerance meant accepting with equanimity the right of every person to be a moron as long as he didn't harm himself or others, you were still free to regard your neighbor's ideas as wrong. No more. In religion especially, we are encouraged not to think of "truth" as a criterion at all. Even among those who regard themselves as "spiritual" types, to say you want to know what's true about God invites the charge of bad taste. In a vital area, we are turning our brains to mush.

But there is something worse than relativism. For what or whom, really, do polytheism and multiculturalism venerate? In fashioning idols to represent the forces of nature—the backside of Reality—the pagans of old chose to depict fire, water, earth, and wind as human beings. They could easily have portrayed these elements in the guise of nature's other creatures, but for the most part they did not. Without realizing it, the ancient pagans were depicting, and bowing to, not nature, but themselves. We do the same.

This is clearly suggested in the books of another best-selling author, Elaine Pagels, who has done so much to revive the ancient heresy of Gnosticism. Readers of The Da Vinci Code learned a bit about the Gnostics, whose version of Christianity was suppressed by Constantine in the fourth century along with, according to Dan Brown, the worship of the sacred feminine. Gnosticism isn't about the Goddess, but it lends itself very well to modern Goddess spirituality. The point of it was that rather than looking to some authority outside yourself for knowledge (gnosis) about God, you could look within yourself.

Pagels's 2003 book, Beyond Belief: The Secret Gospel of Thomas, spent thirteen weeks on the New York Times best-seller list. The apocryphal text, which claims to present Jesus' "secret sayings," was among those discovered near Nag Hammadi, Egypt, in 1945. Pagels thinks it dates to the first century of the Common Era, and she offers a Gnostic alternative to the orthodox Gospel of John. In the latter, the Jews are depicted as assailing Jesus for "making yourself God." In the Gospel of Thomas, Jesus deputizes his followers not to think of him as the Deity but to make *themselves* God. "Thomas's gospel encourages the hearer not so much to *believe in Jesus,* as John requires, as to *seek to know God* through one's own, divinely given capacity." This is not the same approach to religious experience that other mystics, both Jews and Christians, have adopted: "Christian mystics, like their Jewish and Muslim counterparts, have always been careful not to identify themselves with God. But the Gospel of Thomas teaches that recognizing one's affinity with God is the key to the kingdom of God." Thomas himself puts it this way: "Jesus said: 'If you bring forth what is within you, what you bring forth will save you. If you do not bring forth what is within you, what you do not bring forth will destroy you.' "

Today's neopagans similarly think they have discovered their inner god. Janice Van Cleve of Seattle's Women of the Goddess Circle, a Dianic Wiccan and lesbian activist, offered me her own taxonomy of world religions. In her opinion, they are divided between those faiths that locate God inside the believer and those that locate Him outside: "People who look without write books about God—Bibles, Qurans. Only the three major monotheist religions look without, but a majority of the world's peoples look within for their spirituality. All deity is within ourselves." She cited Buddhism, Taoism, and paganism as examples of inward-looking religions.

So then the Goddess that Janice venerates is to be identified with . . . Janice? "Yeah," she says, "she's me."

Still another best-selling author, Neale Donald Walsch, has written a series of remarkable books (*Conversations with God,* 136 weeks on the *Times* best-seller list, published in 1996 and followed by five best-selling sequels), in which he claims to have talked with God and received brand-new information about Him. His fans attend five-hundred-dollar weekends—the "Meeting of Messengers": "If you are one of the many people who experience that you are also having Conversations with God," says his Web site, "and have been longing for a 'safe place' in which to tell others about your experience, you will be very happy to know that such a space has now been created." Walsch's perfectly nonjudgmental God is definitely not the God of Scripture. His most recent book asserts that within the next thirty years mankind will create and embrace a totally new God, much along the lines of the deity that Walsch says has been talking to him.

Silly? Harmless? The rabbis of the Talmud saw the danger posed by the little "god" that lurks within the self. They pointed to a cryptic verse in Psalms: "There shall be no strange god within you, nor shall you bow before an alien god" (81:10). Rabbi Avin explained, "What is this 'strange god' that is literally inside a person? It can only be the evil impulse" (Shabbat 105b). The rabbis understood that a person is subject to the influence of a good impulse and an evil one. When he obeys the evil impulse, it is the "strange god" within him that he serves.

This is the third thing you need to know about the modern tendency to dismiss the warning of the second commandment: that as moral beings, we are eternally balanced between good and evil, and that self-worship may anoint the evil impulse as our guide and master. In some people, this impulse is stronger than in others. I worry about people in whose heart the balance tilts toward evil, and about our own wider culture, where that balance seems unsteady.

It has happened before, paganism descending to barbarism. And why should it not, when popular American morality makes reference to no objective canon of criteria for judging our actions (such as you will find in the Bible)? Even when in theory restrained by the strictures of orthodox religious tradition, men can treat one another abominably. When they are constrained only by their own inner voice, the possibilities become still more terrible.

Jewish tradition preserves memories of what real paganism was like before Christianity erased it. In the Mishnah, compiled around 200 C.E., the rabbis laid out detailed rules for dealing with polytheists. Their practical advice can be summarized in three words: Watch your back. "A man should not be secluded with them, because they are suspected of bloodshed" (Avodah Zarah 2:1). Simply getting a haircut from an idolater was deemed too risky if there was no one else around to make sure he didn't slit your throat. You should not even allow your animals to be secluded with them, because they are suspected of committing the grossest sexual immorality—bestiality.

James Frazer's classic *The Golden Bough* (1922), a treasury of arcane information about the world's premonotheist past, is beloved by critics of Christianity for its tracing of Christian customs to pagan antecedents, but the truth is that Frazer is much more devastating about paganism itself. His section on human sacrifice makes for an eye-opening read. To ensure a plentiful harvest, the ancient Mexicans slaughtered "new-born babes at sowing [of the maize], older children when the grain sprouted, and so on till it was fully ripe, when they sacrificed old men." The Pawnee, those ecologically sensitive souls, were not above sacrificing children. This was still going on as late as 1837 or 1838, when white men brought back the tale of how a fourteen-year-old Sioux girl was offered up for the success of the maize crop:

> Her body having been painted half red and half black, she was attached to a sort of gibbet and roasted for some time over a slow fire, then shot to death with arrows. The chief sacrificer next tore out her heart and devoured it. While her flesh was still warm it was cut in small pieces from the bones, put in little baskets, and taken to a neighboring cornfield. There the head chief took a piece of the flesh from a basket and squeezed a drop of blood upon the newly-deposited grains of corn. His example was followed by the rest, till all the seed had been sprinkled with blood; it was then covered up with earth.

When Frazer wrote his book, the British in eastern India were still trying to suppress human sacrifice to the goddess Anna Kuari, "who can give good crops and make a man rich. . . . The victims are poor waifs and strays whose disappearance attracts no notice."

In his *Rise and Fall of the Third Reich*, William Shirer tells of the Nazi plans for the churches of Germany. The intention was to "exterminate irrevocably . . . the strange and foreign Christian faiths imported into Germany in the ill-omened year 800." The Christian churches would be replaced with a "National Church," enshrining what historian Michael Burleigh calls "the dark irrationalist world of Teutonic myth." Where did such a mad idea come from? Another scholar, Harvard's Richard Noll, has blazingly depicted an earlier eruption of neopaganism, at the turn of the twentieth century, purporting to revive the ancient race-centered tradition of Teutonic spirituality. Hitlerism flowed directly from the neopagan impulse in its most recent previous incarnation.

To take the second commandment lightly is to risk opening up the darkest channels in the human soul, allowing them to flow through our own streets, offices, and homes. What seems benign, mundane— Wiccans frolicking on the bright, sunny shores of Puget Sound— conceals the dark terror of what can be unleashed if the time and conditions are ripe. At such a time, as in Nazi Germany, the most obscene crimes are permitted because there is no objective force or authority capable of forbidding them. After all, the inner voice that might have restrained us is our own. The smiling, compassionate countenance of modern-day paganism, spreading far beyond the confines of an eccentric Goddess movement, would then be revealed as the feral, snarling face of our own worst selves.

THIRD COMMANDMENT

GOD ABUSE

You shall not take the Name of the Lord, your God, in vain,
for the Lord will not absolve anyone who takes His Name in vain.
(Exodus 20:7)

I'm driving to work one morning, listening to Seattle's NPR station, and a local host is interviewing a scholar who's talking about an exhibition of the Dead Sea Scrolls that's on view at the Pacific Science Center. The scholar is explaining how the ancient Jewish religious sect that produced the scrolls took the greatest care in writing God's name, which they would not dare to speak outside the sacred precincts of Jerusalem's holy temple. The professional guest tells the genial host that no one today is really sure how God's name was pronounced, that Jehovah is certainly not correct, but that most scholars think it was pronounced as—and then he blithely says the name with all the reverence of a Starbucks barista calling out the name of the guy whose tall mocha latte is ready. He explains that some religious people even today hesitate to say this name, whether in a sacred or profane context, and then he himself pronounces it again—casually.

"But you said it," comments the host, interrupting, and we can hear the sly smile in his voice. The guest makes no reply. Of course he said it. And why not? No sophisticated person, the kind who listens to NPR, takes the third commandment seriously.

Later, I'm exiting Interstate 5 to downtown Seattle at the Madison Street ramp, where inevitably there is a homeless person stationed at the stop sign immediately off the freeway where you turn left. A grimy cap slouches down over an unshaven face; accusing eyes appraise each driver who passes by. A hand-printed cardboard sign is propped up beside him. The sign reads GOD BLESS. STRANDED. BROKE. HUNGRY. PLEASE HELP. Some days there's a different vagrant, a different sign, but always, in some form or another, the invocation of the Deity.

In New York, more of a pedestrian's city, the calculation that bestowing God's blessing means a better shot at getting a donation is also well known. There, panhandlers more commonly say it to your back—"God bless you!"—once you've walked by without giving, which functions either as a euphemistic curse or as a guilt inducer.

Americans—still a religious people, or greatly impressed by the notion of religion anyway—understand the advantage of having God's brand name attached to your enterprise. The urban homeless share a keen appreciation of this. There is little difference between this and the politician's calling down of the Divinity's approval upon his campaign for office. It's always Republicans who are tarred by the media with dragging God into the muck of electoral politics. Pundits guffawed at George W. Bush when he named Jesus as his favorite philosopher. We need to consider what if anything is wrong with using your Savior's name in such a way. Certainly, however, it is *not* only conservatives who do this. When campaigning for the presidency, Bill Clinton was not shy about giving the impression that God blessed his candidacy. I recall being present at the 1992 Democratic Convention in New York when the Arkansas governor gave his now largely forgotten "New Covenant" speech, in which he appeared to assume upon himself the visionary mantle of biblical prophecy, quoting a scriptural verse:

"Where there is no vision, the people perish" (Proverbs 29:18). The phrase "New Covenant" was intended to recall the New Testament, which means the same thing.

The ancient peoples of pre-Christian Europe and the Middle East handled the names of their gods with trembling wariness. A city would have a patron deity, but, whether in Rome or Assyria, this god's personal name was kept shrouded in secrecy. A name, it was understood, was a mystic, powerful thing. Whether belonging to a man or a god, it could be used to overcome the will of the person or being, forcing him into virtual slavery. If the city's foes possessed the secret name, they could call the god out of the city he protected, rendering the place defenseless.

The Jews treated their Deity's name, or names, with greater reverence than any other people of antiquity. *God* is not God's name, but merely the anglicized version of the Old High German *got*, referring generically to any god. In Hebrew, God's primary personal designation is represented by a word comprising four consonants, a *yud*, a *heh*, a *vav*, followed by a *heh*. The word thus formed is called the Tetragrammaton, from the Greek for "four letters." The Hebrew of the Bible was originally written without vowels, so that there are any number of possible ways the Tetragrammaton could have been vocalized. In printed Torah texts to this day, the word is still written without vowels. When Jews pray or read from the Torah in a formal synagogue setting, they pronounce the word as if it were written "*Adonai*," a euphemism, which simply means "my Lord." Outside the context of chanting and liturgy, Jews call God "*Hashem*," Hebrew for "the Name."

The mystification that surrounded the Name was not always a feature of Jewish religious life. Very early on, in biblical times, its pronunciation was widely known. Then boorish and unscrupulous individuals began to abuse the name, uttering it indiscriminately. So it was taught only to the worthy and the pious. The sacerdotal hierarchy in the Jerusalem Temple knew how the name was pronounced. It was uttered in the daily blessing of the people by the priests, and again on the year's holiest occasion, the Day of Atonement (Yom Kippur), by the high priest. God's name was lost from memory, or almost, following 70 C.E., when the Temple was destroyed by Roman forces. As a second-century rabbinic sage Abba Saul warned, anyone thereafter who knew the Name and treated it lightly would have his soul extinguished upon death and thus would enjoy no reward in heaven.

The Talmudic rabbis understood a verse in Exodus (3:15) as an instruction from God to conceal the name. While the verse is customarily translated one way, "This is My Name *forever*," in fact the Hebrew word taken to mean "forever," *l'olam*, is written as if it meant something totally different, "to hide," *l'alem*: "This is My Name *to hide*." A few kabbalists down through the centuries preserved the hidden name, so that even today it is known to certain mystagogues, who, however, decline to identify themselves. It may even be that the name is not merely forbidden to be uttered. It may literally be unpronounceable, in the sense that without supernatural help, the human tongue cannot by nature give voice to it.

Biblical traditions have preserved other personal names of God, similarly shrouded in bafflement. One name, no fewer than 216 letters in length, is said to be coded in three consecutive verses of the Torah (Exodus 14:19–21). According to the Zohar, the Jewish mystical work that interprets the Bible, the entire text of the Torah can be read as one long text string, without the usual breaks between words and, of course, without vowels, which then comprises other names of God—or possibly one very, very long name. When Jews read publicly from the Torah, they are in effect calling upon God by His most comprehensive, data-rich name. Every name represents a different way that God manifests Himself to people.

The Tetragrammaton is sometimes called "the Ineffable Name." Ineffability means being impossible to grasp or express in language. Just as the name is ineffable, so is God Himself. He infinitely exceeds our ability to express anything definitive about Him. All we really know is what He asks us to do with our own bodies, souls, selves. That's what commandments are.

The pious men and women of the ancient pagan societies knew the power that comes with knowing a very special name. Biblical tradition, too, perceives in God's names a transcendent source of miracles and wonder-working. The person who wields the Name can do tremendous good, or tremendous violence. In the Book of Exodus, before Moses embarks on the God-given mission to liberate the Hebrew people from Egyptian slavery, he has a curious experience. One day, while going about his business, he happens upon a disturbing scene. An Egyptian man is abusing a Hebrew man, striking him viciously for no apparent reason. Looking about to make sure no one is around, Moses kills the Egyptian and hides the body in the sand. How did he strike the death-blow? With a fist? With a club? From linguistic evidence, Jewish tradition teaches that he spoke the Ineffable Name and the Egyptian fell dead. The Name could be used for other, happier purposes, as well. The kabbalists of medieval Spain said that by combining and meditating upon letters of various divine names, they could ascend through levels of heaven and encounter God in a manner beyond normal human experience.

An American missionary in Sri Lanka told of saving twenty-eight children from the 2004 Indian Ocean tsunami that killed more than 100,500 people. The missionary, Daylan Sanders, spoke on CNN about the thirty-foot wave that was bearing down on his Samaritan Children's Home, about how he gathered children into a motorboat, then called on the wave "in the name of Jesus Christ to stand still. And I thought I was imagining at the time that the massive wall of water, it stood. I'm not one given to exaggeration. I saw, as if something was holding it back, some invisible force or hand. It just stood." According to Sanders, villagers nearby who survived by clinging to coconut trees witnessed and later confirmed what he saw.

God's name has powers that go beyond the seemingly magical. We know this from our mundane experience. Simply bringing up God in an ordinary human conversation can send the interaction spinning off in unforeseen directions. Merely hearing the word *God* rouses our passions. Speaking of Him can make people mad. It can also bring them to tears—of joy or gratitude or longing or disappointment. It certainly catches people's attention. That's why politicians and others find it so useful to be able to speak of Him comfortably, naturally. Americans would have a hard time electing a president with a stiff, at-arm's-length way of dealing with the subject of God when, as always happens, it comes up in an electoral season. For a candidate, simply being able to say "God" in a convincing fashion—just that word—can mean the difference between victory and defeat. In the most powerful country in the world, *that's* power.

This power is related to the authority it conveys. Being able to name God as your patron, your sponsor bestows a seal of approval from the ultimate authority. Moses knew this. He met God for the first time, well before the Exodus and the giving of the Ten Commandments, during the incident of the burning bush. He was then a shepherd in the land of Midian. He had fled there to escape Pharaoh's henchmen, who sought his life for killing the Egyptian who had assaulted Moses' fellow Israelite. One day when he was grazing his flock beside a lonely desert mountain, Mount Sinai, he caught sight of a bush that burned with a strange, unearthly fire, by which it was not consumed. God spoke to him from the fire. In the course of their conversation, the Lord instructed Moses that he was to call his people, the Jews, out of Egypt to come worship Him at this very mountain. But Moses asked what he should do if they balked: "Look, when I come to the Israelites and say to them, 'The God of your father has sent me to you,' and they say to me, 'What is His name?' what shall I say to them?"

God replied, in Robert Alter's recent translation, " '*Ehyeh-'Asher-'Ehyeh*, I-Will-Be-Who-I-Will-Be." He continued: "Thus shall you say to the Israelites, ' '*Ehyeh* has sent me to you.' " Evidently, Moses was too bewildered to reply, because God said further, "Thus shall you say to the

Israelites: 'The Lord God of your fathers, the God of Abraham, the God of Isaac, and the God of Jacob, sent me to you. That is My Name forever and thus am I invoked in all ages" (Exodus 3:13–15).

In other words, if the Israelites challenged the claim Moses made of his right to lead them, he was to answer by citing God's permission to use His name, verified by the three names God now revealed to him: 'Ehyeh-'Asher-'Ehyeh, 'Ehyeh, and "the Lord," which is the way English translators conventionally represent the Tetragrammaton. In the Hebrew text, at the climax of the passage, God reveals to Moses the Ineffable Name.

Messing with God means trifling with His ineffability, His power, and His authority. Do modern Americans fall afoul of this imperative? To see that they do, and how, we need to take a closer look at the language of the third commandment.

From the translation I've given in the epigraph for this chapter, you'll see that the phrase "in vain" appears twice: "You shall not take the name of the Lord, your God, *in vain*, for the Lord will not absolve anyone who takes His name *in vain*." Both instances of the adverbial use of the phrase are translated from the Hebrew *la'shav*. But a Bible translation dating, according to tradition, to the second century of the Common Era, does something interesting with this double use of the same language. The translation, attributed to an aristocratic Roman convert to Judaism named Onkelos and composed in an ancient Semitic language, Aramaic, has a special authority. According to one account, it was revealed to Moses on Sinai along with the Ten Commandments and the rest of the Torah but was only written down, much later, by Onkelos. In rendering the third commandment, Onkelos translated the first *la'shav* one way, and the second in a different way, signaling that the Hebrew word has two meanings. The first *la'shav* he translated more or less as we do in English: "for nothing, for foolishness." The second, he translated as "falsely." That is, a person may violate this commandment either by "lifting up" God's name "for nothing" or, alternatively, by "lifting up" His name "falsely."

Broadly, "lifting up" has two meanings that correspond respectively with the two meanings of *la'shav*, "for nothing" and "for falsehood."

First, in Biblical Hebrew, "lifting up" can simply mean "speaking," because speaking requires lifting up your voice. This would convey much the same sense as the conventional English translation of the third commandment. In other words, "You shall not speak God's name for nothing, for foolishness." This would include using a divine name to express your annoyance at stubbing your toe on a rock, crying out "Goddamn it!" which literally means "May God damn this rock!" Cursing a rock is pretty foolish. Strictly considered, to be in violation of the commandment, you would have to needlessly use and thereby profane an actual name of God, like the Tetragrammaton. But more loosely, even using a word like *God*, which refers to God without being His name, is something that a sensitive person would avoid if there is no good reason for it. In English, we call this first kind of "lifting up" of God's name "profanity."

The second kind is more interesting, more reprehensible, and more dangerous. It involves lifting up His name "for falsehood" as you would lift up a banner or a flag. A ship at sea may hoist up a national flag. If the ship flies the flag of a country under false pretenses—identifying itself as American when it's really registered as a Canadian vessel, or vice versa—we say it is "sailing under false colors." People often sail under false colors, claiming a distinction or an affiliation they don't actually possess. An example would be comporting yourself in a very religious, pious fashion, impressing others with the outward appearance of godliness either because you find this useful or because it tickles your vanity, when, in fact, you are not godly, or when you are less pious than you pretend. The commandment would then be translated, "You shall not lift up God's name for falsehood."

There is no concise English term for this sin. To violate the third commandment in this manner is really to use God for your own purposes, ones that have nothing to do with Him. It means abusing His name. For want of a better term, let's call it "God abuse."

While profanity and God abuse may sound like different sins, the second is just an intensification of the first. For both arise from the same attitude, which is the real, underlying problem—namely, that it is acceptable to trifle with God. When we don't take God seriously, while at the same time refusing to dislodge Him entirely from our consciousness, inevitably the result is a violation of the third commandment. In a way, this is even more of an insult than it is to break the first commandment (denying His power to shape our destinies) or the second (setting up other powers in your own mind to rival His). It trivializes Him. That's why the penalty is so severely worded: "for the Lord will not absolve anyone who takes His name in vain."

A mericans are champions at messing with God, maybe because, unlike Europeans, we still say we believe in Him.

In a vulgar culture where "f**k patois" (as Tom Wolfe calls it) pervades to the extent that the word itself—rarely denoting sexual intercourse—barely even registers as obscene, it may seem quaint to worry about people saying "Goddamn it." Yet the transgressiveness of that phrase remains dimly evident to most of us.

Thus in 2001, when TV producer Aaron Sorkin wanted to boost his "controversial" NBC drama series, The West Wing, to new levels of sophistication, he broadcast in a New York Times article that he planned to assault an ancient network taboo: "he wants a character to curse in a way that uses the Lord's name in vain." He already had had the show's lead character, Martin Sheen playing a fictional U.S. president, curse God. When President Josiah Bartlet's personal secretary succumbed to an untimely death and Bartlet had learned that he himself had contracted MS, he let loose with a profane prayer addressed to God, whom he called a "son of a bitch" and a "reckless thug." In a bizarre touch, however, to avoid offense, the prayer was delivered in Latin.

Thanks to the influence of shock radio and racy cable shows, the 1990s saw a dramatic coarsening of language used on network TV. Between 1990 and 2000, according to the Parents Television Council, the average number of vulgarities of all kinds per hour on network broadcasts quintupled. Between 2001 and 2004, overall complaints of broadcast indecency soared from under a thousand in a year to over a million. If TV characters taking God's name in vain isn't quite routine yet, we can assume that, based on the overall trajectory, it soon will be. The flood of vulgarity is such that no pious custom, however venerable, like respecting the word *God*, can withstand being swept away.

Yet speaking of God for no sacred purpose, but, rather, for nothing, for foolishness, isn't always the grave sin that some, not fully understanding the subtleties of the third commandment, would depict it as. One thinks of a little news item out of Orlando, Florida, from 2004 about a billboard for Moe's Southwest Grill. The billboard, promoting Moe's Southwestern-style tacos and burritos, carried God's endorsement:

WELCOME TO MOE'S!

—GOD

A local pastor fumed, "You just don't use God's name that way. It should not be taken lightly and casually. It is sacred. There are consequences to doing something like this. Judgment can come on those who use the Lord's name in such a vain fashion."

The offense involved in some trifling uses of God's name, especially if it's not really His name, can be mild. That this is the case is made clear when you consider *why* it is we swear profanely.

There is a whole literature addressing the enigma of swearing, a universal human phenomenon. Or almost universal: Japanese, American Indians, and most Polynesians do not have swearing in their native cultural background. Ashley Montagu wrote the most sweeping and historically informed study of the subject, *The Anatomy of Swearing* (1967).

What exactly constitutes swearing? As Montagu uses it, *swearing* is a generic term encompassing *profanity* (calling out the name of your deity in a moment of sudden anger—e.g, "Jesus H. Christ!"); *cursing* (a more serious endeavor, calling down divine wrath on another person or even an inanimate object, such as "Goddamn you!"); *blasphemy* (cursing the Deity himself, à la Martin Sheen's execration on *The West Wing*); *obscenity* (using dirty words, not a violation of the third commandment at all); and *vulgarity* (using crude words, as in the English *bloody*).

In Montagu's interpretation, we swear for the same reason babies cry—to relieve stress. He traces the history of this cultural form back to prehistoric days. The heart of ancient man might suddenly swell with anger at his fellow man, but killing the other person presented a problem. Bands of human beings tended to be small in their number of members, so the loss of one person could be catastrophic for the survival of the group as a whole. Some substitute for physical assault needed to be found, and it was: cursing. You invoked the gods, calling on them to punish your opponent. This provided some degree of emotional relief. Cursing could also take as its object the person himself doing the cursing. That is, by way of lending credibility to a sworn statement, you might provisionally invoke the god against yourself, as in "So help me God," which really means, "If I'm lying, then God will not help me; that is, He will abandon me." To swear falsely in this manner would be a prime example of the second of our two senses of "taking God's name in vain"—that in which you utter His name falsely. Later, with the secularization of most human cultures, when God's anger was not feared as much, cursing in the name of a deity was downgraded to something less serious, profanity, which means no genuine harm to its object. This is the difference between "Goddamn it!" (profanity) and "Goddamn you!" (cursing).

Profanity and cursing, much like laughing and crying, Montagu writes, "have in common the function of acting as relief valves for sudden surges of energy that require the appropriate form of expression.

What these separate forms of behavior also have in common is the reestablishment of the psychological equilibrium of the organism." He compares swearing to "an emotional orgasm," which may even result in "improved health."

There is reason to doubt this. For one thing, experts on swearing don't all agree that it alleviates emotional strain. Robert Graves, who wrote his own small book on the subject, *Lars Porsena: Or the Future of Swearing* (1927), took the exact opposite view to that of Ashley Montagu. Graves thought it works as "a nervous stimulant in a crisis," a far cry from an orgasm.

When swearing in response to a burst of stress, what we are really doing is making an eye blink–fast judgment that the swearing will relieve the stress. But it doesn't. Anyone who suffers from anger knows that in working your way up to a full fit of temper, there is a point you pass in which you choose to give vent freely in words to your feelings. The decision to vent pumps up your anger still more. The stress chemicals are then released into your blood, and recovering will take some time. If you had resisted the temptation to voice your frustration, it would have passed much more quickly. You think you are releasing anger just as you might release steam from a vent. But you are not a vent and your anger isn't steam. So it is with swearing. Giving in to the impulse, while this seems healthy, actually ensures that your negative emotion will take longer to pass.

In such a situation, taking God's name in vain is in a way its own punishment. It really is for nothing, for foolishness. It's like overindulgence in alcohol, which similarly holds out the promise of draining off stress. But a hangover brings its own emotional costs, as an addiction to liquor certainly does, so that the alcoholic ends up chasing his stress with a medicine, the administering of which only results in more and more stress.

Even if modern profaners, vainly seeking escape from distress, had the Tetragrammaton itself on their lips, the abuse would be small compared with the abuse of God's name in the other sense we noted earlier: not for nothing or for foolishness, but for falsehood. The Bible often speaks of God's name as a synonym for His reputation in the world. Jeremiah pleaded with God to forgive the Jews, save them from their enemies, because otherwise the world would think that He lacked the power to rescue His people. God's name was at stake: "Though our iniquities testify against us, O Lord, act for Your Name's sake" (14:7). "You are our Father, our King, and Your Name is proclaimed upon us— do not set us aside" (14:9). Given the power of God's reputation even in our secular world, there is a temptation to cloak oneself in it, to profit from it, enjoy its prestige. This typically results in a falsification of what God intends His name to stand for in the world.

The Talmud has a name for this, *hillul Hashem*, "desecration of the Name." It is one of the most heinous sins, because messing with God's reputation turns other people away from Him. Judaism has traditionally discouraged outward displays of piety, where avoidable, for just this reason. To be outwardly, obviously "religious" is dangerous business. When a religious person wears God's name, figuratively, on his person, and then proceeds to falsify the name by doing something publicly that hurts other people or merely seems uncultured or distasteful, those who observe him will naturally think, If that's what a religious man or woman does, who needs religion? Who needs God? Anyone looking for an excuse to dismiss religion will find a ready justification.

Jeremiah had something like this in mind when he urged his listeners to use God's name in taking oaths only if they personally merited doing this: "If you swear, 'As the Lord lives!' in truth, in justice, and in righteousness, the nations will bless themselves through [Israel]" (Jeremiah 4:2). If you live in a manner consistent with truth, justice, and righteousness, then by all means attach God's name to yourself. You will thus cause other peoples to bless themselves in *your* name. If that is not how you live, then don't let God's name pass your lips.

One thinks of the Catholic priests whose sexual abuse of teenage boys has come to light in such massive numbers. According to the John Jay College of Criminal Justice, over the past half century some 4 percent of the U.S. priesthood engaged in this form of abuse of vulnerable young people—and of God's name. The Catholic Church's claim to represent God on Earth has been gruesomely mangled, through its own neglect. Meanwhile, every month seems to bring some new media report of various crimes, molestations, grotesqueries committed by clergy members of other denominations, Protestants and Jews, or by showily "religious" laymen.

Yet, while these desecrators of God's Name do incalculable spiritual harm, usually you can at least say in their defense that they never meant it to happen. They thought their misdeeds would never come to light or be noticed, remaining strictly between the offender and God. The sinners worked hard not to get caught, which counts for something. In a different category is the God abuser who sets out deliberately, publicly, and falsely to use God's reputation, and in doing so deploys all the arts of self-promotion at his disposal. Desecrating God's Name is central to his purpose. This ultimate God abuse is committed for the sake of personal prestige, career advancement, to assuage a guilty conscience, to promote a favored vice or addiction. In our culture, it's alarmingly common. It is tolerated, smiled upon, even admired.

It is done in political advocacy, in intellectual life, in journalism, in theology. By cherry-picking and twisting real scriptural verses, you can construct an intelligent-sounding "biblical" argument for just about any perverse or just plain silly opinion one may imagine.

A frequently heard view ascribes the violation of the third commandment mainly to political and religious conservatives, who, it's said, use religion to promote their agenda. And what is that agenda? Well, say critics, it's religion. They point to an unscripted statement by President George W. Bush five days after September 11, in which he called the country to join him in a "crusade" against Islamic terrorism. They cite the president's remark that "freedom is not America's gift to the world, it's the almighty God's gift to humanity," which seemed to place America in the role of God's agent on Earth. As Bruce Bartlett, a veteran of the Reagan and the first Bush administrations, told the *New York Times Magazine* in October 2004, Bush "truly believes he's on a mission from God." He has, Bartlett said, "this sort of weird, Messianic idea of what he thinks God has told him to do."

Even if a president really did believe he was channeling the Almighty, using religion to advance the cause of your religious beliefs in the public realm doesn't violate the third commandment. Sometimes, however, liberals will argue that actually Republicans employ God to promote a *secular* agenda. As one liberal Texas clergyman, Pastor Howard Batson of Amarillo's First Baptist Church, somewhat hyperbolically declaimed during the 2004 presidential race, "I can think of no evil more evil than using God's name in such a way as to gain secular political power." This opens up a big philosophical and religious question: that of the role of faith in public life.

C. S. Lewis, a revered name with religious conservatives, argued much the same point as did Pastor Batson. In a 1941 essay titled "Meditation on the Third Commandment," Lewis urged fellow Christians to resist the temptation to enter politics through the medium of an officially Christian party. Such a party, he said, either would remain doctrinally pure and thus be politically ineffective or it would compromise on principles in order to attain power and thus cease to be Christian. In his 2000 book *God's Name in Vain: The Wrong and Rights of Religion in Politics*, Yale law professor Stephen L. Carter updates Lewis. Carter, too, emphasizes the need for purity if religious folk are to get involved in political life. To remain pure, he writes, they should beware of the ugly scrum of electoral politics and instead concentrate on broadcasting broadly formulated principles to the voting public, who can then decide for themselves how to apply the principles in casting their votes. Any other strategy would risk taking God's name in vain.

To anyone who takes the Hebrew Bible seriously, this will seem much too precious a picture of religion. The Bible's first scene of high-level politics, the first of many, has Joseph, son of the patriarch Jacob, advising Pharaoh, king of Egypt, on how the latter's administration should deal with a coming cycle of agricultural plenty followed by catastrophic famine. Impressed by Joseph's acumen, which the Hebrew modestly attributes to God's inspiring wisdom, Pharaoh appoints him to the number-two job in all the land: "Since God has informed you of all this, there can be no one so discerning and wise as you. You shall be in charge of my palace and by your command shall all my people be sustained; only by the throne shall I outrank you" (Genesis 41:39–40). The biblical narrative intends us to cheer this welcome turn of events.

The Hebrew prophets, too, are full of detailed commentary on the foreign and domestic policy of their day. Ezekiel, among other prophets, harangued his fellow Jews not to rely on Egypt as their political ally in the struggle against Babylon. This was in the run-up to Babylon's destruction of Jerusalem and the First Temple. Ezekiel argued that Egypt would not come through in a crunch: "They [Egypt] were a reed-like support for the House of Israel. When they grasp you in [their] palm, you will be snapped, and you will pierce their every shoulder; and when they lean upon you, you will be broken and will force their loins to stand straight" (Ezekiel 29:6–7). The same type of argument was made in 2003 against relying on allies like France and Germany in the run-up to the Iraq war.

From the Bible's perspective, bringing religion to bear on politics is only natural. The problem comes when religion is falsified to meet political needs.

Who, then, is guiltier of falsifying God's name? Conservatives or liberals?

Extreme religious language, the hysterically belligerent calling down of God's wrath on opponents, has become almost the exclusive domain of the American Left. Calling the fellow who opposes the candidate or bill you support a "blasphemer" or "idolater" is something conservatives in reality—as distinct from the daydreams of those who dislike them—could never get away with. But there is a Methodist minister here in Seattle, Pastor Rich Lang of Trinity United Methodist Church, who calls President Bush the "Antichrist." And he's serious. His hatred of the "religious right" drives him to such paroxysms that in a sermon—which landed him on the cover of the local alternative weekly paper—he declared that "the power and seduction of this administration emerges from its diabolical manipulation of Christian rhetoric . . . the mirror opposite of what Jesus embodied. It is, indeed, the materialization of the spirit of Antichrist: a perversion of Christian faith and practice."

On the national scene, the Reverend Jim Wallis, influential editor of the liberal *Sojourners* magazine, jumped on the statement by President Bush that "Our responsibility to history is already clear: to answer these attacks [of September 11] and rid the world of evil." Wallis writes, "To confuse the role of God with that of the American nation, as George Bush seems to do, is a serious theological error that some might say borders on idolatry or blasphemy."

A lot of things border on idolatry or blasphemy. The liberal group Americans United for Separation of Church and State finds that the "religious right's" interest in seeing the Ten Commandments posted in public places "borders on blasphemy."

The country's top Reform Jewish rabbi, Eric Yoffie, found the same moral stain on those who don't share his taste for gun control: "Our gun-flooded society has turned weapons into idols, and the worship of idols must be recognized for what it is: blasphemy." Reform Judaism, the most liberal Jewish denomination, has a political arm, the Religions Action Center (RAC), which rules that driving a gas-wasting SUV may constitute idol worship. The RAC demands legislation mandating higher fuel-economy standards, warning that ". . . when we become obsessed with ever bigger and more powerful chariots and forget their impact on the world around us, then . . . our technological achievements and the pleasure of convenience they bring becomes our ends, our idols, with dire consequences for our souls, for our society and for the earth around us."

For all their inherent silliness, at least these pungently expressed views, which surely falsify the Bible, don't run smack up against scriptural verses that say, in the clearest terms, the precise opposite. Overturning biblical norms is exactly what the current drive to normalize homosexuality, instituting gay marriage and celebrating gay sex, is all about.

The same God who gave the Ten Commandments stated His opposition to homosexual intercourse, directing Moses to instruct the people: "You shall not lie with a man as one lies with a woman, it is an abomination" (Leviticus 18:22). Yet for many progressive-minded Americans, lending the prestige of God's reputation, His name, to homosexual acts has become a priority. For these folks, it's insufficient or unacceptable to say, as atheists do, that ancient morality needn't constrain modern people. Simply dumping the Bible as a source of American values at least would not violate the third commandment, but these enlightened souls understand that we live in a culture where many people care about what God says. Thus a certain leftish perspective, among Christians and Jews, will settle for nothing less than the scriptural stamp of approval on gay sex.

A relatively mild instance was the TV ad produced in 2004 by the United Church of Christ, showing a gay couple being turned away from the doors of a church by burly bouncers. A voice-over declares, "Jesus didn't turn people away. Neither do we."

Bernice Powell Jackson, executive minister of the United Church of Christ's Justice and Witness Ministries, recruits Jesus as a pro-gay spokesman: "I believe that those of us who are Christians must take back Jesus and those of us who are people of faith must take back our ability to frame our positions on critical social issues in the context of faith. . . . The Jesus I am talking about never said one word about homosexuality." Which is true enough, but Jesus' most important interpreter, the apostle Paul, was clear on the subject. In his letter to the Romans, he wrote of those who indulge "dishonorable passions. Their women exchanged natural relations for unnatural, and the men likewise gave up natural relations with women and were consumed with passion for one another, men committing shameless acts with men" (Romans 1:26–27). To set up the Christian Savior as a defender of homosexuality makes nonsense of Christian tradition.

Some Christians go further, turning the announcement of one's homosexuality into a Christian ritual. Writes Chris Glaser, former director of the Lazarus Project, a Los Angeles ministry for gays, "Coming out is an experience best understood on the other side of the closet door— in other words, by those who have experienced it, like a sacrament." In his book *Coming Out as Sacrament*, Glaser turns God Himself into a homosexual: "We need, in a sense, to make love with God, the perfect Lover."

Another strategy, for the pro-gay religious left, is not to ignore Scripture but to turn it on its head, aiming biblical or biblical-style language against the Bible's own proscription. Reform Judaism, for example, offers "congregational honor" (sort of marriage lite) for gay couples. Since Reform rabbis can't claim to be unfamiliar with Leviticus 18:22, they instead try to deploy the authority of other verses, from the same biblical book, to overrule the proscription of gay sex. Rabbi Marc Israel, director of congregational relations at the Reform movement's Religious Action Center, gives three verses from Leviticus, which he translates: "You must not oppress your neighbor" (19:13), "You must judge your neighbor justly" (19:15), and, somewhat comically, "You shall love your neighbor as yourself" (19:18). Rabbi Israel even tries to make out as if it is religious opponents of gay marriage who violate the third commandment: "We condemn any and all campaigns by those who, *in the*

name of God and under the cloak of religion, preach intolerance, hatred, and bigotry." Rabbi David Ellenson, president of Reform's Hebrew
Union College–Jewish Institute of Religion, defends same-sex marriage
by pointing to a verse in Exodus, "You shall not taunt or oppress a
stranger, for you were strangers in the land of Egypt" (22:10).

If there is little evident logic in mindlessly piling biblical verses atop
one another, there's even less sense in adducing the simple fact of someone's desire for members of the same sex to justify, in God's name, homosexual intercourse.

"I feel that God created me a lesbian," the Reverend Irene Elizabeth
Stroud has said by way of justifying an openly gay lifestyle despite her
job as a United Methodist minister in Germantown, Pennsylvania. At
New York City's Gay, Lesbian, Bisexual and Transgender Pride Parade,
a crowd of marchers down Fifth Avenue is generously dotted with GOD
MADE ME GAY signs. "I'm gay because God made me gay," explains
Steve Wickson, executive director of the Gay and Lesbian Community
Center in Las Vegas, in an interview with the *Las Vegas Review-Journal*.
"God made me gay. I'm going to embrace it," says Meg Bechter, a psy-
chology student at the University of Akron, speaking with the *Akron
Beacon-Journal*. "God made me gay. Why should I feel bad about that?"
asks New York University freshman Matt Hadley in the NYU student
paper, the *Washington Square News*.

People have been acting against the dictates of their conscience as
long as there have been consciences. But seeking to rope God into our
efforts to assuage guilt, using His name to tell ourselves that what we do
is just fine in His eyes, when His own words say otherwise, is something
new. It indicates an increasing willingness not only to diminish God
(first commandment) and not only to relativize Him (second commandment) but to mess with Him, which rises to still higher levels of
disrespect.

When people feel free to mess with God, it indicates that society's
moral foundation has or is about to become unstable. A culture needs
rules of behavior—clear, objective rules that don't change with the

blowing breeze of personal whim, lust, greed, and ambition. In theory, the rules can come from any source. The ancient Roman Stoics had their own moral code, in its way no less rigorous than the Christian religion that displaced Stoicism. Confucianism has its firm morals. So does Islam. In a thought experiment, you could imagine America exchanging its Judeo-Christian sense of ethics with that of Stoicism. It could work. What doesn't work is when the members of a society feel free and easy about editing the ethical system to suit themselves, on an ad hoc basis, while claiming they are following the same old system their ancestors did. When that happens, what they are really doing is following not the objective moral system to which they still profess loyalty, but, rather, their own desires, clumsily masked in "religious" language.

You start to see why Jeremiah took the doleful view he did of the real-world impact of oaths uttered falsely in God's name: "because of [false] oaths the land has become desolate, and the pastures of the wilderness withered; their course is evil and their might is in untruth. For even the prophet and the priests are insincere; even in My Temple I find their evil—the word of the Lord" (Jeremiah 23:10–11). Could it be that countries suffer such regrettable fates—reduced to such a state of degradation—because of taking God's name falsely? Yes, because it's not the false oath per se that is the problem, but the lack of mooring in a firm ethical system. This is a prescription for chaos, with the mutilation of our beliefs about right and wrong limited only by our creativity in thinking up new ways to justify doing whatever we please. When "even the prophets and the priests are insincere," self-serving, and dishonest, what hope is there for the rest of us?

NO REST FOR
THE WEARY

*Remember the Sabbath day to hallow it. Six days you shall work and you
shall do your tasks, but the seventh day is a Sabbath to the Lord your God.
You shall do no task, you and your son and your daughter, your male
slave and your slavegirl and your beast and your sojourner who is within
your gates. For six days did the Lord make the heavens and the earth,
the sea and all that is in it, and He rested on the seventh
day. Therefore did the Lord bless the Sabbath day and hallow it.*
(Exodus 20:8–11)

I t is Sunday in Seattle, the day set aside for contemplating God's
creation of the world. How do Seattleites hallow what Christians
call the Lord's Day? Well, the malls open an hour and a half later
than on a weekday, at 11:00 A.M. instead of 9:30 A.M. On a recent Sunday morning, my family was waiting with many other locals for the
opening of the Bellevue Square mall (motto: The Best of Everything)
on the Eastside. We were there to buy shoes. As soon as the mall doors
opened, the place was flooded with customers, from the Nordstrom
department store anchoring the enormous commercial complex in
the north to the JCPenney in the south. I don't know what everyone
else was there for, but with worship services customarily beginning at

11:00 A.M., I can say with confidence that whatever it was must have been something they needed so urgently as to push aside any thought of attending church.

What would be an appropriate Sabbath-afternoon activity? How about a viewing of twenty-one skinned Chinese cadavers preserved in plastic with all the muscles and organs showing? Sounds good. On this Sunday, I fight the downtown traffic, struggle to find a parking spot near the Convention Center, and pay my $24.50 to experience "Bodies: The Exhibition." The exhibition space is packed, since it's a Sunday. The show has been advertised on the city buses (REAL HUMAN BODIES) since it opened a couple of months ago, with a photo of a polymerized corpse cut in two down the middle to reveal the internal organs. The bodies on display belonged to Chinese individuals who, upon their death, were somehow "unclaimed" and thus made available to a Chinese medical school.

Expected to draw 400,000 viewers before it leaves town, "Bodies" is basically a traveling freak show, with a medical gloss because you can see the internal organs (some diseased), arteries (some blocked by plaque), as well as evidence of illness (breast cancer), which will supposedly help you "partner with your personal physician."

Medically educational it may possibly be, but reverential? Not exactly.

Three young friends, two women and a man, are gaping at a display case featuring a severed and polymerized upper limb with all the ligaments and muscles clearly delineated.

"It looks like chicken," says one.

"It looks like salmon," says another.

"It looks like beef," says the third, "like what you'd buy in a grocery store."

There is nothing unique about this scene, or about the Sabbath in Seattle, that would set our city apart from the rest of the country, which similarly treats Sunday (or Saturday, if you're Jewish) with as much awe for the wonder of creation as "Bodies: The Exhibition" does the wonder of the human creature. The fact that my Sunday of shopping and ogling at corpses with fellow Seattleites would hardly seem exceptional in any American city is exactly the point. The secularization of the Sabbath is so complete that we take it for granted, never noticing what we have lost.

By contrast, a taste of the old reverence for the biblically mandated day of rest was heard shortly after the devastating tsunami that swept the Indian Ocean on December 26, 2004. The disaster came on a Sunday, as the Reverend John MacLeod, a Scottish Presbyterian minister, pointed out in comments that sent waves of outrage across the English-speaking world. "It has to be noted," MacLeod declared to fellow Christians, "that the wave arrived on the Lord's Day, the day that God has set apart to be observed the world over by a holy resting from all employments and recreations that are lawful on other days." He observed that it was no coincidence that many of the worst-struck coastal localities included beach resorts patronized by vacationing Westerners and other "pleasure seekers from all over the world." He pronounced the wave to have been a divine punishment.

Keeping the Sabbath may be the least respected of all the Ten Commandments. In recent decades, Americans as a whole have seemed hell-bent on erasing the slightest hint of Sabbath rest from our weekends, and we have been paying for it. Rabbi David Lapin points out the irony that many of us think of Sabbath observance as old-fashioned, better suited to the days when people rode horses and wagons on dirt roads and read at night by candlelight—when the reality is that in our age of overwork and overstress, a time of technology-induced social isolation, of BlackBerrys and iPods, the idea of a weekly rest with friends and family has never been more relevant, more a blessing waiting to be grasped, than it is today. The surprise isn't that some modern people do, in fact, earnestly keep the Sabbath. The real wonder is that premodern Jews and Christians preserved the weekly rest as a heritage—though they couldn't fully appreciate the necessity of it—for us, who truly need it.

We are overdue for a Sabbath revival. The good news is that on the horizon of Christian religious culture, just barely discernible, there may be one coming. The bad news is that the Sabbath has a unique meaning for Jews, beyond resting from labor, that all too few Jews even realize.

The origins of the Sabbath remain clouded, rendering even professional scholars of biblical history strangely silent. From the end of the nineteenth century, secular historians advanced theories about how the institution, far from being the revealed will of God from Mount Sinai, had actually been borrowed (or stolen) by the ancient Israelites from one or another neighboring people—Babylonians, Arabs, Kenites. More recently, the historians have had to admit that these theories all fail on the evidence.

Could it be that the Sabbath really was given to Moses—the seventh day, Saturday, as a time to withdraw from creative activity, to enjoy the company of family and community, to reflect on timeless truths—as the Bible indicates?

These various purposes behind the observance of the seventh day were assumed by later generations to be no less crucial to the spiritual life of the people than Moses in his day held them. The prophet Jeremiah had a special concern about those who violated the rest day by carrying articles out of their homes, whether for commercial or personal reasons, which he considered an exemplary indication that you were going normally about your business as if it were not the Sabbath. For this the holy city, Jerusalem, would be destroyed if the Jews kept up their desecrations: "But if you do not listen to Me, to sanctify the Sabbath day and not to carry a burden and enter the gates of Jerusalem on the Sabbath day, then I shall set a fire to its gates, which will consume the palaces of Jerusalem and not be extinguished" (Jeremiah 17:27). Evidently, the people didn't heed the warning, because Jeremiah lived to see the burning of Jerusalem and her glories by the armies of Babylon.

The Sabbath had definite rules, like not carrying things outside of one's home, that were not specified in the Five Books of Moses. Indeed, Moses never defined what Sabbath observance actually means. What is "work," and therefore forbidden, and what isn't? The Hebrew word translated as "work" or "task," *melachah*, really means a creative act, not necessarily a physically taxing or tiring one. After all, in observing the Sabbath we are imitating God, who "rested" on the seventh day of his creating the world—God, who, needless to say, "never grows faint or weary" (Isaiah 40:28). God was not taking a breather from strenuous labor, but, rather, abstaining from creativity. What, however, defines creation? Evidently, the ancient Israelites knew of rules, clear and distinct. Jeremiah alluded to this when he admonished, "Neither shall you take a burden out of your houses on the Sabbath day nor shall you perform any work, and you shall sanctify the Sabbath day as I commanded your ancestors" (Jeremiah 17:22). Evidently, the prohibition of taking things out of your home on the Sabbath was "commanded [to] your ancestors." But we find no reference to such a prohibition in the text of the Torah. So how and where was it conveyed?

These detailed Sabbath regulations, according to Judaism, were taught by oral tradition, originally to Moses at Sinai by God Himself and then passed down from generation to generation, not to be written down until they were in danger of being forgotten, about 200 C.E. in the Mishnah, a cryptically written rabbinic text in which one finds the tractate Shabbat, dealing extensively with the Sabbath regulations. But not only with regulations. The orally transmitted data conveyed by the Jews includes insights that fit no legal definition, such as that Shabbat is no less than one of God's secret names; that Shabbat is the mystic bride given to the Jewish people, her groom, which is why the Sabbath is sanctified over a cup of wine, as in a Jewish wedding; that the Sabbath is a taste of the World to Come (precisely one-sixtieth of our future heavenly rest, if you want to be exact); that ultimately the Sabbath is not a law at all, a demand imposed from on high, but, rather, as the Talmud puts it, a "beautiful gift."

The prophets, far from feeling oppressed by rules, regarded the Sabbath as a source of joy. The foremost poet of the hallowed day is Isaiah. He assumed that not only Jews but also non-Jews would be drawn to its observance: "And the foreigners who join themselves to the Lord to serve Him, all who guard the Sabbath against desecration, and grasp My covenant tightly—I will bring them to My holy mountain, and I will gladden them in My house of prayer; their elevation-offerings and their feast-offerings will find favor on My altar, for My house will be called a house of prayer for all peoples" (Isaiah 56:6–7). Everyone who observes the seventh day will find reward: "If you restrain your foot because it is the Sabbath; refrain from accomplishing your own needs on My holy day; if you proclaim the Sabbath 'a delight,' and the holy [day] of the Lord 'honored,' and you honor it by not engaging in your own affairs, from seeking your own needs or discussing the forbidden—then you will delight in the Lord, and I will mount you astride the heights of the world . . ." (58:13–14). At the end of history, says Isaiah in concluding his prophetic book, Jews and non-Jews will join together to worship God on this most exalted day: "It shall be that at every New Moon and on every Sabbath all mankind will come to prostrate themselves before Me, says the Lord" (66:23).

By the time of Jesus, doubt had crept into the thinking of some Jews about the need for rules in Sabbath observance. The Christian Savior respected the Sabbath itself, but he dismissed the oral traditions, including those dealing with regulations of the seventh day, that Jeremiah had known. He once healed a man who had been sick for thirty-eight years, then told him, "Rise, take up your pallet, and walk." Some observers felt this was wrong and told the healed man so: "It is the Sabbath, it is not lawful for you to carry your pallet" (John 5:8,10).

The other rules included not cooking, writing, using money, traveling, or lighting a fire—a total of thirty-nine categories of creative activity, with many subcategories. The difficulty in dispensing with these seemingly minute, picayune details is that without them the Sabbath tends to get eaten up by the call of responsibilities and impulses that follow us from the workweek. Without definite rules, we have little cause to resist the importuning of activity. This is simply human nature. Rules give us the courage to say no, both to ourselves and to other people. This is why Hebrew, a language that works also at the level of mathematical code, uses the same three-letter verbal root to represent the words *freedom* and *engraved* or *incised,* in the sense that the Ten Commandments were engraved on the two tablets. Law, permanently incised in stone, not only binds but also frees us.

The apostle Paul, then, was in a sense only drawing a logical inference from Jesus' perspective on the Sabbath when he, the apostle, dissolved the obligation of its observance altogether. In his letter to the Colossians, he wrote, "Therefore let no one pass judgment on you in questions of food and drink or with regard to a festival or a new moon or a Sabbath. These are only a shadow of what is to come; but the substance belongs to Christ" (Colossians 2:16). A few centuries later, Saint Augustine was scolding Jews for missing the point of the Sabbath—for having too good a time and generally kicking up their heels. They "observe their Sabbath by a kind of bodily rest, languid and luxurious. They abstain from labor and give themselves up to trifles . . . ; it is better to plough than to dance." The Greek biographer Plutarch, a pagan priest, condemned the Jews in a similar vein for loosening up with a few drinks on their Sabbath.

This demotion of the actual Sabbath observance to a merely symbolic role was accompanied by moving it forward in the week, to Sunday, recognized by pagans as an appropriate day to take time off from exertions. Already in the first century, Christians observed the "eighth day" (Sunday) in commemoration of Christ's Resurrection. Saint Ignatius, who died as a martyr in 107, wrote of how Christians were "no longer observing the Sabbath, but living in the observance of the Lord's Day."

I have just reviewed about fourteen hundred years of religious thinking on the question to explain why Americans have been of two minds about their Sabbath and how to observe it. On one hand, there is our country's historically Christian culture. On the other hand, more

specifically, there is the heritage of English and Scottish Puritanism
from which our roots spring.

The Puritans looked back longingly to the Old Testament and saw
themselves as a new Israel. A shrewd historical thinker, David Gelernter, has argued that far from disappearing by the late 1700s, as it has
been conventionally assumed, the religious worldview of our country's
original Puritan settlers, the Pilgrims, was actually absorbed into the de-
veloping, distinctive ethos of the new republic as a whole. In other
words, "Americanism" is merely the continuation of Puritanism. No
surprise, then, that as Gelernter writes, "From the 17th century through
John F. Kennedy and Martin Luther King, Americans kept talking
about their country as if it were the biblical Israel and they were the
chosen people."

No surprise, either, that taking the Sabbath seriously—not only as
"a shadow of what is to come" but as a vital social institution in the
here and now—was a priority of the nation's earliest legislators. Before
and after the Revolution, it was taken for granted that, as a statute
passed in Massachusetts in 1797 put it, "the observance of the Lord's
day is highly promotive of the welfare of a community," specifically of
"a Christian society." A book called *Blue Laws: The History, Economics,
and Politics of Sunday-Closing Laws*, by David Laband and Deborah
Hendry Heinbuch, provides a detailed account of the subject. In
colonies and states as diverse as Virginia, Maryland, and New York, you
could be fined up to twenty shillings or the equivalent in tobacco (a
couple hundred pounds or so) for "travel[ing] upon the road" (Virginia), doing "any manner of labor, business or work" or being "present
at any concert of music, dancing, or public diversion, show or entertainment" (Massachusetts), "laboring, working, shooting, fishing, sport-
ing, playing, horseracing, frequenting of tippling houses" (New York).
There are records of citizens in Arkansas being prosecuted and fined in
the 1800s for Sabbath violations, including shooting squirrels ($22),
digging potatoes ($26.50), or hoeing in one's garden ($30.90).

Statutes like these are called "blue laws"—the term apparently deriving either from the color of the paper on which Connecticut printed a set of ordinances in 1665 or from the term *true blue*, meaning steady, faithful, sober. The Supreme Court has found them to be constitutional—notably, in a 1961 decision, *McGowan v. Maryland*—provided that the purpose has a secular aspect, conferring a practical benefit on citizens, not only an exclusively religious one.

From their high point, the Sabbath blue laws have been in a slow but steady decline, with their only really noticeable legacy remaining in those states that forbid liquor sales on Sunday. This has to do with the secularization of American society, but not only that. As the decline sped up precipitously from the 1970s on, it became evident that one major contributing factor was a trend toward mothers working outside the home. Women who once might have done the family shopping during the week now could only realistically hope to do it on weekends. Stores that could open on Sunday stood to benefit from the demise of the traditional family structure.

I'm not arguing that we should go back to fining people for puttering in their garden on Sunday (or Saturday). But consider what this says about where American culture is headed: In one eighteen-month period in 2002–2004, six states relaxed laws against Sunday liquor sales, bringing the total to twenty-seven states that have done so.

The state of voluntary observance of Sunday on the part of businesses is telling. Nationally, the only major chain that still closes on Sunday is Chick-fil-A, the curiously named fast-food chicken restaurant that is KFC's main competitor. The chain's founder, Truett Cathy, is a Christian, and he says he was willing to give up the millions of dollars he might otherwise make on the Sabbath—a day when other restaurants typically do 20 percent of their business. Even in Mormon and otherwise religiously traditional Utah, a huge majority of the state's major stores—84 percent in 2005, according to the *Deseret Morning News*—now do business on Sunday. Fifty years ago, the percentage was near zero. "To a majority of Utahns," the paper commented, "the Ten Commandments may have shrunken to just the Nine Commandments." Today, 40 percent of Utah's household breadwinners work on Sunday.

All this might not be so terrible if we had other days off in which to regroup and regain our energy. But we are severely and increasingly overworked. In 2002, despite a dip in the previous two years, due to a recession, average work hours for men and women were up 11 percent since 1975. Between 1979 and 2000, men and women in the hard-pressed second-to-bottom quintile increased their average annual hours by up to 20 percent. Juliet Schor, author of the 1991 best-seller *The Overworked American*, calls it a "crisis of leisure time" and observes that "Americans are literally working themselves to death—as jobs contribute to heart disease, hypertension, gastric problems, depression, exhaustion, and a variety of other ailments."

Recently, employers have taken notice of this, providing office time and space for free massages and classes in yoga and tai chi to help workers relax, contributing to a $11.7 billion stress-management industry. But the purpose seems to be primarily to make it possible for employees to keep working ever harder without keeling over. The *New York Times* quotes a public-relations officer for Armani Exchange, Wendy Rothman, who complained, "I love the yoga class, but I just can't get to it anymore; I'm running all day." The irony is painful: We're so busy, thus we need to relax, but we can't because we're too busy.

A better solution to the problem of the leisure crisis comes from the Christian world. On my desk I've got a little pile of recent documents and volumes recommending the rediscovery of the Sabbath.

Pope John Paul II released a 1998 apostolic letter, "Dies Domini," urging a Sabbath revival, and the Presbyterian Church of the United States followed up with a report to its General Assembly entitled "An Invitation to Sabbath: Rediscovering a Gift." Lauren Winner, an evangelical Christian who went through a Jewish phase in college, writes endearingly in *Mudhouse Sabbath* (2003) of the Torah practices she fondly remembers: "Shabbat is, without question, the piece of Judaism I miss most." Paul and Augustine might have a bone to pick with Pat Robertson. In his 2004 book, *The Ten Offenses: Reclaim the Blessings of the Ten Commandments*, the Christian right leader joins the chorus for a renewed commitment to Sabbath rest and endorses the old blue laws. At the opposite end of the political spectrum, in his best-selling cheerleading book for the Christian left, *God's Politics* (2005), the Reverend Jim Wallis offers a prediction for the new millennium: "The concept and discipline of the Sabbath will see a great comeback in the lives of overworked and overstressed people."

Wayne Muller's *Sabbath: Restoring the Sacred Rhythm of Rest* (1999) is a lovely book that helped spark the Christian movement to revive the Sabbath. When I read Muller, I was struck by how many insights he had arrived at from his practice of the Sabbath that I had reached by approaching it from my own different, Jewish vantage. He writes of the liberation that comes with following rules: "While many of us are terribly weary, we have come to associate tremendous guilt and shame with taking time to rest. Sabbath gives us permission; it commands us to stop."

Yes, there is no contradiction between Christian Sabbath keeping and discipline, as a Christian friend of mine reminds me. Michele and her husband, Paul, used to live in Lynden, Washington, a farming town that at the time they resided there, in 1993, boasted the highest number of churches per capita in the country. In Lynden, there were strict Sunday-closing laws, but not only that: You couldn't even mow your lawn on the Sabbath. And this was in the town where it was also a finable offense to let your lawn go unmaintained. Says Michele, "The whole point was that since you could not mow your lawn on Sundays, then you had to make sure that you got this thing done in the six days you had before Sundays. Paul loved that idea and has maintained that we need to have that day as our Sabbath since those early days of our marriage."

The point of the day certainly is not simply to *stop* but, rather, to stop in order *to do* other things. I find that the Jewish Shabbat is a particularly fertile space, intellectually and spiritually, when ideas arise from what seems to be nowhere and illuminate me. Conversations are better on Shabbat, and sometimes I wish I could take notes of particularly keen observations from friends and loved ones. In fact, a Jewish tradition has it that at the conclusion of the Sabbath, God tallies up the new thoughts and insights we have had during the previous twenty-five hours, hoping that our time has been spent in fruitful meditation.

Dorothy C. Bass, in her book *Practicing Our Faith* (1997), notes the blessing of the Christian Sabbath not only for the individual but also for the community. If the Pilgrims had their saying that "Good Sabbaths make good Christians," Bass widens the scope of the idea: "Good Sabbaths make good societies." It's true that in ancient Hebrew society breaking the Sabbath was a capital offense, and Bass, perhaps inadvertently, puts her finger on why. If good Sabbaths make good societies, then bad Sabbaths make bad societies—or at least bad Sabbaths are the gauge of a society that has gone off the rails. To the extent a culture fails to build into its customs, and its laws, a break in the week to relax and abstain from creativity, to contemplate, and to appreciate what we have to be thankful for, that culture suffers from an illness, that of Sabbath deprivation. And note that the ailment isn't merely at the individual level but also at the societal. Flagrant Sabbath breaking by enough people will affect the tone of how life is lived by others in the same culture.

Here are some ways that Sabbath deprivation reflects, feeds on, or aggravates cultural breakdown:

Sabbath and motherhood. We've already observed one way that mass Sabbath breaking measures the distance we Americans have traveled in our own exodus from the better way of living our ancestors knew: Businesses now routinely open on Sunday in large part because working mothers otherwise would have no opportunity to do the family shopping. The demise of the Sabbath is a function of the demise of the traditional family. In this connection, I was struck by the irony of a rave review in the *New York Times Book Review* of a 2005 best-seller, *Perfect Madness*, Judith Warner's plaint over the distress of the high-achieving woman who gives up work for children. Warner advocates a system of European-style subsidized child care so that upper-middle-class mothers can more comfortably go back to their prestige jobs and leave mothering to surrogates. According to the reviewer's biography printed under the article, the admiring author of the review, Judith Shulevitz, "is working on a book about the Sabbath." Praising the day of rest, that is—even as she endorses the further undermining of the family that the discarding of the Sabbath enables.

Sabbath and social isolation: Shulevitz once wrote an article in the *New York Times Magazine*—fascinating as much because of the thoroughly secular venue as because of the content—about the peace and beauty she found in her personal rediscovery of Jewish Sabbath observance. As an unmarried woman without a synagogue affiliation, however, she related that spending Friday night and Saturday by herself could be painfully lonely. Of course it is! That's because one of the most fundamental purposes of Shabbat is to glue a community together. For twenty-five hours—from before sundown on Friday to just after dark on Saturday night—traditional Jews refrain from traveling except on foot. This, along with other Jewish Sabbath traditions, compels families to spend the whole day together, including festive meals night and day. Meanwhile, groups of families come together for synagogue worship and typically visit with one another over long dinners and lunches. Table fellowship flourishes. By contrast, liberal Jewish denominations that have permitted the use of automobiles on Shabbat have found the experiment to be a dismal failure. What happened was the dissolution of previously functioning Sabbath communities as families moved too far from the synagogue to make walking practical. After services concluded on Saturday morning, instead of spending time with each other over meals, everyone in the congregation dispersed to go their separate ways. Further liberalization resulted in shopping, TV watching, exercising, and other solitary habits entirely replacing the ancient community-creating laws of Shabbat. Judith Shulevitz discovered what generations of her ancestors knew: that the Sabbath works best when celebrated with others.

The converse is also true. When a culture, like our own, gives up the Sabbath, one result is increased social isolation. Fifty years ago, it was not uncommon for American families to spend Sunday together. Even though, unlike religious Jews, American Christians rarely gave up driving on the Sabbath, the rooting of the day in the sacred custom of church attendance, followed by a family meal, still joined individuals together. With Sunday fast on its way to becoming just another day of the week, the atomization of the American people has been helped along.

Our isolation from one another is partly a function of communication technologies that weren't widely in use even fifteen years ago—technologies that, not by coincidence, are forbidden on the Jewish Sabbath. When the Internet was new, there was a lot of wide-eyed talk about how the world had become a global village, linked by packets of digital information zipping through the ether. Everyone was now joined together electronically, allowing countless specialized communities to flourish. It hasn't worked out that way. Staring at your computer monitor by yourself isn't really so different from staring at your TV by yourself.

Sabbath and work: Another subject, work, may also at first glance seem to be about as unrelated to Sabbath rest as could be—indeed, its polar opposite. Isn't the whole point of the Sabbath to restrain yourself, as Isaiah put it, from "engaging in your own affairs, from seeking your own needs or discussing the forbidden"? How could the Sabbath make us better at, or more fulfilled in, our work?

The answer is not merely that the Sabbath provides a respite from the weariness of labor. In fact, the whole concept of work as wearying labor—a burden of drudgery we would evade if we could—is foreign to biblical tradition. The Mishnah records a rabbinic saying that the world itself is supported by three noble kinds of undertaking: religious learning, acts of loving kindness, and work. The Hebrew word for work or service, *avodah*, can equally mean human creativity and the activities of the priests in the Temple relating to divine service. In other words, human creativity—that which is forbidden on Shabbat—is a form of divine service. The rabbis instructed their followers to "love work."

How could this be? If work is divine and beloved, how could it also be forbidden on the Sabbath?

It turns out that, the way God made us and made His universe, creativity depends on a vital, ongoing tension between activity and rest. The *New York Times* recently ran a feature that puzzled over the seeming irony that all the new self-help books stress either one of two contrasting themes: the need to slow down or the need to speed up: "The how-to-live movement has split into two camps: those who believe the key to contentment is to do more every day and those who say we should all be doing a lot less." On one hand, you have titles like *In Praise of Slowness: How a Worldwide Movement Is Challenging the Cult of Speed,* by Carl Honore, and *The Lazy Way to Success: How to Do Nothing and Accomplish Everything,* by Fred Gratzon. On the other hand, you have *TurboCoach: A Powerful System for Achieving Breakthrough Career Success,* by Brian Tracy, and *Getting Things Done,* by David Allen. The idea of the Sabbath says that between these two apparently contradictory approaches there is no contradiction. The Sabbath is for slowness. The week of *avodah* is for getting things done. Jewish law mandates that everyone's workday should begin upon first awakening by his leaping out of bed "like a lion"—no snooze buttons, please—to serve God. This explains why the fourth commandment was phrased as it was. It doesn't just say, in its opening words, "Remember the Sabbath day to hallow it"; it immediately continues: "Six days you shall work and you shall do your tasks." In other words, fulfilling the commandment completely means not only resting on the seventh day but *working on the other six.*

The insight that our work has deep meaning, that it is a commandment unto itself, that by working we are doing divine service by emu-
lating God—who in creating the world also worked and rested—is a
teaching that couldn't be timelier. Americans not only are missing
downtime in their week; they also seem to be missing meaning in their
work. That's the message of recent films like *Jerry McGuire* (1996),
about a sports agent (Tom Cruise) who realizes he needs to think of his
work not as a high-paying *job* but as something more like a *mission* or a
calling, and *In Good Company* (2005), about a fifty-one-year-old advertising salesman (Dennis Quaid) for a sports magazine who against all
odds retains the old-fashioned idea that selling his product has value
independent of the bottom line. Because of his outdated belief in the
nobility of work, Quaid's character is made the subordinate of a twenty-
six-year-old smart-aleck who says things like "Cell phones, ad space, it's
all the same crap," and the older man nearly loses his job.

The assumption that the products of our work are interchangeable,
fungible, meaningless has been implicitly challenged by a Christian
movement to turn workplaces into so many interlinked ministries—so
far, about thirteen hundred around the country. As the Reverend Billy
Graham has foreseen, "One of the next great moves of God is going to
be through believers in the workplace." A founder of a group in the
Chicago area, Business Leaders for Excellence, Ethics, and Justice, Gre-
gory F. A. Pierce asked in *Fortune* magazine, "Why would we want to
look for God in our work? The simple answer is most of us spend so
much time working, it would be a shame if we couldn't find God there.
A more complex answer is that there is a creative energy in work that
is somehow tied to God's creative energy." That is the biblical concept
of *avodah* in a nutshell.

A country unconscious of the fourth commandment not only will
be overworked but will undervalue the work it spends all that time doing. The growing faith-at-work movement seeks to answer a need that,
one may speculate, was fueled by the dissolution of the American Sabbath. So, too, does a seemingly related push by an organization that has

garnered some media attention, a coalition called Take Back Your Time. The group rightly observes that overworked Americans need more free time to nurture their family lives. As a solution to the problem, the group has focused on urging states to pass laws dictating that employers give employees paid sick days and family leaves to attend to new babies and ill family members. But this misses the point. Without a fundamental reorientation of the culture, in the direction of taking the Sabbath seriously once again, such well-meaning legislation will only result in workers calling in sick and taking off time, at their employers' expense, to do errands, watch TV, vacation—virtually anything but observe the Sabbath. New laws won't change anything about how we conceptualize the seventh day. Only a fundamental reconsideration of religious truths, embodied in the Ten Commandments, will do that.

So far, we've mostly been considering the fourth commandment in the context of Christianity. If we shift the focus to Jews and the specifically Jewish Sabbath, which, after all, is what this commandment originally pointed to, two problems emerge. First, the authentic Jewish Sabbath is a remarkably detailed affair—its laws a vast topic for contemplation in their own right—which many uninitiated Jews find daunting, never mind Christians. I am not going to try to sell the Jewish Sabbath here. That would require a book for Jews, which this book is not. Also, to understand Shabbat, to appreciate why it is the day I and so many other Jews look forward to above all others each week, really requires experiencing it, rather than writing or talking about it.

The other challenge raised by the contrast between the Jewish and Christian Sabbath is that the Talmud, in theory, forbids the observance of the seventh day (Saturday) to non-Jews (Sanhedrin 58b). Which doesn't mean Gentiles can't take a day off, but they mustn't do so as a religious act if their Sabbath includes all the manifold regulations stipulated by Jewish law. To do so, in fact, would, according to the Talmud, be an offense against God worthy of death. There is an aspect of Shab-bat, a secret about the spiritual elevation associated with it, that Jews are not even supposed to divulge to non-Jews—and which, accordingly, I won't specify. (See the Talmud's tractate Beitzah 16a.) The fact that it is highly unlikely a believing Christian would attempt observing Shabbat as Jews traditionally do doesn't resolve the awkwardness of the point.

What's this all about? Why is Shabbat uniquely tied to the spiritual destiny of the Jewish people—a fact, incidentally, that is recognized even beyond the limits of the biblical religons? In February 2005, dur-ing the modernization of post-Saddam Iraq, some Muslim Iraqis were outraged at the introduction of Saturday as a day off. The first Saturday when the new weekend schedule was to go into effect, students showed up at high schools and colleges anyway and chanted against "the Zion-ist holiday," "the Jewish holiday." Muslim radicals issued death threats against teachers who declined to teach on Saturday.

I didn't understand until I read Abraham Joshua Heschel's little book *The Sabbath*, which reminds you in a very moving way that the Jewish Sabbath isn't merely about desisting from work. It's about meet-ing God in a "sanctuary in time," a day created to serve much the same function that the Jerusalem Temple did before it was destroyed in 70 C.E.

Sabbath observance in all its complexity is defined by those thirty-nine *melachot*, which are the same forms of "work" that the Jews, after the Exodus from Egypt, used to build the desert Tabernacle, forerunner to the Temple. Shabbat is a temple—not in space but in a holier dimen-sion, time. Heschel observes the seeming irony that the Decalogue says nothing of an earthly habitation for God, no temple or other holy place—or does it? Yes, it does: the eternal Sabbath. It is the special do-main of the Jews because we serve uniquely as the priests who minister there. The Talmud's seemingly harsh prohibition of Gentile Sabbath observance seeks to depict a reality: When non-Jews fill the role or-dained for Jews, something has gone wrong.

I worry about the function God assigned to the Jewish people three thousand years ago at Mount Sinai. There He called us to be a "kingdom of priests" (Exodus 19:6), and many passages in the books of the Hebrew prophets make clear what this should mean. We are called to act as ministers to the world, which is meant to be our congregation, teaching other peoples about God.

It is a pity that, in the eyes of our congregation, the most serious moral message we Jews have to impart has nothing to do with the Torah or with God. It's about something else entirely. Yes, a generalized paranoia, an ingrained habit of issuing mistaken alarms about phantom anti-Semitism.

Do you doubt it? Do you remember a sadly illustrative story from early in 2005? It's tempting to let the Prince Harry Nazi-uniform episode pass from memory as a moment of meaningless comedy—tempting, but wrong.

Twenty-year-old Harry, third in line for the British throne, attended a costume bash dressed in a khaki military shirt and swastika armband. He was photographed in this get-up, cigarette and drink in hand, and London's *Sun* newspaper splashed the picture on its front page. An upper-class twit had acted like an upper-class twit. The horror! It was hardly a big serious deal, in truth, because who cares anymore about the British throne? Yet the story occasioned days of melodramatic media coverage. The *Sun* reported "worldwide anger over Harry's gaffe" and highlighted what it called the "hard-hitting" comments of Rabbi Marvin Hier of the Simon Wiesenthal Center in Los Angeles.

CNN also brought on Rabbi Hier, who denounced Harry's behavior as "shameful," demanded that the prince tour a death camp, and more: "He should visit Auschwitz to be part of the British delegation to show the world that he can be serious, that he understands the great atrocity that occurred there. He could be at his grandmother's side when she greets the Holocaust survivors at Buckingham Palace, rather than remove himself from the scene and expect the world to forgive him because he's a kid."

Much more dispiriting than anything Harry had done, the episode reinforced the world's impression that the chief moral purpose of Jews is to denounce trivial instances of purported anti-Semitism. Recall the role the Torah asks Jews to fill, that of the "kingdom of priests" who minister to and teach others about God. Few Jewish voices are raised in this capacity today.

The most broadly recognized "moral" voices on the American Jewish scene, the purported authorities on Jewish values best known outside the Jewish community, concern themselves not with illuminating other people with the beauty and wisdom of the Torah, but mainly with ferreting out either imagined or meaningless acts of Jew bating. The Anti-Defamation League hounding Mel Gibson for making *The Passion,* the Simon Wiesenthal Center hounding Prince Harry—this is what we are reduced to.

Meanwhile, American Christians are continuously stepping into the breach, acting as the moral leaders Jews should be. One thinks of James Dobson or Chuck Colson, the country's most distinguished evangelical Christian voices.

Naturally, Christians have little choice but to take up our responsibility when we drop it. But the fact that we discarded our priestly role is not acceptable. Not to us, if we know what a Jew should be. But neither should non-Jews amiably allow Jews to get away with our dereliction of duty. The Christian understanding that the specifically Jewish Sabbath isn't for them indicates that, perhaps unconsciously, they feel this.

The time has come to acknowledge our mistake, even to apologize. Jews have a job in the world, which the God of Israel gave us, related to the Jewish Sabbath. We're not doing it now, but if we chose to reconsider where our community spends its money, how we assign our priorities, we could get down to our real work, our true *avodah*.

SUPERNANNY AND THE CULTURE WAR

*Honor your father and your mother so that your days will be
long upon the land that the Lord your God gives you.*
(Exodus 20:12)

Sometimes the overturning of the fifth commandment presents
itself as tragedy, sometimes as comedy, sometimes as both. I
recall a story from the *Seattle Times* about Dale Ray Frank, a
sixteen-year-old boy in Renton, a bland middle-class community by the
Boeing plant south of Seattle. Dale Ray Frank was playing video games
with two others boys, according to police, when he suddenly unbur-
dened himself of a guilty secret: "Dude, I think I killed my mom." He
thought about this for moment, then said, "There, I said it, I told someone. Dude, the body is too heavy. I can't pick it up." But reportedly he
had managed well enough, having strangled her, to somehow pick up
and move the body of his forty-three-year-old mother out to a recycling
bin, where it was subsequently found.

Of course the real frontier, the leading indicators in parent-child relations, do not involve murdering parents. Take my neighbors Paul and

Michele, who have been raising their teenage daughter in the permissive atmosphere of our upper-middle-class Seattle suburb, where children now cross boundaries that, when we were their age, a little more than twenty years ago, we wouldn't have dreamed of. We didn't dream, for example, of addressing friends' parents by their first names, a practice now common. We screamed at our parents, sure—but not in front of other people, a practice now taken for granted among kids with "nice" parents. Paul and Michele, who think of themselves as traditionalists and disciplinarians, were taken aback when their fifteen-year-old daughter resented a gentle reprimand from Paul about putting her feet up on the pew ahead of her in church. "You're so freakin' stupid," the daughter hissed back, her voice loud enough for those around to hear.

There are no figures available on the incidence rate of fifteen-year-old girls calling their dads "freakin' stupid" while in church. The point I want to underline here is that such an outburst doesn't really shock us anymore, although it would have done even in the notorious 1960s. I want to ask why it doesn't. I shall argue that when children disrespect parents, with all that implies by way of the direction the culture is headed, it isn't the kids' fault.

By the middle of the new millennium's first decade, the respect shown to American parents by their children had sunk to such a low point that the only way the honor of mothers and fathers nationwide could possibly be rescued was through foreign intervention. In the spring of 2005, about ten million television viewers weekly were tuning in to *Supernanny* on ABC, and about ten million were watching *Nanny 911* on Fox, a pair of "reality" programs whose entire premise was that American kids are so out of control that no one in the country, and certainly not their own parents, have the faintest idea how to rectify the situation. For this reason, every week the producers of the two hit shows would call to the rescue one or another of a group of about six British women of various ages, professional nannies, who had agreed to be dropped into a selected U.S. household, one per episode, to establish control on behalf of the bewildered, helpless adults in the home.

In one San Diego family, the father of the household, a young and seemingly healthy man as he appeared in a photograph, had "passed away." His widow, a chubby, sweet-faced woman, was being terrorized by their two preadolescent children, a boy and girl. The ten-year-old daughter was particularly vicious. Also chubby, she was shown repeatedly pummeling her mother with both fists. The mother not only did not push or hit back; she could do absolutely nothing else to protect herself physically. All she did do was implore her daughter to behave—to no effect, of course.

Cut to Nanny Headquarters, a studio mock-up of a proper British-looking living room with a fireplace crackling cheerfully under a mantel and five nannies sitting in a circle of straight-backed chairs, holding counsel on what to do about the distressing situation. The group then decided to send in one of their own to help get things under control—which the woman proceeded to do over the course of the show's hour-long duration.

Around this time, thousands of parents in similar straits were writing in each week to the producers of Nanny 911 and Supernanny, begging for help in establishing some hint of parental authority in their own homes. Other Americans were buying the book version of the ABC series, Supernanny, offering parenting tips from author Jo Frost, aka Supernanny herself, sending the volume to the top of the New York Times self-help best-seller list.

If children are increasingly "out of control," there must be a reason, and the reason cannot be attributed to the children themselves. It must be because the adults chiefly responsible for children's behavior have released them from the control to which mothers and fathers once routinely subjected children. That control was always based upon honor.

The fifth commandment suggests some of the darker consequences of a continuation of this trend toward the breakdown of respect for parents—consequences that include unhealthy outcomes not only in the everyday physical realm but also in the metaphysical, the spiritual. Its place on the list—the fifth of ten—forms a kind of transition point between the first four commandments, which all unambiguously have to do with humanity's relationship with God, and the last five, which have to do with our relationship with other people. The fifth commandment is about both—how we relate to God, and other humans.

W hat exactly does it mean to "honor" parents? Would it suffice to confer upon them a decorative medal or a commemorative plaque ("World's Best Mom")? If not, then what would suffice? The difficulty is compounded when you consider that another verse in the Pentateuch, in Leviticus, the book that immediately follows the one (Exodus) in which the Ten Commandments are first recorded, contains a commandment that says, "You shall each revere his mother and his father" (19:3). Why the apparent redundancy? Or is it a redundancy at all? A contrast immediately suggests itself not only in the choice of verb (*honor* versus *revere*) but in the order of the persons to whom the honor (Hebrew, *kibud*) or reverence (*morah*) is to be directed. In the fifth commandment, we are told to honor "your father and your mother." In the verse in Leviticus, however, a person is directed to "revere his mother and his father."

In any other literature, we would hardly pay much attention to such redundancies or discrepancies. After all, when people write books, imprecision naturally creeps in. But the only reason we pay as much regard to the Ten Commandments as we do is that many of us are willing to grant, at least for the sake of argument, that they were not authored by our fellow human beings, but by God, who chooses His words carefully. So the curious authorial choices must convey some significance.

The concluding phrase of the fifth commandment also requires attention. It promises that if we obey, then "your days will be long upon the land that the Lord your God gives you." Why does this commandment come packaged with a reward, whereas the others don't, and what does that reward entail? Long life? How long? What kind of life—in this world and in this life, or maybe in the next "life," after we die? On what land? The promised land of Israel, to which the Jews were headed when they received the Decalogue at Sinai? But then has this commandment lost some of its relevance for those, including non-Jewish Americans, who never entertained a thought of living in Israel?

There are no ready solutions to these critical problems if all we have to rely upon is the form of deep thinking called biblical "interpretation." That activity very often simply means seeing such meaning in the text as you are inclined to discover there because that meaning overlaps with beliefs and values you have picked up from the environment you live in, the cultural air you breathe. The fifth commandment, like so many other verses in the Hebrew Bible, simply has no obvious meaning that would lend itself to applying the commandment in any objective, practical way. The words on the page prompt questions, to which they don't necessarily offer answers. How do you know if you are really giving proper *kibud* (honor) or *morah* (reverence) to your parents?

The Talmud devotes an extensive but typically meandering discussion to the meaning of *kibud* and *morah*. Maimonides systematized the subject, clearly detailing the relevant laws, in a book of his legal code, the Mishneh Torah, called "Hilchot Mamrim"—the "Laws of Rebels." This book deals with many ways in which people inappropriately throw off the controls imposed by authority. The rebels in question are those who shrug off the authority of God. To disrespect parents is to disrespect one's Creator.

In brief, the distinction between *honor* and *reverence* is a distinction between positive and negative ways of observing the same comprehensive responsibility to respect mother and father. Honor means doing the right things. Reverence means not doing the wrong things. Thus, honoring parents entails serving them in various ways, mostly when they have grown old and are unable to do these for themselves: To bring them food and drink, and feed them if necessary. To dress them. To escort them wherever they need to go. To stand when they enter the room. On the other hand, reverence entails taking care not to do anything that would detract from their honor. It means refraining from sitting in a chair your parent is accustomed to sitting in, or from standing in a place where he normally stands; from contradicting your parent in conversation; from calling your parent by his or her name, even after the parent has died; and the like. When we combine honor and reverence, they add up to respect.

Biblical tradition makes clear the somewhat shocking connection between respecting parents and respecting God. Shocking? Yes, because it almost appears that we owe the same deference to the one as to the other. In Scripture, the very same language is used to describe both the proper relationship to the eternal Creator and to our mortal creators: "Honor your father and your mother" (Exodus 20:12), and "Honor the Lord" (Proverbs 3:9). "You shall each revere his mother and his father" (Leviticus 19:3), and "You shall revere the Lord your God" (Deuteronomy 6:13). This partly explains why honoring parents appears on the first tablet of the Ten Commandments. How we relate to them is one side of the coin, the other side of which is how we relate to God.

That's why biblically informed cultures have seen the relationship with parents as an extension of that with God, not as an independent good as in Chinese Confucianism. According to the latter, as Francis Fukuyama writes in his book *Trust* (1995), "The central core of this ethical teaching was the apotheosis of the family—in Chinese, the *jia*—as the social relationship to which all others were subordinate. Duty to the family trumped all other duties, including obligations to emperor, Heaven, or any other source of temporal or divine authority." The "moral obligation of *xiao*, or filial piety . . . is Confucianism's central moral imperative."

To be precise, when we speak of "parents," it might be better to refer instead to "father and mother" or, as the case may be, depending on whether we're talking about honor or reverence, "mother and father." The Talmud explains the difference in the way the Bible orders them—with father coming before mother when the context is honor, and mother coming before father when the context is reverence—by noting that children naturally relate to the male parent in a different way than to the female. Children have a harder time honoring their father than their mother. The tenderness of feeling for her that goes with honoring is more natural than for the father, so the Bible counters our nature, adjusts for it, by placing father ahead of mother—to remind us of the greater challenge. On the other hand, children have a harder time revering their mother than their father. Reverence has an element of fear, or at least awe. The fact that in traditional societies a child spends more time, when growing up, with mother than with father tends to make reverence a tougher challenge with her. Familiarity undermines awe. When commanding us to revere our parents, the Bible again counters our nature by placing mother ahead of father.

When society disintegrates, one of the inevitable casualties is the fifth commandment: "For son spurns father, daughter rises up against mother, daughter-in-law against mother-in-law—a man's own household are his enemies" (Micah 7:6). "Fathers and mothers have been humiliated within you; strangers have been cheated in your midst; orphans and widows have been wronged within you" (Ezekiel 22:7).

Matricide and patricide would seem to be the most extreme form that disrespecting parents could assume, with other forms of physical abuse taking a second place. Not surprisingly, it is the oldest and most vulnerable parents—not young, healthy ones like Dale Ray Frank's mother—who bear the brunt of what turns out to be a surprisingly wide swath of child-on-parent violence. The National Center on Elder Abuse in Washington, D.C., reports statistics showing that from one to two million Americans over the age of sixty-five have been "injured, exploited, or otherwise mistreated by someone on whom they depended for care or protection." A study released by the National Center in 2000, "A Response to the Abuse of Vulnerable Adults," using information from state Adult Protective Services programs, found 101,000 substantiated cases of such abuse in 1999 alone. Of course, not all those

abused older people are parents, and not all the abusers are their children. However, a solid plurality (42.5 percent) occurred at home, as opposed to in institutional settings (retirement homes and the like). The
victims were mostly women (56 percent)—the power of our once-
instinctive sense of honor did not apparently save those mothers among
them—and almost half (46.5 percent) were above eighty years old. In
almost a fifth of the cases, the abuser was the grown child of the victim
(17.6 percent). There were even some cases of abuse by a grandchild
(2.5 percent).

Some brief narratives of cases churn your stomach as you read them.
There is Ruby, a "71-year-old widow who lived with her son Wayne. A
neighbor stated that her friend Ruby seemed more and more depressed
as time went by. In a recent conversation between the two women,
Ruby told her friend that, at night, after she was in bed, Wayne sat next
to her bed and read to her. After turning out the light, he slipped his
hand under the bed covers and into her pants."

Not all the accounts from Adult Protective Services involve physical abuse. There is Harry, who at age seventy-two was "hospitalized due
to the amputation of his leg. He signed over a power of attorney to his
son, John. John did not have a job nor did his wife. Harry had an estate
of $400,000, plenty of money to support all of them. The son and his
wife moved in and took over, including remodeling the house and
spending significant amounts of money on luxury items."

But the evidence about the fate of the fifth commandment is not all
so readily quantifiable. There is, instead, for those sensitized to it by
contemplating the biblical text, simply a pervasive, undeniable sense
that the number of children who hold their father and mother in anything vaguely resembling awe has dwindled, diminished to the vanish-
ing point.

A friend of mine, Cary Kozberg, who serves as the rabbinic chaplain
at a Jewish retirement home in Columbus, Ohio, speaks of the way
grown children infantilize even their mentally unimpaired aged par-

ents, addressing them as if the parents were small children: "Come on, Mom, let's eat. How are we feeling today?" It is not so much the words spoken, he says, as much as it is the tone of bored condescension associated with child care—more specifically, with the way people care for other people's children. Rabbi Kozberg describes the way adult children correct their parents, in the same tone, when the latter experience a lapse in memory. He notes a lovely teaching in Talmud that tells how people who have lost their memory really should be treated. Referring to the two sets of tablets of the Ten Commandments (the first of which Moses shattered in anger when he came from Mount Sinai and found the Jews engaged in worshiping the Golden Calf, the second of which was their replacement), it says, "Be careful with a person who has lost his memory . . . since it is said that the holy tablets and the broken tablets both lay together in the Holy Ark" (Berachot 8b).

With Americans living longer lives than ever before, long enough to develop mentally debilitating diseases like Alzheimer's, grown children will be confronted in increasing numbers by parents who are broken tablets. How many of these adult children will recognize the holiness in the shattered stones?

The key to understanding what's going on has to do with what we may call "the mystique of parental authority." Some institutions and people have a mystique that compels our respect. Almost mystically, it protects them from attacks on their honor, and from physical attacks, as well. This is why America was so ill prepared for the attacks of September 11. We never saw them coming because previously America's mystique had made the idea of such a massive, audacious attack unthinkable, for us but also for non-Americans. After the attacks, we became vigilant against further spectacular violent acts because we realized that, in a single morning, our protective mystique had disappeared. We were revealed as a country that is as vulnerable as any other.

Parents are the same way. Once, their authority was such that most children, whether young or grown, truly hesitated to challenge it. Then something happened, and the mystique evaporated.

My peers in Generation X, prior to having children ourselves, received the message over and over that as parents we would have no moral right to be honored, much less revered. In his book *Hollywood vs. America: Popular Culture and the War on Traditional Values* (1992), critic Michael Medved wrote about the way movies educate viewers to regard fathers and mothers as ridiculous, pathetic figures—fathers especially.

During the 1980s and 1990s, Hollywood was producing a string of top-grossing films seemingly calculated to undermine the fifth commandment. Medved gives examples of the genre in which it's kids who teach important lessons to foolish, incompetent, or malignant parents. Steven Spielberg, with his recurrent "kids-good, adults-bad theme," was responsible for three of these films: *E.T.*, *Back to the Future*, and *Hook*, each of which features children who save the day by evading, disregarding, or otherwise condescending to the wishes of their parents. Commenting on Homer Simpson as Hollywood's foremost icon of the father as genial moron, Medved mused, "In today's climate, a television series called *Father Knows Best* would be absolutely unthinkable—it would be deemed too judgmental, authoritarian, patriarchal, and perhaps even sexist. A program entitled *Father Knows Nothing* would stand a far better chance." A few years after Medved's book appeared, ABC put a new show entitled *Father Knows Nothing* into production.

The program was never put on the air, but anyone who's seen an episode of one of the most popular sitcoms to have aired in the present decade may think it ultimately made its way to our small screen under a different name: *Everybody Loves Raymond*. Today, parents may consider themselves lucky if they can get away with being portrayed not as their children's inferiors but as their equals—in the manner of *The Gilmore Girls*, a TV series on the WB about a woman and her college-age daughter, who, despite the generation gap, are best friends, buddies, peers.

It doesn't help that in some sectors of the culture, parents are literally their children's peers—because the mother is herself a child, a "Baby Mama," as a celebratory tune popular in 2005 put it in reference to the widespread phenomenon of African-American teens giving birth out of wedlock. At the other end of the socioeconomic spectrum, upper-middle-class parents feel unworthy of wielding parental authority.

Any married couple today who have children are quickly absorbed into the modern culture of parenting. We depend on this culture to know how to be mothers and fathers because our parents, affected by the "Don't trust anyone over thirty" ethos of the 1960s, were for the most part uncertain themselves about their own parenting roles. They were hardly role models of the mystique of parental authority. And what the new parenting culture tells us is that we have no right even to self-respect, much less respect from our kids. The question is, In a family, who rules? The parents, or the children?

I first came across the idea of the "childcentric home" when I was single, in a conversation with a girl I was dating. She asked me what I imagined our home life would be like if we got married. I hadn't thought about it, so I asked how *she* imagined married life. She had thought about it and launched into an enthusiastic description: "At the center of our home would be children. Children would be everywhere, laughing, playing, running. You would come home from work and play with the children. The children would be our life."

Happy children are, of course, what every parent wants, but the notion of children being "at the center" of things in the home is problematic. A family may center either on the parents and their relationship or on the kids. The latter has produced *Perfect Madness*, as the journalist Judith Warner puts it in the title of her 2005 book.

Warner writes of " 'dedicated' mothers who spent their evenings and weekends driving to and from soccer, attending Girl Scout cookie meetings, uber-momming, generally, twenty-four hours a day. . . . I was amazed at the breakdown of boundaries between children and adults and the erosion, for many families, of any notion of adult time and space. . . . In Washington and its suburbs, many houses were being built or had been renovated to eliminate formal living and dining rooms altogether. Instead, the focal point of most houses was the 'family room,' where a TV and a computer occupied center stage. . . . I found the pressure to breast-feed for at least a year, to endure natural childbirth, and to tolerate the boundary breakdowns of 'attachment parenting'—baby wearing, co-sleeping, long-term breast-feeding and the rest of it—cruelly insensitive to mothers' needs as adult women. And I was amazed by the fact that the women around me didn't seem to find their lives strange. It appeared normal to them that motherhood should be fraught with anxiety and guilt and exhaustion." Today's mother is the iconic "minivan mom": "As her wheels implied, she was a mom on the move, driving to school, piano, fencing, violin practice, Brownies, Cub Scouts, Sunday school, PTA meeting, volunteer work, *and* some kind of part-time, vaguely edifying, remunerative activity [that is, a job]."

It's not hard to see why a child growing up today would find revering her mother to be such a bizarre idea. After all, if you grow up in the environment of most plush American suburbs now, the working assumption is that parents serve children. Whoever heard of revering your servant? In relationship to my own three small children, for me to put on the role of the authoritative father who "knows best" is an acting exercise requiring a conscious decision and applied willpower. As it would not have done to a father a century ago, it feels very unnatural.

But working against me is not only the parenting culture with its associated publishing arm—Barnes & Noble shelves stacked with parenting books with titles like Penelope Leach's *Children First* (1994)—but, depending on where you live, the political culture, too. Parenting has become one of those issues that divide red states from blue.

Nothing illustrates this more clearly than the spanking issue. There's a lot to be said for a *potch* (the Yiddish word), which in our home means one swat with a bare hand on a clothed butt. If you were to map the

states that allow corporal punishment in public schools and those that
don't—blue for nonspanking states, twenty-seven in all, plus the District of Columbia, and red for spanking states—you would arrive at a
map closely overlapping with the map showing the results of the 2004
presidential election. In our Seattle suburb, I know virtually no parent
who admits to spanking his or her own children. Oh, they do it, in de-
spair, often in rage, against their principles when all else fails—which,
incidentally, makes the act far more potentially damaging to the relationship with your child than a coolly delivered *potch* followed by a
warm hug later. The latter is only possible when the *potch* is more a first
resort administered dispassionately like medicine than a last resort administered in fury.

I remember a National Public Radio personal commentary about a
couple of liberal baby boomers on a driving trip with a recalcitrant
three-year-old in the backseat. Finally, after pleading with the boy to be
a civilized traveling companion, the dad gave one warning, which was
disregarded, then pulled over to the side of the road and gave the boy
his first spanking. The narrator, his wife, who previously had associated
spanking with child abuse, recalled her amazement that "the rest of our
trip [was] unusually cheerful. . . . The hard part was realizing that
maybe, just maybe, a type of discipline once used by our parents had actually worked." But in the rarefied atmosphere of our big coastal cities,
rarely is spanking seen as a rationally derived policy to drive home the
occasional lesson that in family decision making, children don't come
first. The lesson it sends kids isn't in the negligible pain, but in the act
itself: It signifies parental authority.

In some places, giving a spanking could get you arrested. A parent
reads stories in the newspaper like that about Charles S. Enroe, age
forty-two, of Plymouth, Massachusetts, and it has to give you pause. According to the *Boston Globe* (May 12, 2005), he was picked up by the police on charges of domestic assault and battery with a dangerous weapon.
The "weapon" was a belt, which he used to "lightly strike his son for forgetting his homework." The paper reported that the Plymouth police

department "has some leeway on corporal punishment if it involves an open hand and there are no injuries . . . but once an instrument—a stick, a club, a belt is introduced, the police are required to react to the situation." If I lived in Plymouth, Massachusetts, the idea that the police have "leeway" when dealing with a spanking using "an open hand," that such a thing could even potentially enter into police jurisdiction, would certainly make me think hard before giving a *potch*.

One thing that all parties in the spanking controversy agree on is that the Bible has no problem with the practice. In fact, Scripture recommends it. "The strongest support for the practice of hitting children, in school or at home, comes almost solely from the Bible," commented in the *New York Times* in an editorial that denounced spanking as "primitive and unconscionable" (May 7, 2001).

The "primitive and unconscionable" scriptural verses in question include these, all from the Book of Proverbs: "He who spares the rod hates his son; but he who loves him disciplines him early" (13:24). "Chasten your son while this is still hope, and let not your soul spare for his crying" (19:18). "Do not withhold discipline from a child; if you beat him with a rod he will not die. Beat him with a rod and you will save him from the grave" (23:13–14).

W hat may not be clear yet is the larger purpose behind establishing parental discipline. Do traditionally minded mothers and fathers establish order in their home simply to satisfy their inner Mussolini? Can discipline truly be said to serve the interests of children?

That is the Bible's promise when it uses the alarmingly frank language in Proverbs. The fifth commandment says the same thing when it assures us, "Honor your father and your mother *so that your days will be long upon the land that the Lord your God gives you.*" It's possible to create the mystique of parental authority in a home without corporal punishment. The point the Bible is making has to do with whether the atmosphere of the home is one in which parents rule or one in which

children dominate. It is telling us that children brought up to honor
and revere their parents will live better, longer lives—"your days will be
long." Respect for mother and father is established not for the parents'
sake, because they deserve it, but for their children's.

Is this remotely credible?

The words in Scripture were chosen carefully. Had the words meant
to imply a supernatural reward, they should have been phrased differently. Instead, the Bible is pointing out the way the world works.

There are a few different ways of understanding this idea. After we
die, for instance, we live on through the legacy of our children, who
carry our values into the future. If we revere our aged parents, and our
children see us doing this, then they will honor us when we are old and
after we have died. They will pass on our values to their children, rendering to us a certain immortality. The cultural commentator Dennis
Prager was saying much the same thing when he wrote of his own up-
bringing: "When I saw how my father treated his extremely difficult
mother, I understood that I would have obligations toward my parents.
When your children see you totally ignore your parents, what precedent are you setting for them?" To disrespect parents is, in this sense, to
extinguish your own immortality.

Not everyone cares about continuing on after death through his
children. One prominent psychologist, Alice Miller, is on record as vig-
orously arguing that observance of the fifth commandment *shortens* life.
(She calls it the fourth commandment, in line with the way some Bible
translations divide up the Decalogue.) Writes Miller in her 2005 book,
The Body Never Lies: The Lingering Effects of Cruel Parenting, "It is my
firm and considered opinion that one specific and extremely well-
established behavior norm—the Fourth Commandment—frequently
prevents us from admitting to our true feelings, and that we pay for this
compromise with various forms of physical illness." The "true feelings"
in question stem from the abuse many, if not most, of us sustained from
parents in their efforts to discipline us.

In Miller's scenario, repressing the pain that necessarily accompanies the establishment of parental authority results, when the child has grown up, in deep psychic stress. Citing a 1990s research project in San Diego, the Adverse Childhood Experiences Study, she argues that this stress leads to somatic symptoms—physical illness—even early death. This accounts for Dostoevsky's epileptic fits, Kafka's tuberculosis, Nietzsche's rheumatism, Proust's asthma. It all goes back to Moses, abandoned as a child when his mother cast him in an ark of bulrushes into the Nile to save his life from Pharaoh, Moses, who sought to justify his parents' actions by commanding his fellow Israelites to respect their parents no matter what: "We see that the Fourth Commandment contains a threat, a kind of moral blackmail that has lost none of its potency: If you want to live a long life, you have to honor your parents, even if they do not deserve it; otherwise you will die an early death," Miller writes.

Moral blackmail? No. The mystique of parental authority is really about creating a certain atmosphere in the home, where children have their place, which is not the same place as that of the adults. Biblical tradition symbolizes this by instructing the child not to sit in his father's seat, not to contradict his parents, not to call them by their first names. This is a long way from modern "attachment parenting," which, in creating the "democratic family" with its "floor time" and its "family bed," seeks to break down barriers between adults and children.

When those barriers fall, one of the results is a transformed relationship between the parents themselves—transformed for the worst, with consequences for their children. When we had our first baby, my wife would tell me about the conversations she had with other women in her PEPS group. PEPS is an organization for mothers that offers bonding sessions at one another's homes, with occasional instruction from parenting experts for enrichment. Small groups of mothers get together and talk about what's on their minds.

In the suburban communities of Seattle's Eastside, what they talk about involves primarily two things. They talk about children's gear of all kinds: what style of jogging stroller to buy, what car seats have been recalled, what minivan got the best side-impact-collision safety rating. And they talk about sex: how their husbands want it but they don't. At the thought of intimacy, they roll their eyes and hope he won't ask for it. They are young and healthy, frequent gyms, dress well, have not descended to frumpiness in any way that would be outwardly observable. But these are women whose lives are defined by being mothers. Simply, they are giving all they have to their children. Consequently, they have little left for their husbands.

This was my first inkling of the "sexless marriage," a phenomenon *Newsweek* broke out into the open in 2003 by reporting that 20 percent of American married couples were having sex on only ten or fewer occasions yearly.

In a *New York Times* "Styles" section essay (March 27, 2005), the novelist Ayelet Waldman wrote about her own experience in the equivalent of a PEPS group—elsewhere called Mommy and Me or Second-Times Moms—about how the conversations always circled back to how the moms were "so physically *available*" to their kids that "how could they bear to be physically available to anyone else?" While Ayelet Waldman wished to point out that this wasn't the case in *her* marriage, which remained red-hot, she wondered about the effect all this overparenting will have on the sacrificed-for children:

"I wish some learned sociologist would publish a definitive study of marriages where the parents are desperately, ardently in love, where the parents love each other even more than they love the children. It would be wonderful if it could be established, once and for all, that children of these marriages are more successful, happier, *live longer and have healthier lives* than children whose mothers focus their desires and passions on them," said Waldman.

Waldman had put her finger on a reason that the fifth commandment promises, as a natural outcome, longer lives to children who respect their parents. Respect, honor, and reverence require a certain distance between parent and child, in the absence of which the relationship of the parents suffers, and so do the children. A November

2004 article in *Psychology Today* ("A Nation of Wimps") suggested the ways that overparenting may lead to neurotic or other undesirable behavior by children as they grow up. "I wish my parents had some hobby other than me," a young patient was quoted as telling his doctor, who observed that parents who try to solve their children's problems end up raising kids who later in life can't tolerate modest levels of adversity. Harvard psychologist Jerome Kagan has observed a direct causative relationship between parental hovering and the later development of anxiety in the grown child. Anxiety certainly makes life less enjoyable. Is that all it does?

The costs of overparenting begin with anxiety. They spiral upward from there, with unknowable ultimate results. Could smothering kids, figuratively, even contribute to the kind of lifetime neurotic behaviors that shorten life spans? That is entirely possible, and it is something that well-meaning but hypervigilant mothers and fathers should consider. It does neither you nor your children the good you hoped it would. In a home where parents are honored, that cost may be avoided.

W hen the fifth commandment associates giving honor with enjoying long life, there is an additional level of meaning. It appears, you remember, not on the second tablet, where we would expect it—among the commandments that deal with relationships between people—but on the first tablet—among commandments that deal with our relationship to God. When fathers and mothers fail to establish the mystique of parental authority in the home, they undermine their children's relationship with God, which, in turn, affects the life of the society around them. Cultures that trifle with parental honor do so at great risk.

The primary beneficiary of the promise of long days "upon the land that the Lord your God gives you" is not the individual, but the society. After all, it was to the Israelites as a nation, not to individual Jews, that the Lord gave the land.

When children honor and revere parents, that makes it much more likely that the parents—the father in particular—will pass on beliefs about God and the ways in which He asks us to walk. This tradition goes all the way back to ancient Israelite society, where the *bet-av*, or "father's house," the extended family, including grandparents, parents, and children, along with *mishpacha*, or clan, were the institutions responsible for many of the functions that we associate today with the state: military, economic, judicial, and educational. Of these, the last was arguably the most important. The father, not the government, was responsible for educating his children.

Of course, this education included religious values. The Jewish prayer Shemah, including verses from Deuteronomy, makes this point explicit: "Take to heart these instructions with which I charge you this day. Teach them to your children" (6:6–7). Again from Deuteronomy: "Therefore impress these My words upon your very heart: bind them as a sign on your hand and let them serve as a symbol on your forehead, and teach them to your children—reciting them when you stay at home and when you are away, when you lie down and when you get up" (11:18–19). The same biblical book makes explicit the promise of long life on the land: "Take to heart all the words with which I have warned you this day. Enjoin them upon your children, that they may observe faithfully all the terms in this Teaching. For this is not a trifling thing for you: it is your very life; through it you shall long endure on the land that you are to possess upon crossing the Jordan" (32:46–47).

Obviously, it wasn't government-paid instructors who were teaching the children "at home and when you are away, when you lie down and when you get up." It wasn't even instructors in religious schools, but what today we would call "home schooling." Jewish law, in fact, discourages sending children to formal school at all until they reach the age of about seven. When Americans in the nineteenth century entrusted the education of young children to the government, they were undermining the mechanism the Bible envisions for passing along values to the future generations.

The teacher was the father. When I say the father has a special role, this doesn't mean the mother has none. Yet his role is crucial in a way hers may not be. The Bible, we saw, phrases the commandment of revering parents so as to suggest that for a child, revering his father comes more naturally than revering his mother. This is because, says the Talmud, "his father teaches him Torah" (Kiddushin 31a). A father's teaching values to his children increases the likelihood they will revere him, which, in turn, increases his effectiveness as a teacher.

It also seems to be the case that he is the more effective teacher of such matters, which have about them a certain edge. They make non-negotiable demands. By contrast, as the Talmud puts it, the mother "coaxes [the child] with words." She's a soft touch, when what may be needed, especially with boys, is a harder presence. This is why it might be seen as an ominous sign that religious life in the United States is becoming, to a much larger extent than the demography of the sexes would predict, a women's affair. As David Murrow reported in his book *Why Men Hate Going to Church* (2005), according to one survey after another, women make a huge majority, 60 to 80 percent, of participants in almost every type of church activity.

American fathers are abdicating what we may call "their priestly roles." In biblical tradition, mother and father (again, the father especially) act as priests in a temple, the home, where the children are the congregation. Like priests in any religion, their main role is to teach. Even the great Jerusalem Temple was simply a larger-scale model of the home temple that the ancient Jewish patriarchs, Abraham, Isaac, and Jacob, had established and bequeathed to their descendants. When the Jerusalem Temple was destroyed, the Jews reverted to the older domestic sanctuary, with its religious and didactic functions.

Jews to this day regard the homely dining room table as a kind of altar, where on the Sabbath especially the sanctification of bread and wine, the ritual hand washing, and other symbolic acts all have parallels in the rites of the fallen great Temple. The Talmud even teaches that the table brings atonement just as the Temple's altar once did.

However, all this is impossible in the absence of parental authority, which translates into parental *teaching* authority.

James Dobson, for one, has it right in his book *Dare to Discipline* when he points out that, on Earth, in many ways, parents in their child's eyes stand in for God Himself. This, too, of course, is a priestly role. "Young children typically identify their parents . . . and especially their fathers . . . with God. Therefore, if Mom and Dad are not worthy of respect, then neither are their morals, their country, their values and beliefs, or even their religious faith." He argues the point persuasively in the arena of sex. If parents don't impress their ethical values on their children, no one will. And society will suffer, for sexual indiscipline has consequences outside the bedroom: "When a man is devoted to one woman and one family, he is motivated to build, save, protect, plan, and prosper on their behalf. However, when his sexual interests are dispersed and generalized, his effort is invested in the gratification of sexual desires." Providing historical confirmation of this, Dobson cites the research of a British social anthropologist, J. D. Unwin, who studied how eighty different civilizations rose, declined, and ultimately fell. Unwin found that, as a rule, while the rise to prosperity and power was associated with a culture of sexual restraint, the end was always preceded by a drifting toward sexual libertinism.

Respect for parents, in other words, is a necessary condition for moral education, which is a necessary condition for a society's thriving, perhaps for its very survival. To put it another way: "Honor your father and your mother so that your days will be long upon the land that the Lord your God gives you."

A culture like ours that so discourages parents who want to engender respect in their children, a culture that doesn't even consider what the impact will be on its own longevity—the longevity of American civilization—has written for itself something that looks very much like a suicide note.

A DEATH SMELL

You shall not murder.
(Exodus 20:13)

In search of the wonderful style of moral reasoning of our Seattle neighbors, a friend of mine, local radio talk host Dan Sytman, exhaustively interviewed "activists" protesting the Iraq war outside the Federal Building in downtown Seattle. At one point, the subject of murder came up in a conversation with a woman with a French accent, a fellow who sounded like he was from New York, and a third gentleman with a harsh and grating voice. The Q&A exchange, which Dan recorded, is worth savoring.

Q: Is there such a thing as right and wrong?

A (woman with French accent): I don't think so. I would like you to hear me. What I'm saying is that it is not working to call people names and make them "wrong" and then think "we are right."

A (man with New York accent, interrupting): I would suggest that good and evil and right and wrong, when you look at them in a broad perspective, are simply another way of saying "like" and "don't like." So I would say, when you ask me about murder, I would say "I don't like murder."

A (man with harsh, grating accent): I don't believe that people should murder other people because I don't want to be murdered. So I'm not going to kill anybody. So other people should not want to kill other people.

Q: Is murder wrong?

A (French woman): You keep wanting me to, to . . .

Q: Is murder wrong?

A: I do not like it.

Q: You don't like murder. . . .

A: I do not support it.

Q: What about mass murder? Is mass murder wrong? Yes or no?

A: You keep asking me the question. Obviously you haven't heard me. Evil, good, wrong, right—this is how tyrants make people follow them.

Q: How about George W. Bush?

A (harsh-voiced man): I don't believe he's evil. He's not evil. There's no such thing. There's no such thing as inherent right or wrong.

Q: What should be done with a mass murderer? Someone who kills, say, a hundred thousand people, two hundred thousand people, a million people. What should the punishment be?

A (New Yorker): Don't reelect him.

If some Americans can't think of anything worse to say about murder than that they don't "support it," don't "like it," would not want it to happen to them, and wouldn't knowingly elect a murderer, that is a discouraging fact.

Yet is there not good news to tell about murder? If we are grading modern American culture on a scale of one to ten—the scale of the Ten Commandments—isn't it true that, when it comes to the sixth commandment, forbidding murder, the bad news of the previous five chapters of this book must now give way to a cheerier mood?

Since 1991, the nation has enjoyed a steady decline in homicide, as in every category of violent and property crime. By 2000, the murder rate had fallen by 44 percent—to 5.5 per 100,000, a figure not seen in forty years. To put this in terms of the absolute number of deaths, in 2002, about nine thousand fewer people were murdered than in 1991. Is this not something to be pleased about?

Recently, economist Steven D. Levitt has (very controversially) explained the drop in crime in a word: abortion. The 1973 Supreme Court decision Roe v. Wade, which legalized abortion nationwide, naturally led to a surge of women ending their pregnancies. The group of women most likely to do this—those who, owing to poverty, lack of education, or being too young themselves, were most unprepared to raise their children—is also the group of mothers most likely to give birth to future criminals. By 1980, the abortion rate had reached 1.6 million yearly, or about 1 in 2.25 live births. That means that from 1973 on, there was a whole cohort of young Americans who were simply missing from the population. Given the circumstances of their mothers' lives, a disproportionate number would have grown up to become criminals, including murderers. It was about 1990, when the first of the missing cohort would have been turning seventeen, that the effect of their nonexistence began to be felt.

We were buying a relative freedom from the fear of murder by eliminating potential lives. It starts to sound like a science-fiction movie. In fact, something very much like this idea provides the seed of a couple of recent films: Steven Spielberg's Minority Report (2002), with Tom Cruise, about a futuristic law-enforcement agency that can determine who may commit murder; and Batman Begins (2005), in which Liam Neeson leads an apocalyptic vigilante group that specializes in wiping out whole cities that include too many criminals.

Ask yourself: Cui bono? Who benefits? It turns out that we all do. In a given year, by destroying up to a million and a half potential lives through abortion, we had saved nine thousand others—a gruesome calculus. The erasure of those tens of millions of lives is a fact whose benefits we are implicitly willing to accept because the meaning of those deaths hardly registers with us.

Americans seem able to stomach the intentional taking of innocent life so long as it is suitably disguised as "choice." The subject of this chapter is the sixth commandment's prohibition of murder, but the theme I want to bring out is the extent to which murder may be hidden from us through our own denial of it. The theme is the increasing acceptance and mainstreaming of murder, why this is happening, and why it's not unrealistic to worry about the problem getting worse.

On one of the nights in March 2005 when Terri Schiavo, the severely brain-damaged Florida woman, lay dying at the insistence of her husband, I happened to be giving a speech at a large suburban synagogue with a liberal congregation, near Seattle. Michael Schiavo had won the legal right to have his otherwise-healthy wife starved and dehydrated to death. The events in Florida, which were convulsing the nation in bitter controversy, weren't related to what I had been invited to speak about. But in the course of my speech, I had mentioned something about the need to appreciate the vital and ongoing contributions of Christianity to the civilizing of the Western world. During the Q&A period afterward, the rabbi asked if I could give an example of what good Christians do nowadays, and I had responded that, for one thing, "at this moment there are tens of thousands of Christians who are trying to save Terri Schiavo because her husband is trying to kill her."

I hadn't expected that what I regarded as a simple factual statement would get the reaction it did. As soon as the words "kill her" were out of my mouth, there was a gasp from the audience and a fluttering movement of bodies in seats. Several people said, "No, no," as if to deny the obvious truth: that Mr. Schiavo was intent on killing his wife. The reaction was so impassioned that an anxiety wire somewhere in my brain was briefly tripped and I was ready, if someone rushed the podium, to defend myself physically.

Such was the level of emotion, and of self-deception, stirred up across the country by the Schiavo case. Many, many Americans, like my audience in Seattle, were intent on not seeing what was happening, and they would passionately assail anyone who tried to dispel the pleasant illusion.

Then there came the months following Terri Schiavo's death. Few families were not touched by her ordeal. Suddenly, it seemed, preparing for "death with dignity," a wonderful euphemism, was on everyone's mind. After Terri died, hundreds of thousands of mostly older Americans filled out "living wills," also known as advance directives, instructing how they should be treated—whether they, too, should be dehydrated to death—in the event of a catastrophic illness that rendered them comatose and where there was no realistic hope of regaining consciousness. The phrase you kept hearing in the media was "around the dining room table." "Around the dining room table," sometimes "around the kitchen table," millions of Americans were discussing what kind of death they would like to have. My father called me on the phone to say he had decided to sign over another kind of advance directive, called "durable powers of attorney for health care," to his wife, my stepmother, rather than to me. This provides that such wrenching decisions about a person's life or death should be made by the party stipulated in the powers-of-attorney document. My father explained that I would not be the one making such decisions for him because he and my stepmother shared the wish "not to be kept alive on a tube." In other words, they would, under certain circumstances, prefer that someone kill them.

There are a couple of reasons to worry about the number of killings that occur under the reassuring aegis of a living will. First, it's not unrealistic to imagine that a dependent senior citizen could be influenced by a family member who is not inclined to be the one waiting by the hospital bed as the loved one on the feeding tube fights a prolonged battle for life.

Second, there is what journalist Wesley Smith calls the "gotcha" concern. A living will, like any legal document, locks in the preferences of the person signing it. But unlike business contracts or wedding licenses, once it has taken effect, due to a catastrophic stroke or the like, it may leave no possibility for being amended or escaped. In one case, a stroke victim by the name of Marjorie Nighbert was in the process of being dehydrated to death. Not yet dead, she unexpectedly recovered a will to live, raised her voice, and said, "Please feed me. I'm hungry. I'm thirsty." Smith, who retells this and other troubling stories in his book *Forced Exit*, concludes, "Her earlier expressed sentiments ended up costing the non-terminally ill Nighbert her life."

Apart from living wills, there is a sizable portion of the citizenry that would like to have the option of being killed by a physician under circumstances of their choosing, not limited by any end-of-life document they might draw up. This is the concept behind physician-assisted suicide (PAS), currently legal only in Oregon but whose wider legality would be favored, according to 2005 polling data from Gallup, by 58 percent of Americans. One notable fact about PAS is that while it has been typically presented to voters and in the media as a remedy only for the terminally ill who are in excruciating agony and who beg for release, its practical application has proven to be considerably wider. The very first patient to poison herself under Oregon's Measure 16, after it was passed in 1994, had breast cancer but had chosen to take her own life not because she was in agony—she was not at this point, though her condition was judged terminal—but because she wished to "be relieved of all the stress I have."

Smith reports that "the starving and dehydration of cognitively disabled patients has become almost routine in hospitals and nursing homes all around the country." The vast majority of these people are unable to speak up for themselves about their own wishes one way or the other. But sometimes a "cognitively disabled" person, on the verge of being killed, will find a way to express his true wishes.

Such was the case of Robert Wendland. As Terri Schiavo reportedly did before falling ill, Wendland, when he was still healthy, had expressed to his wife (or so she said) a desire to die rather than be kept alive as something less than a fully competent and able human being. Tragically, a 1993 auto accident reduced him to just the circumstances he had once called worse than death. He woke from a coma but remained severely disabled. Though he participated in physical therapy, presumably evidence of a wish to live, and improved to the point where he could drive his own electric wheelchair, his wife insisted on following what she presented as his previously expressed will to die, notwithstanding that it was based on a casual statement. His doctors and the hospital ethics committee agreed that he should be dehydrated to death. The case was fought all the way to the California Supreme Court, with Robert's mother and sister pleading that his life be spared. In the end, he died of pneumonia.

What happens when the people being killed aren't adults at all, but children, babies who, by definition, could express no preference in the matter?

"Euthanasia for Babies?" was the frank title of a *New York Times Magazine* article in the summer of 2005. The author, Jim Holt, held up for our admiration a pair of Dutch doctors who had written an article in *The New England Journal of Medicine* about the protocol for killing babies they had established at the Groningen pediatric hospital. In certain extreme cases involving birth defects resulting in "unbearable and unrelievable suffering" in an infant, the Dutch physicians advocate administering a lethal drip of morphine and a sleeping drug called midazolam. One of the doctors, Eduard Verhagen, described how "beautiful" it is to see a baby die this way, and Jim Holt assured readers that the procedure is done only with the "informed consent of both parents."

In fact, it's not true that all such cases in the Netherlands, which account for about 8 percent of infant deaths in that country, or between eighty and one hundred such deaths a year, include "informed consent of both parents," as a 1996 study in the British journal *Lancet* found. But never mind. The Dutch have accepted infanticide, and with the implicit approval of *The New England Journal of Medicine* and the *New York Times*, we Americans are being invited to do so, too.

W e are increasingly hard to shock. Ideas about killing, and images of it, that would have seemed beyond the pale only a decade or two earlier now appear utterly mundane. Think of the way murder is turned into a live-action cartoon in cultural vehicles like Quentin Tarantino's two *Kill Bill* films. Bumper stickers that might once have been dismissed as a cartoon version of moral thinking—MEAT IS MUR-DER, for example, on a car whose driver supports the work of People for the Ethical Treatment of Animals (PETA)—appear increasingly likely to represent mainstream American attitudes.

When we aren't trivializing murder, we are crowning murderers as heroes. Consider the list of movies nominated for the top 2005 Academy Awards. There was *Million Dollar Baby*, the boxing-cum-euthanasia film from Clint Eastwood about a trainer who makes the heroic decision to end the life of a boxer whom a catastrophic injury has reduced to a paraplegic. There was *The Sea Inside*, a Spanish film about a quadriplegic who begs to be killed. There was *Vera Drake*, which made a heroine of a 1950s British matron who performed illegal abortions by injecting women with soapy water.

In short, however pleased we may be by the fact that the murder rate stands at its lowest level in four decades, our satisfaction should be tempered by the transformation of American attitudes about the value of a human life—a transformation from which the happy news about crime statistics tends to divert our attention.

How did we come to this point?

Remember what I said earlier about how the commandments on the first tablet—the first through fifth commandments—relate to those on the second tablet—sixth through tenth. The Decalogue forms not only a list of ten independent items, or two lists of five items each; it also forms a matrix, where the first item on the first tablet aligns with the sixth item on the second tablet, the second item on the first tablet aligns with the seventh item on the second tablet, and so on. As long ago as about 200 C.E., Jewish tradition, as recorded in the rabbinic text Mechilta, taught that the items on the two tablets can be read not only down but across, as a series of if/then statements. Grammatically speaking, the Ten Commandments are not really formulated as commandments at all—"Don't do this," "Don't do that," "Do this"—but as a comprehensive description of spiritual and social reality. In Hebrew, for example, lo tirtzach, usually translated as "You shall not murder," means literally, "You will not murder." Strictly speaking, it is not a "commandment," but an affirmation, a promise, a prediction.

The Decalogue, in other words, offers a series of predictions. The first five "commandments," as we've seen, have to do with the way people relate to God. The second five have to do with the way we deal with other human beings. The Ten Commandments predict the specific ways that departures from right thinking about God will result in wrong ways of thinking about other people.

So let's try to read the first commandment in conjunction with the sixth. What is the prediction here? The first commandment, "I am the Lord your God, who has taken you out of the land of Egypt, from the house of slavery," has to do with rejecting materialism, the view that material reality is all there is, that the universe has always been able to get along perfectly well without the interventions of a deity. So here is the if/then statement: If a culture takes to heart God's teaching that "I am the Lord your God," then "You will not murder," meaning your culture will be the kind where people don't murder, or at least where they take murder seriously. The converse is also true: If a culture embraces materialism, then its members will take murder lightly, and possibly commit a great deal of it.

To see why this should be so, we need to understand why murder is wrong in the first place, in the Bible's system of morality, and why people nevertheless take one another's lives without good cause.

As for the first question—"Why not murder?"—the Book of Genesis reports God's words to Noah. The latter had just emerged from his ark following the Flood to repopulate the ravaged world. Said God, "Whoever sheds the blood of man, by man shall his blood be shed; for in the image of God He made man" (9:5). There is something special a human being possesses that is defiled if another person kills him, or, indeed, if he kills himself.

What is that special something? In Hebrew, the mysterious and impossible-to-translate phrase is "*tzelem Elokim,*" the "image of God" that was somehow imprinted upon the first man, Adam: "So God created man in His image, in the image of God He created him; male and female He created them" (Genesis 1:27). It is some kind of presence, aura, effulgence, or spirit that pervades a person, and it partakes of the divine. The exact moment when man received the "image" appears to have been when God breathed life into him: "And the Lord God formed man of dust from the ground, and He blew into his nostrils the soul of life; and man became a living being" (2:7).

When he received the *tzelem,* Adam was unconscious. Today, we might say he was in a persistent vegetative state. And then he "became a living being"—he woke up. But before he awoke, he already glowed with the aura of God's image. Had someone killed him after he received the imprint of the *tzelem,* but before he awoke from his vegetative coma, obviously this would have been an attack on God's image.

The problem with murder is that it assails the image of God, the possession of which is not a function of consciousness, but simply of being human. There would be nothing wrong with taking the life of a terminally ill patient who wished to die or a persistently vegetative one, but for the fact that the patient is imprinted with God's *tzelem* and thus neither he nor anyone else has permission to obliterate his Maker's image in this way.

Why, then, do people violate the sixth commandment? The Bible presents some answers in the story of the first murder. Adam and Eve had two sons to begin with, Cain and Abel. After the family was expelled from the Garden of Eden, Cain killed Abel. Cain's motives, alluded to in the Bible and clarified in ancient biblical tradition, happen to coincide with the analysis of murder and its motives offered by some of today's criminal psychologists.

Cain was a materialist. One of the tenets of materialism holds that, because matter is all that there ever was or ever will be, human beings are locked in a zero-sum game. Believers in God assume that creation ex nihilo, from nothing, is a possibility for people. In the biblical worldview, this is the promise of infinite human creativity. However, the believer in nothing but material reality is denied this hope. Because there is only so much material stuff, a definite finite quantity that can be apportioned more or less equally or fairly, any material possession of mine must be something that I denied to you. I cannot really have created it, only taken it. In a materialistic world, acquisitiveness and jealousy will naturally be rampant.

Cain's character was hinted at in the name his mother, Eve, gave him. In Hebrew, the name Kayin is built on the same grammatical root as the verb *kana*, "to acquire," a root related to the noun *kina*, which means "jealousy." The plain text of the Bible (Genesis 4:3–8) is cryptic about what drove Cain to slay his brother, but it appears to have been an outpouring of jealousy.

> After a period of time, Cain brought an offering to the Lord of the fruit of the ground; and as for Abel, he also brought of the firstlings of his flock and from their choicest. The Lord turned to Abel and to his offering, but to Cain and to his offering He did not turn. This annoyed Cain exceedingly, and his countenance fell.
>
> And the Lord said to Cain, "Why are you annoyed, and why has your countenance fallen? Surely, if you improve yourself, you will be forgiven. But if you do not improve yourself, sin rests at the door. Its desire is toward you, yet you can conquer it."

Cain spoke with his brother Abel. And it happened when
they were in the field, that Cain rose up against his brother Abel
and killed.

Why did God reject Cain's offering? What did Cain say to Abel
just before he killed him, a question heightened by the literal phrasing
of the Hebrew—not "Cain *spoke* with his brother Abel," but "Cain
said to his brother Abel"—and what does that have to do with the murder? The story makes little sense without the explanatory scriptural
traditions supplied in sources like the Talmud and Midrash. From
them, we learn that Cain's offering was from the inferior portion of his
crop, whereas Abel's was from the "choicest." For Cain, the challenge
to humans of sustaining ourselves is a zero-sum game. Naturally, he
withheld the best he had, because once it was gone, it could never be
re-created.

Tradition adds additional layers of meaning, as well. One medieval
commentator, Rabbi Moses ben Nachman, called "Ramban," explains
that Cain's intention "in killing [Abel] was that the world should develop from him [alone], for he thought that his father would not have
further offspring." Here is the theme of the zero-sum game again. It dis-
tressed Cain to be forced to share glory and dominion with his brother.
Another medieval exegete, Rabbi Abraham Ibn Ezra, highlights God's
choice of words in questioning Cain shortly before the murder: "why
has your countenance fallen?" As Ibn Ezra notes, in the Bible, a "fallen
countenance" always signifies shame, the loss of status. Cain was
ashamed, his status crushed, because God highly regarded Abel's offering but not his. Still another tradition holds that Abel had a sister
whom Cain wished to marry. To acquire the woman, he jealously killed
his only competitor in the world.

There is no reason to assume these explanations are mutually exclusive. Biblical tradition gives a complex picture of human motivations,
so most likely we should assume that all these factors worked in Cain's
mind as he drew closer to the moment of murder. In short, the first and

therefore exemplary homicide was committed because of jealousy, an excessive attachment to status, and acquisitiveness in regard to possessions, reputation, and a woman.

It's interesting to note that a recent book by an evolutionary psychologist, David M. Buss, explains the psychology of murder in exactly this way. In *The Murderer Next Door: Why the Mind Is Designed to Kill* (2005), Buss brings to bear the Darwinian doctrine that people are, after all, nothing more than sophisticated animals. The mechanism of natural selection determines what traits are likeliest to lead to the successful propagation of offspring. From this perspective, a main evolutionary-psychological impulse that drives males in particular is the impulse to fight off rivals. For rivals threaten to reduce our access to reproductive assets (women) by lowering our status in a social hierarchy. In certain neighborhoods, all it takes is a disrespectful look or word, a "dis," especially in front of women, to get a man killed. In evolutionary psychology, as in common sense, it is apparent that males highly value whatever source of status or prestige they have managed to secure.

We value status so much that some are willing to kill over it. Others are willing at least to wound, if only with words. Material goods, in so far as they convey prestige, are like movable sources of status, which serve the same purpose.

Indeed, a shattered sense of personal prestige contributed to the careers of serials killers such as Ted Bundy. Just before he embarked on a string of bold and gruesome killings of young women in Washington State, Utah, Colorado, and Florida, Bundy had been rejected by a woman. Almost every one of his victims fit the physical profile of that woman—long straight hair parted down the middle—as if he were taking his revenge on her over and over again. In her biography of Bundy, *The Stranger Beside Me*, Ann Rule makes clear the role that status played in his mind:

> Like a little boy who yearns to be important, to be noticed,
> Ted played perverse games with policemen. . . . Although he

often called policemen stupid, he needed to know that he was
important to them, if only in a negative sense. . . .

When Ted confessed his escape [from incarceration in
Colorado] and his intricate credit card thefts, when he discussed
his terrible fantasies, it was to policemen. His voice on the tapes
made in Pensacola is excited and full of pride. He is triumphant
and in his element on those tapes, doing exactly what he wants to
be doing as if he were laying a gift before them, expecting praise
for his cunning.

Bundy hoped, like Cain, that this time his offering would be accepted. When he gave a final videotaped interview—to conservative
Christian psychologist James Dobson the day before his execution in
Florida's electric chair in 1989—he was at it again, looking for approval
now from God's representative. With a little smile playing over his face
the whole time, he told Dobson exactly what he knew the other man
wanted to hear: how it was all because of hard-core pornography and
violence in the media that he had committed these unspeakably awful
murders—notwithstanding that Bundy's biographer found no evidence
of such influences in the killer's personal history.

A more obvious way in which a picture of the universe defined by
the material rather than the spiritual leads to homicide is as obvious as the nose—or rather, the *tzelem*—on your face. That happens to
be where Ramban locates the primary physical manifestation of God's
image: the human face and its expressions. There is something dead
about an ape's face in comparison to a person's. Even when asleep, a human has an aura that may sometimes be discerned. The special horror
connected with murder is a function of our intuition that the countenance of a human being reflects the essence of his Creator. There is
nothing comparably horrendous about the killing of an animal. This is
because, however intelligent and sympathetic, neither a dog nor a cat,

neither a whale nor a dolphin, ever received the *tzelem Elokim*. In a materialist universe, however, there is no Creator and therefore no image of God flickering in a man's face.

We should expect, therefore, that in a culture that has repudiated the biblical idea of God's image imprinted in humanity, the estimation of the value of a human's life and that of an animal will change relative to each other and approach equality.

It has happened before. When the Hebrew prophets wished to depict humanity fallen to the uttermost depths of immorality, the image they chose was that of Gehenna, or Ben-Hinnom, a valley under the slopes of the southwestern corner of Jerusalem where from ancient days children were burned on the altar of Baal, also called Molech, a god with the face of the tenderest animal, a calf. The place of slaughter was also called Tophet, apparently a reference to the drum (*tof*) music employed to drown out the child's cries. Jeremiah prophesies, "And they built the high places of Baal to burn their children with fire as burnt offerings to Baal, which I did not command, neither did I speak nor did it enter My mind. Therefore, behold days are coming, says the Lord, when the place will no longer be called Tophet or Ben-Hinnom valley, but the Valley of Slaughter. And I will frustrate the counsel of Judah and Jerusalem in this place, and I will hurl them down by the sword before their enemies and into the hands of those who seek their lives, and I will give their carcasses for food to the fowl of the heaven and to the beasts of the earth" (Jeremiah 19:5–7). Nothing could be worse than letting children die to sate an animal, so the appropriate punishment is that the malefactors will themselves be consumed as food for animals. Gehenna would later become, in the terminology of biblical tradition, another word for hell.

For many centuries, the tradition of the West, in religion and philosophy, insisted that there was something unique about the spirit of man, relating him to God, whereby murder retained the status of the ultimate crime. On this point, biblical tradition was organized and codified into law in the most comprehensive manner by Maimonides, also called "Rambam," who later influenced Aquinas. In his encyclopedia-length Mishneh Torah, Rambam detailed the legislation of biblical tradition with its exquisite sensitivity to protecting the image of God infused in a human being, whatever condition that person may be in, whether he is sick or well, whether he wants to die or not. "One and same is the man who kills a healthy person or a sick person who is likely to die, even one who kills a person who is entirely moribund"—in Hebrew, a *goses*, someone on the verge of death—in each such instance the killer "is subject to capital punishment" (Hilchot Rotzeach 2:7). Suicide is forbidden, according to Maimonides, because God in Genesis had commanded, "However, your blood which belongs to your souls I will demand" (9:5)—that is, if you shed your own blood, I will demand it from you.

To these propositions, Christian theologians could agree. In the nineteenth century, however, our culture was rocked in its certainties on such matters. Given what we've said about the centrality of the idea of *tzelem Elokim*, the unique gift of God to man, you won't be surprised that the morality of taking a life was undermined when the uniqueness of man began to be doubted.

Casting into doubt man's uniqueness was the contribution primarily of Charles Darwin, whose *Origin of Species* (1859) and even more his *Descent of Man* (1871) bore this out. While Darwin's *Origin* left mostly untouched the subject of man's origins, the *Descent* took this up forcefully. "If man had not been his own classifier," wrote Darwin, "he would never have thought of founding a separate order for his own reception." The reality, he showed to his own satisfaction, was that man bears overwhelming similarities to other animals not only in physical but in intellectual and moral endowments. Ethical instincts, even the most passionately insisted upon—for example, against incest—were the product mainly of natural selection: "We may, therefore, reject the belief, lately insisted on by some writers, that the abhorrence of incest is due to our possessing a special God-implanted conscience."

According to Darwin, there is nothing absolute about our ideas of right and wrong, including the subject of murder. Had our species evolved under other conditions, he maintained, we might have very different ideas:

> I do not wish to maintain that any strictly social animal, if its intellectual faculties were to become as active and as highly developed as man, would acquire exactly the same moral sense as ours. In the same manner as various animals have some sense of beauty, though they admire widely different objects, so they might have a sense of right and wrong, though led by it to follow widely different lines of conduct. If, for instance, to take an extreme case, men were reared under precisely the same conditions as hive-bees, there can hardly be a doubt that our unmarried females would, like the worker-bees, think it a sacred duty to kill their brothers, and mothers would strive to kill their fertile daughters; and no one would think of interfering.

Another potent materialist, Professor Peter Singer of Princeton University, recounts the influence of Darwin's ideas about killing in his book *Rethinking Life and Death: The Collapse of our Traditional Ethics* (1994). Singer rightly sees that Darwin was laying siege to the "Hebrew view of creation," with its solemn and central theme: "And God said, 'Let us make man in our image.'" According to Singer, the "Hebrew view" hung as if suspended in the air by the slenderest string for about a century: "its foundations had been knocked out from under it, and yet it remained upright." Some of the impact of Darwin's thought on the valuing of human life didn't appear in full until the 1970s. One of its flowerings was the animal rights movement, of which Singer has become today's leading icon.

Singer's philosophy may be summed up by the statement, "There are other persons on this planet." That would include dolphins, monkeys, pigs, and other intelligent, sympathetic, seemingly self-aware creatures. In his view, since no "person," human or otherwise, has been stamped with God's image, none has an *absolute* right to life. "Once we remove the assumption that an animal must be human in order to have some kind of right to life, then we will have to start looking at the characteristics and capacities that an animal must possess in order to have that right." For bioethicists like Singer, those capacities include rationality and self-awareness, to which a newborn infant may have a lesser claim than a dog or a monkey. The latter would then be considered a "person" with a right to life, while the former would be no more a person than is, for instance, a salmon.

This is the sort of logic to which a willed blindness about seeing God's image in man naturally leads. Singer's utilitarianism makes it a priority for society to maximize the happiness of as many "persons" as possible. This would mean that if newborns with certain defects—hemophilia or autism—could be shown to be net drains on society, by diverting funds or other resources from the needs of others, then it would be ethical to kill such babies: "When the death of a disabled infant will lead to the birth of another infant with better prospects of a happy life, the total amount of happiness will be greater if the disabled infant is killed. The loss of the happy life for the first infant is outweighed by the gain of a happier life for the second. Therefore, if the killing of the hemophiliac infant has no adverse effect on others it would be right to kill him." In other words, if a nonhuman person—let's say a dog—were to somehow benefit from the killing of a hemophiliac infant, it would be right to sacrifice the baby for the benefit of the dog.

We have, in short, come full circle—from our own times back to the worst of times depicted in the Hebrew Bible. If Peter Singer weren't an atheist, he would be entirely comfortable, at a bioethical level, with the Molech worship that Jeremiah railed against, which killed children to satisfy an animal god. Molech worship was also very mainstream. Kings of ancient Judah, including Ahaz and Menasseh, fully approved of it and personally sacrificed their own children.

Singerism is the inevitable result of compassion uninformed by the first commandment: "I am the Lord your God." The materialism that results, expressed in the belief that humans are distinguished from animals only in degree, not in kind, breaks down the ancient horror once felt at the contemplation of killing another human being.

The widening agreement in our culture that simply being human doesn't entitle a person to protection from harm—even harm invited by the person herself—can only be sustained on a diminished appreciation that man was created in God's image. When that understanding no longer informs a culture, a door has been opened to things much darker than living wills, darker even than physician-assisted suicide.

So far, those things have been suggested only in science fiction—novels like Kazuo Ishiguro's *Never Let Me Go* (2005) and movies like Michael Bay's *The Island* (2005), both of which are about the farming of cloned human beings for the use of their organs. Till they are needed, the clones are kept in comfort and ignorance, treated kindly as children. Of course, when he, or it, has served the purpose for which he was created, the clone is killed and discarded—a used-up "product," nothing more.

As Peter Singer said about Darwinism's impact on the "Hebrew view of creation," for a century, while "its foundations had been knocked out from under it . . . it remained upright." It may take a century for the impact of an idea, or a technology, to be fully realized, its possibilities fully explored in a practical fashion.

The "Hebrew view" has an unusual, somewhat hard to decipher additional perspective to offer on a culture where the infliction of death on the innocent seems increasingly acceptable. In the Book of Numbers, God tells Moses to instruct the people on this theme: "You shall not bring guilt upon the land in which you are, for the blood will bring guilt upon the land; the land will not have atonement for the blood that was spilled in it, except through the blood of the one who spilled it. You shall not *contaminate* the land in which you dwell, in whose midst I rest . . ." (35:33–34). An ancient rabbinic text, Sifri, a commentary on Numbers, reflects on the word *contaminate*, taking it literally. In murder, there is a contaminant—in Hebrew, *tumah*—that can't be tolerated in God's presence. From a land stained by the blood of murder, God will remove His presence.

Tumah, ritual contamination, is the subject of a great deal of detailed legislation in the Five Books of Moses. It's a fascinating subject, partaking of the occult, but in essence in the Hebrew view there is something about the presence of death that actually pervades and changes the reality of its immediate environment. Touching a dead body is a prime source of contamination. When someone dies in a house, objects in the house can be contaminated.

As I was struggling with how to clarify what the Bible means when it associates *tumah* with a culture that tolerates murder, I happened to be attending a homicide trial at the King County Courthouse in downtown Seattle. A thirty-eight-year-old man from South Seattle, Charles Alonzo Jackson, was accused of the murder of a prostitute, forty-six-year-old Julie Ann Sterling. According to the prosecution, he had strangled her over two hundred dollars he thought she had stolen from him. He kept her naked body in a green plastic Rubbermaid tub for a few days, showed it to a friend, then dumped her behind some bushes in the city's Seward Park neighborhood.

One of the prosecution witnesses was Jackson's friend, a soft-spoken man who looked like Spike Lee. He told of how the defendant had invited him into his basement. Jackson then produced the tub and opened it, revealing a foot. The friend immediately ran upstairs in disgust and terror. It wasn't the foot, so much; it was the smell that immediately suffused the basement.

"What kind of smell was it?" the prosecutor asked.

"It was a death smell," said the friend.

Tumah, perhaps, for all its mysteriousness, may best be described by an olfactory metaphor. Unlike other data of the senses—taste, touch, sight, feel—that which we smell has a way of billowing out of control, getting into things, getting stuck where we don't want it. "You shall not *contaminate* the land in which you dwell, in whose midst I rest." A culture that tolerates murder will start to stink. The stink begins as small whiffs in the air—the murder of dysfunctional people, broken people, unborn and potential people, sad people, people who want to die. But the smell, like all smells, is not readily contained. It gets into everything. It becomes very hard to eradicate.

UNITED STATES
OF ADULTERY

You shall not commit adultery.
(Exodus 12:13)

Today, I've driven the forty miles from Seattle southeast to the farming hamlet of Enumclaw to see the famous barn on Southeast 444th Street. The state of Washington has become notorious for a certain case of "adultery"—as translators of the seventh commandment from its original language conventionally but imprecisely render the relevant Hebrew term. What this particular sin means is no simple matter. It doesn't mean exactly the same thing that the word *adultery* does in English.

On this gray December afternoon, the air is heavy with the smell of chickens at the latter stages of their digestive cycle. However, the disagreeable odor is offset by the magnificent up-close view of Mount Rainier in her glory, visible from anywhere in town you look. This week, Seattleites are discussing the news reported in the local papers that the 2005 Enumclaw case will be the subject of a documentary at the Sundance Film Festival. The Sundance judges have hailed the film, *Zoo*, as a "humanizing look at the life and bizarre death of a seemingly normal Seattle family man who met his untimely end after an unusual encounter with a horse."

On the street outside the farm, a woman in an orange reflective jacket is walking a tall brown mare, who suddenly appears to get spooked, as if about to bolt. And no wonder. It's not a nice place for horses. The Enumclaw story involves a ring of men from the Seattle area who enjoyed sneaking into barns here and videotaping themselves while having sex with livestock. This became national news, the most read story ever to appear in the *Seattle Times*, after a man died of a perforated colon inflicted in the act. (Don't ask how.) Thanks to the Internet, the area had become a magnet for people interested in bestiality, since Washington is one of eight states in the country with no law against it.

We've come a long way from the scarlet letter. In historical and, more important, in scriptural terms, what does the word *adultery* mean?

Most of us are pretty sure we know, and we use the word freely—as in discussing recent famous transgressors against marital fidelity, both alleged and proven, a list that is long and diverse. The political world seems rife with reported extramarital affairs. Just ask Rudy Giuliani, Jesse Jackson, former New Jersey governor Jim McGreevey, former California congressman Gary Condit, former U.S. Speaker of the House Newt Gingrich, former Lousiana congressman Bob Livingston, Indiana congressman Dan Burton, and, of course, ex-President Clinton. Or how about murderer Scott Peterson, basketball superstar Kobe Bryant, or Britain's Prince Charles? All these are properly called adulterers—or are they? From a biblical perspective, one notes some curious ambiguities.

The Hebrew word conventionally translated as "adultery" is *niuf*. The typical Bible reader naturally assumes that if that's the way it's translated, then the Hebrew term must be pretty straightforwardly interchangeable with the English. Actually, not so. For how do we know what any word means in ancient Hebrew? It is not as if the language was preserved as the common spoken tongue of a people for all the three millennia separating us from Moses. Looking up a word in a Hebrew dictionary tells you what the editor of the dictionary thinks it means, but how does *he* know? In fact, the meaning is discoverable only from two possible sources: either from the context of the whole Hebrew Bible, comparing how it is used in other verses and deducing the meaning that way, or from the traditions of ancient Jews, who lived closer to the time when Biblical Hebrew was the everyday tongue and who reflected on the ramifications of each verse and passed down the results of their linguistic memories and investigations in the form of oral teachings later written down in the Talmud, Midrash, and in the writing of classical biblical commentators.

The medieval exegete Rashi states flatly that the word *adultery* refers only to a situation where a married woman engages in intercourse with a man other than her husband, whatever the other man's marital status. In this view, a married man carrying on an affair with an unmarried woman would be a sin, fornication, but it would not be adultery. This double standard may shock us. But Rashi has support from Scripture itself. He points to the verse in Leviticus that specifies the penalty for adultery: "A man who will commit adultery with a man's wife, who will commit adultery with his fellow's wife: the adulterer and the adulteress shall be put to death" (20:10). The repetitiveness of the verse— "who will commit adultery with a man's wife, who will commit adultery with his fellow's wife"—indicates that a definition is being given: Adultery means having sex with somebody else's wife. The prophet Ezekiel seems to have had the same idea in mind when, condemning Israel for her wanton idolatry, he spoke of the Jews as if they had collectively cheated on their cosmic spouse, God: "O adulterous wife, who takes strangers in place of her husband!" (Ezekiel 16:32).

Yet other classical commentators take a much more sweeping view. The Babylonian sage Saadia Gaon (882–942) wrote that *adultery* refers to a spectrum of misdeeds ranging—in order of grievousness, starting with the least morally problematic—from premarital sex, to sex with a menstruating woman, on up to sex with another man's wife, sex between a Jew and a non-Jew, homosexuality, and finally, yes, bestiality. The criterion he uses to determine the relative seriousness of each of these has to do with the possibility of making a forbidden sexual combination legitimate through a change of personal status. That is, two unmarried people, a man and a woman, are not permitted to be intimate. But if they marry, which could be accomplished easily, then they are permitted such intimacy. So premarital sex is established as the least sinful form of adultery. Similarly, the Bible prohibits intercourse during menstruation. However, as soon as this condition has passed, the husband and wife are once again permitted to join together. Another man's wife is forbidden as a sexual partner. But should her husband die, she can remarry. Marriage, and hence sexual intimacy, between a Jew and a non-Jew is forbidden. But if the non-Jewish partner converts and becomes a Jew, a process that is not so easily accomplished, then the pair may be joined in matrimony. Pairings with a member of your own sex or with an animal are acts that can never be legitimized under any circumstance. So these last two emerge as the most serious forms of adultery.

What is left of the gravity that once surrounded the seventh commandment—prohibiting marital infidelity, never mind bestiality—could be observed in the important news sensation that compelled the attention of countless Americans during midsummer 2005. No, I don't mean the historic Israeli pullout from Gaza, which garnered some headlines at the time. I mean Brad Pitt's pullout from his marriage to Jennifer Aniston, coinciding with a romance with Angelina Jolie.

Echoed by every tabloid that ever cried out to a supermarket shopper, all the relevant data were delivered in an exhaustive *Vanity Fair* interview under a cover promising long awaited revelations: JEN FINALLY TALKS! Accompanied by photos of a kittenish Miss Aniston modeling interesting underwear, the VF article didn't exactly condone infidelity. But it did not seem to regard it with any particular shock or awe, either.

True, Jennifer Aniston's friends were said to be "horrified" by W magazine's "60-page photo spread featuring Pitt and Jolie as an early-1960s-style married couple with a brood of miniature blond Brads." One friend declared, "He's made some choices that have been tremendously insensitive." As the article recounted: When the Pitts split up, Brad insisted he hadn't slept with Jolie, and Aniston accepted his denial. . . . The moment he and Aniston separated, however, he re-emerged in what looked like a full-blown affair with Jolie." Yet the gravest thing anyone was quoted as saying about adultery came from Miss Aniston herself, who commented on a new movie she had coming out, *Derailed*, about an extramarital affair that ends violently. Said Miss Aniston, "It will be one of those movies you leave and say, 'The affair thing? Maybe not!'"

In the mainstream culture, this is about as weighty a summation as you're likely to see of the seriousness of committing infidelity. The other end of the current spectrum of opinion was indicated in a piece by *New York Times Magazine* columnist Randy Cohen, aka the Ethicist. Cohen answers "ethical" queries from *Times* readers. Recently, a woman with a sexually impaired husband wrote to him about her adulterous affair. She admitted that her Roman Catholic faith told her it was wrong, but she wanted to know what "secular ethics" has to say. The Ethicist replied that while adultery is "dicey territory," the woman had "entered the realm of don't ask, don't tell," and anyway, he said, "Few practitioners of any faith adhere to each of its dictates."

From "You shall not commit adultery," we've descended to "Don't ask, don't tell."

The seventh commandment simply doesn't have the heft it once did. The husband of a friend of mine, a man who cheated many times over the course of their marriage, explained himself with the admission, "I'm not a bad person, I just do bad things." Though we may formally admit that cheating is "dicey," as the Ethicist says, it doesn't make you a "bad person."

It does seem to be the case, however, that in the biblical view, there is something uniquely worrisome or damaging about the adultery of a married woman. Psychologist Shirley Glass warns that we are in the middle of a "new crisis of infidelity." Citing survey information from the National Opinion Research Center, Glass concludes that in the realm of cheating, married women are catching up to married men. Before considering whether or not such a crisis is upon us and, if so, what other cultural tributaries are feeding it, it will help to look back in history at the origins and development of the double standard, and at changing attitudes toward adultery defined in a more general way.

Regarding where the double standard for married women came from, the Bible and modern anthropology say much the same thing. Anthropologists point out that primitive cultures extant today often lack such a double standard, while it is much more common in relatively advanced societies. There seems to be a difference between hunter-gather cultures and those that have made the transition to engaging in agriculture. Hence, the thinking goes, these simpler cultures represent a constellation of attitudes toward sex preserved from a time long ago. It is theorized that women became the objects of sexual control by their husbands about the same time that human beings began to learn how to use a plow, about the year 4000 B.C.E. in what is today Iraq. According to this theory, preplow cultures were relatively egalitarian, because what simple farming was done, with a hoe, which is a lightweight instrument, could be done equally well by men and women. Marriage, such as it was, was also casual.

With the introduction of the plow, hugely heavy and drawn by large beasts, women were shunted to the side. Plowing required brute physical strength, which many men possessed but very few women did. In eking a livelihood from the earth, men became indispensable, while women became less so. Because of their enhanced status, men could exercise control over women, insisting on fidelity, while women were not in a position to demand the same of their husbands. A new kind of relationship, a more formal sort of marriage with distinct roles for men and women, was born.

That is a widely accepted theory in academia, and curiously, it fixes in time a change in the relationship of men to women much as the Bible does. In Scripture's telling of the story of Adam and Eve, the first humans were originally ensconced in a Paradise of egalitarianism. God placed man in the Garden of Eden "to work it and to guard it" (Genesis 2:15), but from the context it is apparent that the work wasn't exceptionally hard—more hoe work than plow.

Woman was placed in the Garden as man's "helper" (2:18), but there is little question that socially the two conducted themselves as peers. After Eve gave her husband the fruit of the forbidden Tree of Knowledge, thus incurring God's wrath, Adam justified himself by explaining that he was, after all, only following orders from his wife. "The woman whom You gave to be with me—she gave me of the tree, and I ate" (3:12). It was only after this primordial sin, as a consequence of it, that the Lord greatly increased the difficulty of Adam's agricultural labor and simultaneously introduced the double standard. God told Adam, "Because you listened to the voice of your wife and ate of the tree about which I commanded you saying, 'You shall not eat of it,' accursed is the ground because of you; through suffering shall you eat of it all the days of your life. Thorns and thistles shall it sprout for you, and you shall eat the herb of the field. By the sweat of your brow shall you eat bread . . ." (3:17–19). To Eve, He said: "Your craving shall be for your husband, and he shall rule over you" (3:16).

The year, according to traditional reckoning, was 3760 B.C.E., within a few centuries of the time frame given by secular anthropologists for the simultaneous transformation of agriculture with the introduction of the plow, on one hand, and, on the other hand, the subordination of women's sexual desires, including the two standards for judging marital infidelity by men and by women.

The seventh commandment, more than merely legislating morality, reflects the reality of a deeply ingrained feature of human life stretching back through the millennia. From Japan and China to ancient Mesopotamia and Hindu India, diverse traditional cultures agreed that a wife's infidelity was a very serious matter—even a capital offense— which wasn't the case if it was the husband who was cheating on her with an unmarried woman.

There were good reasons behind the double standard. Of course it's true that carrying on a man's family heritage becomes impossible when it's not clear if the children born to his wife are his or not. Thus a wife's infidelity endangers cultural continuity in a way her husband's would not, since there is rarely a doubt who a child's mother is. No less important, a man's cheating, while being absolutely sinful on other grounds, does not necessarily spell the end of the marriage as an emotional relationship, or signal that he has stopped caring about his wife. But if a wife takes a lover, then much more often the marriage truly is doomed. Psychologists report that when a wife cheats, it means she has given up on her marriage and she has stopped loving her spouse. Her adultery is a catastrophe far harder to recover from than that of her husband.

The catastrophic nature of wifely cheating explains the literary choice of the Hebrew prophets to depict Israel as an adulterous woman caught in the act of betraying her spouse—namely, God. Of course the Lord has no gender, but to portray Him as a Her with Israel as the cheating husband would have resulted less in tragedy than in comedy. The Jews committed their "adultery" by whoring—so the prophets frequently put it—after other gods. This happens to be one of the commonest motifs in all the Bible's prophetic books. Jeremiah (3:1–2) plaintively spoke in God's name:

> If a man divorces his wife, and she goes from him and marries another man, can he return to her again? Would that not bring profound guilt upon the land? Yet you have committed adultery with many lovers and would now return to Me—the word of the Lord. Lift your eyes to the hilltops and see; where have you not been lain with? On the roads you awaited [your loves], like an

Arab in the desert. You have brought guilt upon the land with
your adultery and with your evil.

T he culture of Christian Europe inherited the seventh commandment from Judaism. However, this didn't stop aristocrats of the
twelfth and thirteenth centuries from singing the praises of love outside
marriage. This ideal of "courtly love" whipped up some love-crazed Europeans to the point where it was felt in some circles that true passion
and Christian marriage were simply incompatible. Meanwhile, the ancient distinction between adultery committed by men and by women
continued to be made.

As the historian Stephanie Coontz writes in her book *Marriage: A
History* (2005), "Few men prior to the eighteenth century seem to have
questioned the sexual double standard, even if they were in affection-
ate marriages." She quotes a seventeenth-century letter from an English
aristocrat to his married nephew, offering sage advice about how to
handle an upcoming extended journey the nephew's wife was planning:
"I presume that once within these 3 or 4 months you will have as fair
an old time of whoring as . . . you are like to have." The uncle later offered the services of a comely maidservant: "Because you writ me word
that you were in love with Dirty Sluts, I took care to fit you with a Joan
that may be as good as my Lady in the dark."

As Coontz argues, however, something in the culture was in the
process of evolving. For thousands of years, marriages had been practical affairs, rather than affairs of the heart. Love, it was hoped, would be
stirred after the marriage had already been established. Such relationships were entered into for economic reasons, political reasons, rarely
because of infatuation. In Europe, between the fourteenth and seventeenth centuries, the ground was prepared for change when newly married couples began striking out on their own, creating independent
households, rather than living with parents and in-laws in extended
family groups. This entailed that couples, rather than wedding as near

children, which had been the custom, would have to wait before marrying until they had matured enough to support themselves economi-
cally. The average marrying age rose, and so did the idea of choosing
your spouse, rather than letting your parents do that for you. Coontz
traces, from the seventeenth to the twentieth centuries, the creation of
a new idea about getting married: the idea that one might, even should,
marry for love.

The romantic marriage cast doubt on the ancient sexual double
standard, which had its origins in the economic relationship of husband
to wife. Unfortunately, marriage for love carried within itself the seeds
of its own destruction. If one chose to marry for the sake of an emotion,
that meant that when love seemed to weaken or evaporate, so did the
rationale for staying married.

The 1950s were a brief calm, a haven for married and family life, before the "disestablishment" of marriage proceeded toward its climax late
in the last century as the U.S. divorce rate doubled between 1966 and
1976, reaching an all-time modern high in 1981. Marriage simply
wasn't the obvious life choice it once had been. Most couples who want
to live together now choose, rather than marrying, to begin with a so-
called starter marriage—"living together." Others, in a booming trend,
feel that even sharing a living space is going too far and unacceptably
hampers their personal freedom to pursue the whims of the imperial
ego. Thus the rise of the hottest new thing in relationship engineering,
the LAT, or "living apart together," nonmarriage marriage in which the
"dual dwelling duo" consider themselves a long-term couple without
troubling themselves even to cohabit.

With the disestablishment of marriage, the impact on attitudes
about adultery was predictable. If marriage is about love, then it follows
that love's dissolution should give us the liberty to pursue other partners
even if the formal marital bond has not yet been dissolved.

In the nineteenth century there had been premature attempts to
shrug off the exclusivity of the marital relationship. John Humphrey
Noyes founded a commune at Oneida, New York, in 1849 devoted to

"Biblical Communism" including the sharing of wives. The Oneida community eventually foundered when it became apparent that the seventh commandment really does describe reality: Men were not ultimately willing to share their wives.

It wasn't until the 1960s and 1970s that the "open marriage" emerged as an acceptable option for thousands of Americans. By this time, according to one estimate from the "swinging" community itself, there were up to a million couples engaged in a mass experiment with mate swapping. In 1972, Nena and George McNeil's book *Open Marriage* was a best-seller. In his book *Thy Neighbor's Wife* (1980), journalist Gay Talese summarized the thinking of one swinger, Barbara Williamson, herself a leading figure in a California open-love community called the Sandstone Retreat:

> Most married people, she said, had "ownership problems": They
> wanted to totally possess their spouse, to expect monogamy, and if
> one partner admitted an infidelity to the other it would most
> likely be interpreted as a sign of a deteriorating marriage. But
> this was absurd, she said—a husband and wife should be able to
> enjoy sex with other people without threatening their primary
> relationship, or lying or feeling guilty about their extramarital
> experiences.

As early as 1977, Nena McNeil was backpedaling on some of the wilder advice given in *Open Marriage*, and swinging seems like a dated artifact of the 1970s. Yet in 1995, Clint Eastwood could be heard intoning, in the film version of the ultra-best-selling novel *The Bridges of Madison County*—a movie that did for adultery what his *Million Dollar Baby* did for assisted suicide—much the same line of reasoning that Barbara Williamson had articulated to Gay Talese. Eastwood's character, a worldly and free-loving photographer who has an affair with an Iowa housewife played by Meryl Streep, states his philosophy of life for our consideration and appreciation: "It seems to me that there's too much of 'This is mine' and 'He or she is mine.' There's too many lines being drawn, that kind of thing, you know?" He says later, "I have a little bit of a problem with this American family ethic that seems to have hypnotized the entire country."

The hypnotism had already begun to wear off. By 1992, in her book *Anatomy of Love: A Natural History of Mating, Marriage, and Why We Stray*, Rutgers University anthropologist Helen Fisher wrote of a return to the sexual mores of the preplow past, when marriage was egalitarian and casual, with partners drifting from one relationship to another: "After many centuries of permanent monogamy among our farmer forbears, the primitive human pattern of marriage, divorce, and remarriage had emerged again." The "ancient blueprint," before the rise of settled agriculture communities, was one of "serial monogamy and clandestine adultery." In modern times, Europeans and Americans were reverting to prehistoric lifestyles. In a biblical sense, we were trying to recapture the way of life in the Garden of Eden, when men and women were equally naked and without shame. But Paradise cannot be so easily regained. As the Bible puts it, the entrance to the Garden is securely closed to us, as it has been since Adam and Eve were expelled for their sin, when God stationed angelic "Cherubim and the flame of the ever-turning sword, to guard the way to the Tree of Life" (Genesis 3:24).

Instead of recapturing Eden, modern men and women have succeeded in introducing renewed sources of pain and disenchantment to the world. And such betrayals may well be on the rise, especially among married women.

Statistics on the topic are notoriously unreliable. Alfred Kinsey estimated in the late 1940s and early 1950s that American spouses were betraying one another at a phenomenal rate—half of husbands and a fourth of wives. His figures, based on interviews with population groups that were far from representative of the rest of the country (for example, prostitutes, prisoners, and mental-ward patients), have since been largely dismissed. In the 1970s, *Playboy* commissioned a poll and found that 41 percent of husbands and 25 percent of wives had cheated. In the early 1980s, *Cosmopolitan* reported—based on a survey of 106,000 readers—that 54 percent of American wives had experienced adulterous sex. Naturally, the accuracy of the polls depended on, among other factors, the randomness of the sampling, a thing not easily achieved.

The most recently reported numbers appear more reliable. The 1994 sex survey from the National Opinion Research Center at the University of Chicago canvassed 3,432 Americans and came up with somewhat reassuring figures: Eighty percent of American wives had been faithful to their spouse, as had between 65 and 85 percent of men. More recently, the 2002 National Survey of Family Growth, conducted by the National Center for Health Statistics, sampled 12,571 men and women between the ages of fifteen and forty-four. Unfortunately, on the topic of adultery, this government study asked only about the twelve months before the survey was conducted. In that year, 4.5 percent of married men had slept with two or more women, while 3.8 percent of married women had been intimate with two or more men.

There are three key points to notice about these figures from 2002. First, because they deal with only one year, they say nothing about infidelities in the slightly more distant past. They are a brief snapshot rather than an extended video, and therefore are of limited diagnostic value. The most egregiously unfaithful husband with whom I am personally acquainted, a dentist who is now divorced, had three affairs over the course of twenty-plus years of marriage. The affairs involved two hygienists and a dental assistant. But were there years when he truthfully could have told an interviewer that in the previous twelve months he had had sex with only one woman, his wife? Certainly. There were at least ten such years.

Second, the frequency with which Americans cheat on their "committed" partners is masked by the fact that such relationships may be marriages or they may be cohabitations. If we consider only the figures for adultery per se, where the context is a formal marriage, we are leav-

ing out the couples who merely live together—and there's a lot more
cheating going on among those who live together. Those who cohabit
are more than three times as likely to be unfaithful. According to the
2002 National Survey of Family Growth, of males currently cohabiting,
15.6 percent had two or more sexual partners during the previous
twelve months; 10.8 percent of cohabiting men had had three or more!
Cohabiting women are equally inclined to cheat, the survey noted, citing that 15.2 percent had had two or more partners during the previous
year.

Third, the National Survey of Family Growth shows that sexual activity outside marriage by married women is catching up with infidelity
committed by husbands. This is new and important.

Psychologists who work with troubled married couples report the
same thing. The face of the adulterer today is almost as likely to be that
of a married woman as it is of a married man. To this extent, our culture has indeed succeeded in reverting to a state of nature. In her 2003
book Not "Just Friends," Dr. Shirley Glass writes, "Today's workplace is
the most fertile breeding ground for affairs. The observed increase in
women's infidelity is because more women are in the workplace and
more women are in professions that were previously dominated by
men." What's dangerous about this, explains Glass, is that the old pattern, a married man having "casual sex with single women who were
not his equal in status or income"—call it "the dental hygienist
model"—frequently did not destroy his marriage. Not so the new pattern, where men and women who are social and economic equals get to
know one another on the job. What begins as a friendship ends up as a
sexual relationship. Or rather, very often, it doesn't end, because the
sex means something rather serious to both adulterous partners precisely because they entered into it as friends. What seems egalitarian—
fair and unexploitative—in the affair turns to be a far deadlier poison
to the sanctified relationship, marriage, with which it competes.

The problem of adultery committed by wives has emerged so far out
of the closet that Newsweek put the phenomenon on its cover in July

2004, asking this key question: "Where do married women find their boyfriends? At work mostly. Nearly 60 percent of American women work outside the home, up from about 40 percent in 1964. Quite simply, women intersect with more people during the day than they used to." No wonder the gap is closing.

That married women are stepping out on their husbands more than ever before was the premise of a book of interviews by Los Angeles journalist Diane Shader Smith. In *Undressing Infidelity: Why More Wives Are Unfaithful* (2005), Smith very unjudgmentally recounts the experiences of women who cast aside the seventh commandment. The value-neutral tone adopted by Smith does tell you a lot about how acceptable this sin now is. Writes Smith of her interviewees, "I offer their stories so that other women can learn from their wisdom just as I have." And just what wisdom can they offer us? One woman, pseudonymously identified as Liz Wilson, a Texas native whom Smith met at a bakery and interviewed at "a coffee shop in an exclusive neighborhood near the beach," tells Smith how not to get caught by your husband. She was too frank in her personal journal, which her husband, Marty, caught a glimpse of. "The moral of that story is, never write down anything that could incriminate you. Of if you do, shred it or set it on fire, but do not save it."

Human beings, when contemplating sin, take courage from other people's blasé attitudes. And you have only to switch on the TV or read the newspaper to measure the culture's indifference to the morality of seeking sex, whether you're a husband or a wife, outside your marriage.

The years of the Clinton administration were a watershed, as shameless philandering turned out to be that president's premiere legacy to the nation. (Maybe to the world, too, if news from China is any indication—a Chinese condom manufacturer now sells, in tribute to Bill Clinton's choice of love partners, two lines of specialty condoms, the Clinton and the Lewinsky.) Surely a potential adulterer would have felt encouraged by the many arguments made in the media that Americans should take a lesson from Europeans and lighten up about sex, all sex, with any partner, including presidents and White House interns. CNBC's Geraldo Rivera asked, "He's a hypocrite. So what? Get over it." Even a feminist pundit like Susan Estrich could find nothing to feel outraged about in the public humiliation of the betrayed wife, Mrs. Clinton: "Should allegedly finding comfort, release, satisfaction, peace in the arms of a beautiful 21-year-old count for more than balancing the budget?"

William J. Bennett called this time in the 1990s the "Death of Outrage," when an NBC/*Wall Street Journal* poll found 66 percent of Americans sticking by President Clinton, opposing his impeachment, even, they said, if everything said against him turned out to be true. The period reminded me of a story from the Talmud about a notorious adultery, featuring the utter humiliation of the betrayed husband, that became well known in Jerusalem in the period before the tragic incineration of the Second Temple. God took notice, not least of the fact that the community failed to protest the grotesque behavior of the adulterers. The sexual partner of the unfaithful wife ended up employing the cuckold as a personal servant for himself and his paramour. Once, the husband's tears fell into the cups of wine he served to the pair of lovers: "Because of [what occurred at] that moment, the decree [of destruction] was sealed [in heaven]" (Gittin 58a).

Many voices in our country have been raised, urging Americans to stop taking the Decalogue's commandment against adultery so seriously. Ted Turner has called the Ten Commandments "a little out of date," especially the seventh: "If you're only going too have 10 rules, I don't know if [prohibiting] adultery should be one of them." When another chief executive, this one in the business world, actually was dismissed because he committed adultery—Boeing CEO Harry Stonecipher, in March 2005—a writer at the *Seattle Times* was befuddled, horrified. The Boeing board had stood up to the spirit of the times and declared, "The CEO must set the standard for unimpeachable professional and personal behavior." Columnist Danny Westneat shuddered, no doubt along with many of his readers: "That explanation gives me the willies. Professional behavior, fine. But personal? When all it's about is consensual sex?"

Being blasé about "consensual sex" had come to be seen as a marker of sophistication, and one got the sense that those who pressed this point, seemingly looking for opportunities to press it, were partly articulating a sincere opinion and partly advertising their own worldliness. I recall overhearing a conversation in the locker room at the downtown Seattle YMCA. An overweight fellow was chatting with a skinny tattooed gay man. Said the tattooed fellow, "I heard a guy on TV the other day talking about how Thomas Jefferson probably had an affair with his slave, and the guy was surprised. He actually seemed surprised. How could he be surprised?"

"Exactly. It's like Bill Clinton. Why be surprised, or offended, that he was fooling around? I don't care who he was sleeping with."

"That's right. Whether it's two years ago, or two hundred years—or, I mean, two thousand years ago. I mean, if Jesus was sleeping with Mary Magdalene, like in that movie? So what?"

"Exactly."

There seems to be a certain narcissistic pleasure many of us take not in the adulterous sexual act itself but in contemplating the image of ourselves, as if in a mirror, as we gaze benignly, without judgment, on those who do commit it.

Oh, the Europeanness of it all. The model for this attitude might be Diane Lane's sleazy French lover in the 2002 movie *Unfaithful,* who explains to her why cheating on her husband is no big deal: "There is no such thing as a mistake. There's what you do, and what you don't do."

Exactly.

For the spread of self-congratulatory worldliness on questions of infidelity we may thank the hyperheterosexual Bill Clinton—or, alternatively, we may thank certain show-business homosexuals, says *New Republic* TV critic Lee Siegel. He pointed out how many of the most popular television shows that depict adultery as a commonplace of American life, and something to be accepted as morally routine, are actually created by gay men. Gay men created the HBO series *Sex and the City*, and they created the ABC series *Desperate Housewives*. On both shows, heterosexuals are portrayed as running wild, engaging in sexual couplings without regard to marital status. On *Housewives*, for instance, there is Eva Longoria straying from marital vows with a high school boy and getting pregnant in the process, while Marcia Cross is accused of poisoning her husband as revenge for cheating on her. Siegel and others have reasonably asked whether it serves the purpose of gays to salve their own consciences by confirming the view among heterosexuals that, after all, everyone is casting aside outdated scruples about sexuality.

This evolution of American sexual mores is the chief reason we can feel confident that adultery is advancing rather than retreating. There is another reason: the Internet.

A beautiful, wise, and heartbreakingly funny novel that came out in 2004, Tom Perrotta's *Little Children*, dealt chiefly with permutations of adultery in a fictional Boston suburb, Bellington, including Internet adultery. The married couple at the center of the story are Sarah, a full-time mom, and Richard, a marketing consultant. Sarah is having an affair with Todd, a good-looking dummy and househusband who's been trying unsuccessfully for years to pass the Massachusetts bar and become a lawyer.

Meanwhile, Richard has found his own ideal partner, Slutty Kay, self-described on her Web site as "*a 36-year-old married bisexual exhibitionist actively pursuing a swinging lifestyle*." Though Richard hasn't yet met Kay in person, he has engaged in Internet commerce with her:

> Slutty Kay had become a problem. He thought about her far too
> often, and visited her web site several times a day. He was
> neglecting his work and his family, and staying up until ungodly
> hours composing lyrical e-mails in her honor that he couldn't

quite bring himself to send. It was as if he were back in high
school, pining after some girl in chemistry class, knowing he'd
never find the nerve to talk to her. Only this time he didn't have
to go to the trouble of fabricating his own fantasies. They were all
right there for him on his computer screen, thumbnailed and
neatly archived.

There are a lot of Richards out there—married Americans who take
courage from the anonymousness of the Internet to act upon desires
and betray their spouses in a way they never would have the courage to
do if it meant interacting with a live person from the start. America has
a $14 billion yearly industry in porn—raking in more money than our
most popular spectator sports (professional football, baseball, and basketball) combined—an increasingly big slice of which is delivered electronically.

In her book *Pornified: How Pornography Is Transforming Our Lives,
Our Relationships, and Our Families* (2005), Pamela Paul reports on the
feelings of many spouses who find themselves the victims of this American obsession—wives who complain, justifiably, that virtual cheating
is still cheating, that it undermines relationships as surely as a flesh-
and-blood mistress. Wives also take advantage of chatrooms for the
"married and flirting" set, electronic forums where on a given morning
you may find a thousand people simultaneously logged in and engaged
in virtual philandering. AOL, Yahoo!, and MSN all provide such services.

I f the USA is now the United States of Adultery, this is thanks above
all to the pervasively casual attitude about being an adulterer.
Cheating on a spouse simply doesn't carry the risk of being vilified by
friends and neighbors that it once did. And that, in turn, is due mainly
to the "secular ethics" that cultural spokesmen like *New York Times*
ethicist Randy Cohen represent. The unfaithful wife or husband has

entered nothing worse than "dicey territory," perhaps "the realm of don't ask, don't tell," and anyway, "Few practitioners of any faith adhere to each of its dictates."

Certainly, in such an "ethical" perspective there is nothing transcendent about the seventh commandment. It has no foundation in God's will. Not that secularism utterly disdains the prohibition, but in our present "ethics" it is transformed, minimized, downplayed, and fitted into the structure of an alternative system of right and wrong, a system deriving not from the Bible but from vaguely defined notions of what it means to be a nice person. In other words, the secular-ethical *discouragement*—and even that may be too strong a word—of adultery probably offers the best explanation of why adultery is on the rise. A desire to be "nice" is hardly an adequate defense against sexual temptations. In short, if you want to know why the seventh commandment is on the ropes, the reason can be expressed in a word: secularism.

The insight comes from the Ten Commandments. As we have seen already, biblical tradition long ago pointed out that the Decalogue, given to Moses on two tablets, is not merely a laundry list, but a matrix of geometric exactness. It is an array of two corresponding lists of five items where the first item on the first list (the first commandment) corresponds to the first item on the second list (the sixth commandment), the second to the second, third to third, and so on. Thus the second commandment (prohibiting idolatry) corresponds to the seventh (prohibiting adultery). The ancient rabbis who conveyed the wisdom of the biblical tradition explained that one leads to the other: Idolatry leads to adultery.

You say there are no idol worshipers around anymore? A line in the principal Jewish affirmation of faith, the Shema, is worth reading closely. It is a verse from Deuteronomy: "Beware for yourselves, lest your heart be seduced and you will turn astray and you will serve other gods and prostrate yourselves to them" (11:16). Commenting on the allusive scriptural verse, Rashi clarifies that text: "Once a person separates himself from the Torah, he goes and attaches himself to idolatry."

There are two possibilities—Torah and idolatry—with no middle ground. Turning away from the Bible as the ultimate source of values results *automatically* in a person's turning toward "other gods"—a mistranslation, really, because elsewhere Rashi defines *elohim* ("gods") not merely as fictional deities but more broadly as any sources of authority (in Hebrew, *marut*) other than God.

Turning away from the Bible's authority necessarily entails turning toward other authorities. We might call those authorities "secular ethics," but the Bible calls them "other gods." The juxtaposition of the second and seventh commandments conveys the relationship between idolatry and adultery, which makes sense in other ways. If we are not prepared to affirm the exclusiveness of our relationship with God, His unique authority, why should the exclusiveness of our relationship with a spouse be sacrosanct?

EIGHTH COMMANDMENT

ABSALOM, ABSALOM

You shall not steal.
(Exodus 12:13)

Defining theft presents as many ambiguities as defining adultery. At 3:00 P.M. on a Wednesday, the parking lot of the Muckleshoot Casino, southeast of Seattle, is crowded with would-be thieves. At 5:00 P.M. on a Sunday, so is the parking lot of the Tulalip Casino up north off Interstate 5.

Both are, of course, tribal-owned venues. While the Tulalip tribe puts on a classier presentation than their Muckleshoot cousins, with an expansive waterfall out front and a vaguely underwater theme inside, one finds otherwise the identical glum eternal twilight atmosphere of a standard casino anywhere in America, with the usual mix of patrons, heavy on senior citizens, smokers, and generally unhealthy-looking individuals. While smoking in a public place would be illegal anywhere else in Washington State, at the Tulalip facility the smoke is so thick, it makes me rethink my previous assumption that "secondhand smoke" causing cancer and other ills is all a big myth. Having strolled the vast space for a mere fifteen minutes, my lungs are already irritated and I smell like I've smoked a whole pack.

Stifling a cough, I scan the cheerful, cartoonish names on the electronic slot machines, of which the Muckleshoot Casino boasts 2,600. The games include Fairy's Fortune, Dolphin Treasure, Gifts of the Gods, Money to Burn, Money Storm, Leprechaun's Gold, and Something for Nothing.

The Talmud rejects gambling as a form of soft theft. Why? C. S. Lewis's wife, Joy Davidman, in her book about the Ten Commandments (*Smoke on the Mountain*) succinctly defines stealing as "getting something for nothing." Gambling is said to be "fun," a "diversion," a "hobby." But the fun is considerably dimmed when there's no real money involved—that is, when it is impossible to get something for nothing. And if anyone doubts that the loser in a bet does not give up his money freely, just try playing poker with friends. If somebody is doing well in the game, especially if it's early in the evening, it is considered unseemly to take your "earnings" and leave the table. You must give your fellow players a chance to win their money back. Because they still consider it their money.

I mention this to illustrate the confusion that surrounds the idea of a stealing—a confusion that happens to be mirrored in the text of the Ten Commandments itself.

During the looting of New Orleans following the devastation wrought by Hurricane Katrina in 2005, there was evidence of considerable lack of clarity about what makes thievery morally unacceptable. That poverty excused stealing—not the stealing of food and water by the hungry, but of luxury goods by the greedy—was the theme of comments made by a variety of celebrities. The Bible may observe that a thief should not be "scorned if he steals to satisfy his soul when he is hungry" (Proverbs 6:30), but a few days after the storm, singer and pianist Harry Connick, Jr., a New Orleans native, explained to a reporter on MSNBC that a thief shouldn't be scorned even if he steals to satisfy a yen for high-end electronic equipment. Things were "very desperate" in New Orleans, explained Connick. "If I grew up in conditions like that with no hope, I might have to go out and steal me a plasma TV. Maybe in some strange way this will be a motivation for the city to be more equal in some way."

Connick later said he was sorry for appearing to endorse lawbreaking. I'm not aware, however, of an apology by Congressman Jesse Jackson, Jr., Democrat of Illinois, for seeming to make light of the theft of, again, television sets. On CNN, Jackson said he was "fundamentally appalled" at how the media shifted focus "from the devastation [of] people's lives—people who only owned one pan, people who lived in a shotgun home, people who had one television set"—to "what people do in desperate circumstances, including steal." Notice the implication that owning only one TV amounts to a circumstance so desperate that if it leads to stealing, nobody should be surprised.

"You know, some people are stealing and they're making a big deal of it," complained the singer Celine Dion, also on CNN. "Oh, they're stealing twenty pairs of jeans or they're stealing television sets. Who cares? . . . Maybe those people are so poor, some of the people who do that, they're so poor they've never touched anything in their lives. Let them touch those things for once."

"Your princes are rebellious," lamented the prophet Isaiah (1:23), "and companions of thieves; every one loves gifts"—and plasma televisions.

The earliest biblical commentators pointed out something strange about the verse (Exodus 12:13) that contains the commandment not to steal. The full verse, making up three independent clauses, reads: "You shall not murder; you shall not commit adultery; you shall not steal." The commentators reasoned that the inclusion of three separate commandments within the one verse meant that the divine Author was drawing a comparison between murdering, committing adultery, and stealing. But in the context of biblical law, one of these offenses is not like the others. The penalty for murder is, of course, death. For adultery, also death (see Leviticus 20:10).

In the Bible, the penalty for property theft is restitution: The thief must pay the value of the property itself multiplied by two, four, or five, depending on the circumstances.

So maybe the crime prohibited by the eighth commandment *isn't* ordinary theft at all. After all, *that* prohibition is clearly dealt with elsewhere in the Pentateuch (Leviticus 19:11). Why repeat it there, in Leviticus, if the same crime is being referred to in both places? The Torah is not given to unnecessary repetitions. From this, the rabbis of the Talmud (Sanhedrin 86a) showed that the eighth commandment in fact has as its primary meaning the prohibition of a very special and grave kind of stealing. That was the stealing of people, kidnapping, compared with which, no other sort of theft could be more serious. For that crime—technically, in Talmudic law, the abduction of an adult or child for the purpose of forcing the "stolen" individual to engage in slave labor—the penalty is indeed death.

Nor is this seemingly novel interpretation limited to Jewish sources. The nineteenth-century American abolitionist Theodore Weld, an evangelical Christian, wrote in his 1837 book, *The Bible Against Slavery,* exactly what the Talmudic sages did: The essential violation of the eighth commandment is to steal another person for the purpose of enslaving him.

Our country's history is entwined with kidnapping. According to historian Hugh Thomas in his massive book *The Slave Trade,* such "'man-stealing' accounted for the majority of slaves taken to the New World" from Africa, slaves who include the ancestors of most African Americans. Some Africans were kidnapped or stolen directly by Europeans. Many, many more were kidnapped by fellow Africans and then sold to European and American traders, making the white men accessories to a truly terrible violation of the eighth commandment.

Yet if we leave it at that, then one-tenth of the Ten Commandments has become little more than a pious relic of the past. If we all were to pay our taxes into a fund from which the government then paid reparations to African Americans, would we effectively have cleared our conscience of ever again having to worry about the eighth commandment?

But if we understand Exodus 12:13 simply according to its generally agreed-upon meaning—as prohibiting property theft—then the commandment also seems increasingly irrelevant. For, as with murder, the officially compiled theft rate is clearly trending downward. The FBI tracks all sorts of crimes. As for theft, it breaks down that category of unlawful behavior into twenty-eight subcategories. Those include forcible entry, unlawful entry, burglary of a residence, burglary of a non-residence, pocket picking, purse snatching, shoplifting, theft of automobiles, theft of trucks and buses. For more than a decade, all these categories have been in sharp decline. Between 1990 and 2002, the robbery-victimization rate measured per 100,000 individual Americans fell from 256.3 to 145.9.

S hould we then conclude the present chapter here and move on to the next? Not at all.

Although the primary meaning of "You shall not steal" refers to stealing people, there are secondary meanings. The classical commentator Ovadiah Sforno explained that these include theft of property but also "theft of the human intellect," alternatively called "theft of the heart," which has the basic meaning of deception for personal gain. So when the patriarch Jacob was preparing to escape with his family from the clutches of his abusive father-in-law, Laban, Scripture says that Jacob's wife, Rachel, "stole" some belongings of her father—certain idolatrous ornaments with a magical power that might have helped Laban track the whereabouts of Jacob's family. In the next verse, Jacob slips away unnoticed before Laban can stop him: "Jacob stole the heart of Laban the Aramean by not telling him he was fleeing" (Genesis 31:19–20). When Laban nevertheless later catches up with Jacob, he

accuses him of stealing not merely his heart but—if the verse is read literally—of stealing Laban himself: "Why have you fled so stealthily, and
stolen me?" (31:27). Laban meant that Jacob had fooled him.

Sometimes in order to preserve one's own life, it may be necessary
to steal. Usually, though, stealing the heart has the same negative con-
notation as stealing property. According to another classical commentator, Abraham Ibn Ezra, the primary Biblical illustration of this crime
may be found in the biblical story of King David's beloved but egotisti-
cal son Absalom. It is a story of political demagoguery, of cynicism and
narcissism.

Absalom took great pride in everything about himself. He was an
extraordinarily beautiful man, his body crowned by a massive head of
hair so gorgeous that he cut it only once a year. Though he married and
had three sons, he felt that none of them was a worthy successor to
himself. So he built a monument in his own honor that would survive
after he died—"in order that my name should be remembered," he
humbly explained (2 Samuel 18:18). Yad Avshalom, or Absalom's
Monument, an ancient and peculiar cone-shaped structure, still stands
in a desolate valley under the walls of Jerusalem.

Not surprisingly, it bothered the young prince that his father, David,
ruled Israel when he, Absalom, was (in his own opinion) obviously better qualified for the job. Absalom came up with a strategy: rebellion.
The trick was to sway the people away from following David and undermine their loyalty to his kingship, then to initiate a civil war. To accomplish this, Absalom stationed himself at the gates of Jerusalem each day
from early morning onward. Whenever a citizen approached the city on
the way to place a legal case before the king—some sort of gripe or complaint in need of mediation—the prince intercepted the litigant and
struck up a conversation. He would begin with friendly chitchat ("Which
city are you from?") and then quickly turn the talk to the litigant's case.
Even before hearing the nature of the case, Absalom would exclaim,
"Look, your words are good and proper, but there is not one before the
king to understand you." Then Absalom would look wistful and lament

that he knew of a better prospective ruler than David: himself. "If only someone would appoint me judge in the land, and any man who had a dispute or a judgment could come to me—I would judge him fairly!"

In truth, Absalom didn't care about the litigant or his litigation, which is why he didn't bother even to inquire about the details of the legal dispute that had brought the man to Jerusalem in the first place. His sole interest was in advertising the superiority of his own wisdom and compassion. Having accomplished this, Absalom would conclude the conversation with a physical demonstration of how warm and full of sympathy he was, hugging and kissing the traveler. The Bible concludes: "Absalom did this sort of thing to all of Israel who would come for judgment to the king; and Absalom *stole the hearts* of the people of Israel" (2 Samuel 15:2–6).

After Absalom absconded with the hearts of his fellow citizens, after he had their sentiments and intellects securely in his possession, his rebellion against his father's kingdom commenced. Absalom forced David to flee the holy city, but the young man would ultimately be killed by a loyalist, prompting David's heartbreaking lament for the beautiful and cherished prince, "My son! Absalom, Absalom, my son, my son!" (2 Samuel 19:5).

In summary, then, we have three definitions of what it means to steal. One may "steal" people, property, or hearts. There are what one may call primary and obvious expressions of all three, and then there are secondary and less obvious expressions. The prevalence of these in our culture is not reflected in those cheerful FBI statistics mentioned earlier.

*S*tealing people—*primary expressions.* I'm driving home from work one winter night and notice the huge LCD sign suspended over the lanes of Interstate 90 leading to the bridge over Lake Washington. Usually, the sign, reflecting traffic patterns, displays approximate times for reaching selected cities in Seattle's eastern suburbs (BELLEVUE, 12

MINUTES; ISSAQUAH, 18 MINUTES). Tonight, it displays a register of grief and terror: AMBER ALERT, the sign laconically reads, alerting drivers to be on the lookout for a 1998 blue Dodge van. The Amber Alert system, named for a Texas girl abducted while riding her bicycle in 1996, was instituted to deal with an epidemic of child snatching. Tonight, another child has been abducted—stolen—and this one is presumed to have been hustled into a blue 1998 Dodge van before being driven off, heading toward a fate that may include sexual abuse, torture, and death.

The Justice Department's most recent report on the subject is called the National Incidence Studies of Missing, Abducted, Runaway, and Throwaway Children (NISMART). According to the NISMART, about 58,200 children yearly become the victims of "non-family abduction." This refers to episodes in which an abductor who is not a member of the child's family uses a physical threat or physical force to transport and isolate the child for at least an hour, or in which a child younger than fifteen, and therefore unable to resist, is taken or detained in secret, either for ransom or to be kept permanently. A darker variant, "stereotypical kidnapping," involves taking the child overnight or beyond a distance of fifty miles, for ransom, to keep, or to kill. Occurring only about 115 times a year, this is much rarer than the "non-family abduction."

Not that the latter is benign. Some examples from the year (1999) that the Justice Department intensively studied include a nine-year-old girl "lured into the perpetrator's camper trailer with an offer of candy. The perpetrator, a 35-year-old male, detained the child by force in the trailer for an hour while he sexually assaulted her." Or: "A 10-year-old girl was lured with candy and money by an 85-year-old male neighbor and long-term acquaintance into his home, where he sexually assaulted the child." An example of a stereotypical kidnapping would be: "A 12-year-old girl left home for a short jog, telling her mother she would be back in 20 minutes. That was the last time she was seen alive. The police were called to report her disappearance. A few weeks later, the body of the victim was discovered accidentally by a man and his son, who were walking their dog. Police believed that the perpetrator used a blitz attack and grabbed the victim while she was jogging to sexually assault her."

Sometimes these stories briefly become paragraph-long newspaper items in the local news column—like the ten-year-old girl who, as I was writing this, disappeared on the walk to her school south of Seattle. The FBI spent a weekend using sonar and divers to search nearby American Lake for her body, to no avail. Months later, her remains were found in an empty lot.

Kidnapping has a long history. The word itself derives from slang terms for the words *child* (*kid*) and *seize* (*nap*). According to the Oxford English Dictionary, it was used as early as 1682. But of course people had been seizing children long before that. The classic biblical example is the abduction of Joseph, favorite son of the biblical patriarch Jacob. Joseph annoyed his older brothers by relating to them dreams he had depicting their social and political subjection to him, and by informing on them to their father, Jacob, when they disobeyed family moral traditions. The brothers first contemplated killing him, but they finally decided to abduct and then sell him to Arab slavers. He later became viceroy of Egypt, second only to Pharaoh himself.

In the Middle Ages, Jews were routinely kidnapped and then ransomed by their communities. In the twentieth century, there were the celebrated Lindbergh and Leopold and Loeb cases. The latter had a sexual tinge to it—the kidnappers, upper-class Chicago youths, were probably lovers and they used acid to burn the genitals of their young victim. But the sexualization of kidnapping is strictly a product of our own sick time.

In her book *Kidnapped: Child Abduction in America* (1997), UC Berkeley historian Paula S. Fass traces the modern phenomenon. As Fass argues, media awareness and child abductions are closely linked.

Not only do abductions lead to media coverage but media coverage may also lead to more abductions. The titillation that forms the subtext of these stories can have the effect of intensifying, in some troubled minds, the sexual aura around young children.

However, this describes only half the problem of stolen people. There is a domestic market—Americans stealing other Americans. But there is also an import trade—foreigners being stolen, literally, and brought to this country as slaves, mostly of a sexual kind. The slave trade didn't disappear with the Civil War and the Emancipation Proclamation; it only went underground. The figures here are from the Central Intelligence Agency, which estimates that every year between 50,000 and 100,000 human beings are trafficked into the United States, mostly women and children, largely from Asia, Latin America, and Eastern Europe.

You hear about the trafficking rings on the occasion that one happens to be broken up. A notorious case involved the Snakehead crime syndicate out of Atlanta, which was smuggling women from China, Korea, Thailand, Malaysia, and Vietnam, shuffling them around among a chain of brothels described by the State Department as "prison compounds." When the Snakeheads were dismantled in 1995, they had in their custody between five hundred and one thousand women.

Stealing people—secondary expressions. A secondary form of person theft—the theft of a person's identity to be exploited electronically or in other ways—could only happen in the modern, and especially the Internet, age.

From the Snakehead Asian crime gang to identity theft may sound like a descent from tragedy to comedy. How else to describe the case of transvestite Robert Domasky, aka Kelly Stein? "The Man Who Stole My Life" (*Glamour*, November 2005) tells the story of hairdresser Kelly Stein. The writer of the article explained that it illustrates a "peculiar twist on the growing crime of identify theft." Kelly Stein's story: "Raised never to judge" other people, she was quite defenseless when cross-dresser "Debbie" (real name: Robert Domasky) entered her beauty salon in Greensburg, Pennsylvania. Kelly ended up taking him on as a regular hair and nails client, later a friend. Unfortunately, "Debbie" developed a raging obsession with Kelly. He adopted her first and last names as his own, obtained identification in her name, including her Social Security card and passport, had all her bills switched to his address, tattooed her name on the back of his neck, everything possible, legal and illegal, to *become* Kelly.

When professional thieves get involved, the costs become staggering.

According to the Federal Trade Commission, this kind of crime victimizes about ten million Americans every year. It can take various forms. There is "phishing," which involves sending phony E-mails supposedly from a bank or a business—say Washington Mutual or eBay—asking for your bank account, credit-card number, PIN, mother's maiden name, and so on. A clever variation pretends to be from the IRS, congratulates you on receiving a tax refund, and requests a Social Security number and credit-card information to speed your receipt of the welcome windfall.

There is also "pharming," another Internet scam, which involves hijacking the victim's own computer and directing him to a fake Web site that looks exactly like the real Web site of, for example, the victim's bank. When you enter your ID number and password, the pharmer now has this information and can go to work emptying your bank account. In 2004, Internet fraud in its various guises cost businesses $2.6 billion.

Sometimes thieves use stolen information—perhaps filched out of your own home mailbox—to open new credit or other accounts in the victim's name, and thereby to obtain goods and services. This costs about $33 billion a year, mostly to the affected businesses supplying the goods and services. If you add to this figure the amount lost when ID thieves misuse credit and bank accounts that already exist, the total cost reaches fifty billion dollars yearly.

*S*tealing property—*primary expressions*. As with ID theft, new forms of electronic communication have similarly given a boost to an old way of stealing.

It is theft of a special kind of property: your words. The Latin word *plagiarus* denoted various kinds of plunder and kidnapping, and the history of plagiarism in the modern sense of the English word goes back to the Hebrew prophets. Jeremiah knew all about this crime. Some false prophets who lived in his day would fabricate messages they claimed to have received from God. Others, like the charlatan Hananiah, son of Azzur, pretended that prophecies received by a legitimate prophet had, in fact, come to them instead (28:2). God told Jeremiah, "Assuredly, I am going to deal with the prophets—declares the Lord—who steal My words from one another" (Jeremiah 23:30).

Today, never does a year go by without some modern Hananiah coming to light, a scholar, journalist, or novelist accused of stealing the words of a colleague. There are reasons for the emergence of a genre of news stories about the exposure of reportedly unscrupulous writers—including popular historians like Stephen Ambrose, Doris Kearns Goodwin, and Joe McGinnis, *New York Times* reporter Jayson Blair, *USA Today* reporter Jack Kelley, Harvard law professors Laurence H. Tribe and Charles J. Ogletree, e.e. cummings biographer Wyatt Mason, Central Connecticut State University president Richard L. Judd, prominent Washington, D.C., clergyman the Reverend Alvin O'Neal Jackson, novelist Kaavya Viswanathan, and others. I believe one reason that so many have been accused is that other journalists and writers make their professional mark by taking down a more successful colleague. But another explanation lies in the easy accessibility of other people's words, thanks to the Internet, in a form that makes simply cutting and pasting this form of intellectual property as easy as any theft could be.

Certainly that explains the explosion of student plagiarism on university campuses. When Rutgers University management professor Donald L. McCabe surveyed more than twenty thousand students and teachers on twenty-three campuses in 2003, he revealed that 38 percent admitted to engaging in unacknowledged word-for-word "cut and paste" copying of other people's work found on the Internet, up from 10 percent three years earlier. About half the surveyed students offered the opinion that such cheating is morally unobjectionable.

Since I began this discussion of property theft with a description of *word* theft, does this mean that we needn't worry about actual bona fide theft of other people's *stuff*?

A lot of stealing goes unreported. In fact, most does—an amazing two-thirds, according to a 2003 study, the National Crime Victimization Survey. That's unlike all other crimes, which are much more likely to be reported to police. Larceny-theft, as it's called when committed not against a person but against businesses and other organizations, may be still more invisible to the eyes of law enforcement. Consider shoplifting.

Altogether, shoplifting costs businesses about ten billion dollars yearly, says the National Association of Shoplifting Prevention, which comes out to $27 million daily. Apart from recent celebrity cases, which have their own logic or illogic—Winona Ryder at the Beverly Hills Saks Fifth Avenue, Shelley Morrison (of TV's *Will & Grace*) at the San Francisco Robinsons-May department store—the shoplifting done by regular people is not only underreported but staggering.

When a team of criminologists monitored a single Atlanta drugstore for a year for a study published in the academic journal *Justice Quarterly* (December 2004), they found that an astonishing 8.5 percent of all those "customers" entering the store were actually there "to commit an act of shoplifting while on the premises." The commonest profile of the shoplifter turned out to be someone who did not steal to survive: "Middle aged shoppers (35 to 54) were the most common shoplifters. . . . These persons are described as gainfully employed, middle-age adults who occasionally steal as a means of acquiring goods that stretch beyond the household budget." Hispanic women were the demographic group most likely to shoplift, while white women were the least likely.

That's disturbing, yet not as much as forms of stealing that are not only fully reported but widely advertised on billboards and television, sponsored by the government, and deeply implicated in the funding of government.

Stealing property—secondary expression. I refer to gambling. Taking money away with you from someone who doesn't give it up freely is unambiguously stealing. But the loser is a thief no less than the winner. Or rather, he is a would-be thief, a failed thief.

Gambling is now legal in forty-eight states (Utah and Hawaii are the holdouts), of which forty themselves run state lotteries. The states are addicted. Five of them (South Dakota, Rhode Island, Oregon, Louisiana, and, of course, Nevada) depend on gambling revenue to pay for 10 percent of their annual budget, while five others (Indiana, Iowa, Mississippi, Delaware, and West Virginia) will soon reach that significant threshold.

The people are addicted. Jon Grant, who teaches psychiatry at Brown University Medical School and wrote a book called *Stop Me Because I Can't Stop Myself* (2003), estimates that 4 percent of the population has, in medical terms, a moderate to severe gambling addiction.

But the number who are flushing their money down Internet and Native American gambling toilets is obviously far higher. How else to explain the fact that yearly Native American gambling revenues since 1995 have soared from five billion dollars to twenty billion? On-line poker, meanwhile, earned—or rather, "earned"—one billion dollars in 2004, which is expected to reach six billion yearly by 2009. The fascination with Texas Hold'Em is fanned by cable-TV poker shows. There is ESPN's *World Series of Poker*, and the Travel Channel's *World Poker Tour*.

The gambler is simultaneously the thief and the victim of theft. But it is often that way with stealing. Let's say you get caught up in a "4–1–9" Nigerian E-mail scam—the kind where you receive an E-mail from a supposed Nigerian government official promising he'll deposit tens of millions of dollars in your bank account if you will just write back with account information, and later pay various fees to allow the pretend official to wire the money to you. Usually, the premise of the scam is that the money is unclaimed windfall from government contractors and you'll get a 30 percent commission for allowing the funds to be deposited in your account. In this way, according to the U.S. Secret Service, whose mission includes fighting computer fraud, gullible and greedy "victims" fork over hundreds of millions of dollars every year in "fees" before wising up. In this 4–1–9 scam (named for the section in the Nigerian law code that forbids it), who's to blame? Just the Nigerian crook? What about greedy you?

S tealing hearts. You could ask the same question about the victims of Absalom's crime, that of demagoguery, the theft of the intellect. Those men of Israel who came before the king to plead their case but were intercepted by the prince could surely have been expected to see through his ruse of compassion and concern. Remember that he didn't even bother to inquire about the details of their complaints, but immediately accepted them as justified. They freely allowed their hearts to be stolen. Why? For much the same reason that gamblers allow their wallets to be emptied: greed, in this case, for recognition, sympathy, the assurance that your gripe is true and right.

"I feel your pain," said Absalom, or something very much like that. There is a class of mostly privileged, mostly white Americans whose political outlook has as its chief feature granting legitimacy to the grievances of others—for instance, domestic racial minorities and resentful Third Worlders—whether there is merit in them or not. You saw this, for example, when wealthy white movie and music stars (Jason Alexander, Anjelica Huston, Tim Robbins, Susan Sarandon, singer Bonnie Raitt, Bianca Jagger, and others) formed the vanguard of supporters of Stanley "Tookie" Williams, founder of the Crips street gang, before he was executed in California in December 2005. The idea was that Williams, a convicted murder, should not die because in prison he had become a changed man, an activist fighting gang violence, and because, more important, many black people feel the criminal justice system is biased against them. The fact that some black people say capital punishment is racist makes it so.

Actually, the word *demagoguery* may be slightly misleading, because it suggests the cynical use of other people's disgruntlements in one's own pursuit of power. But Absalom was not in it for the power per se. As the Bible makes clear, he was a narcissist who fed upon the high regard of other people. Similarly, it is not the case that our modern Absaloms would use minority grievances *solely* for anything so meager as gaining political power. Like King David's son, above all they want respect, adoration, the gratification of the inflated ego.

The subtitle of a book by Thomas Sowell, *The Vision of the Anointed: Self-Congratulation as a Basis for Social Policy* (1995), says it all. Sowell crystallizes what separates the two dominant political philosophies today. One of those philosophies he calls "the Vision of the Anointed." It holds that every gripe is justified, and that every complaint can be adequately addressed, a solution found for every social problem—if only the "anointed" elite are put in charge:

> The refrain of the anointed is *we already know the answers . . .* and
> the kinds of questions raised by those with other views are just
> stalling and obstructing progress. "Solutions" are out there waiting
> to be found, like eggs at an Easter egg hunt. Intractable problems
> with painful trade-offs are simply not part of the vision of the
> anointed. Problems exist only because other people are not as
> wise or as caring, or not as imaginative and bold, as the anointed.

Often the solution of the anointed involves transferring money from one group (usually the middle class) to another (the "disadvantaged"). The Bible considers this a different form of theft: "Charity will elevate a nation, but the kindness of the kingdoms is a sin." On this verse in Proverbs (14:24), Rashi explained that proper charity, where I freely give my own money away, "elevates a nation." But the "kindness" practiced by certain governments—which "steal from this one and give to that one"—is a sin. At the price of such theft, the anointed win the acclaim they seek.

Contrasted with this is "the Tragic Vision," which recognizes that some complaints may have merit and yet be impossible to resolve in a way that's entirely satisfactory to the complainant. To tell people there may be no solutions to their problems is no likely formula for winning the love of an adoring public. While the anointed commit heart larceny, leaders with the tragic vision have a hard time winning votes, much less stealing hearts.

U ndoubtedly, those comforting figures from the FBI understate the derelict condition into which the eighth commandment has fallen. Human cultures have been down this road before.

"Now the earth had become corrupt before God; and the earth had become filled with robbery" (Genesis 6:11). That verse describes the condition of the world in the lifetime of Noah, before the Flood. "God said to Noah, 'The end of all flesh has come before Me, for the earth is filled with robbery through them; and behold, I am about to destroy them from the earth" (6:13).

Two points about Noah's world are worth noting. First, a culture saturated in thievery, like ours, is bound for still worse things. Second, the Bible traces the degeneration of Noah's contemporaries to something very specific: trifling with God's Name. It is my hypothesis that the Ten Commandments offer a moral-cultural diagnostic tool. Where you find evidence of degeneracy in an area of life described by the second set of tablets, look to the corresponding commandment on the first set. The dereliction of the commandment on the first tablet leads to the dereliction of the corresponding one on the second tablet.

The eighth commandment lines up with the third, "You shall not take the Name of the Lord thy God in vain." And sure enough, a couple of chapters before Noah, we have the description of how the culture in his time became filled with robbery. It was only two generations after Adam and Eve, who had a son named Seth. "And as for Seth, to him also a son was born, and he named him Enosh. Then to call in the Name of the Lord became profaned" (Genesis 4:26). Rabbinic tradition explains it as a reference to the trivialization of God's ineffable Name. Things that were not God were called by his Name.

In chapter 3, we saw that taking the Lord's Name in vain means to trivialize it, use it for trifling purposes (not only the Tetragrammaton, which is God's proper Name). An ancient tradition, mentioned by another medieval exegete, Nachmanides, in his introduction to Genesis, regards the entire text of the Torah as comprising personal names of God strung together. In Enosh's generation, they began to abuse the Lord's personal designations, making use of His names for "profane" or secular purposes, much as we saw that Americans are accustomed to abusing the Name. From this beginning, the generations degenerated—only eight generations separate Enosh from Noah in the biblical scheme—producing the thievery-saturated culture that we see in Noah's time, and our own.

We need to understand why trifling with God's Name, specifically, leads to theft. So far, the conceptual link isn't clear.

In the Hebrew Bible, God's Name is associated with a certain awe of Him, sometimes translated as "fear" (*yirah*). There is an awe we feel on contemplating God's majesty. I feel this when I stand before the awesome Pacific Ocean. That awe is comforting; it dispels anxiety by putting my personal struggles and challenges, my failures in the moral realm, in a perspective where they seem small. "Lord, what is man that you recognize him; the son of a frail human that You reckon with him?" (Psalms 144:3).

However, there is a more challenging awe, associated with God's personal Name. It can wrap us in love, but it can also make us fear. This awe was associated by the ancient Hebrews with God's holy Temple, where his Name dwelled. When Jews visited the Temple, they enjoyed sacred meals there: "And you shall eat before the Lord, your God, in the place that He will choose to rest his Name there . . . so that you will learn to fear the Lord, your God, all the days" (Deuteronomy 14:23). This fear or awe is the feeling you have when you realize that God isn't only a cosmic deity but that he is right beside you now, watching out for you but also watching you. In Hebrew, the word for awe, *yirah*, shares a root with the verb that means "to see."

We feel awe when we are aware that God, in a very personal way, sees us. When the feeling is lost, can that lead to robbery? Sociologist Rodney Stark, in a 2001 article in the *Journal for the Scientific Study of Religion*, studied the effects of beliefs about God on attitudes about right and wrong. His research showed that within individual countries, religious belief is a strong predictor of moral rectitude. In almost every nation on Earth, the firmer your faith in a personal God, the more likely you are to regard, for example, stealing as wrong. Writes Stark, "It suffices to recognize that divine essences [the cosmic sort of deity] are unable to issue commandments or make moral judgments. Thus, conceptions of the supernatural are irrelevant to the moral order unless the supernatural is conceived of as a *being*—a thing having consciousness and desires. Put another way, only beings can desire moral authority."

The biblical patriarch Abraham had a similar sociological insight about the way cultures work. Once in his travels with his wife, Sarah, he visited a place called Gerar. This city-state in the southwest of the land of Israel was a cosmopolitan and morally lax sort of town. That made Abraham nervous. His wife was a beautiful woman and he feared that the people of Gerar would steal her, which would be the primary meaning of the eighth commandment. That's exactly what happened. To fend off unwanted challenges for her affection, Abraham had told a lie—that Sarah was actually his sister, not his wife. Somehow, he figured, the Gerar men would respect a brother more than a husband. However, the king of Gerar, Abimelech, did exactly what Abraham had worried about. He abducted Sarah and took her to his palace.

After God intervened to save her, coming to Abimelech in a dream and warning him of her true identity, the king upbraided Abraham: "What have you done to us? How have I sinned against you that you brought upon me and my kingdom such great sin? Deeds that ought not to be done have you done to me!" The king asked, "What did you see that you did such a thing?"

Abraham explained: "Because I said, 'There is but no fear of God in this place and they will slay me because of my wife' " (Genesis 20:9–11).

Abimelech was a man whose type we should all recognize, a well-meaning person, with good manners and even good values. In his view, however, the world turned without the intervention or oversight of any personal God. He was, in today's language, a secular humanist. He possessed ethics, but he could not explain where his ethics came from. As the Bible tells it, he lashed out at Abraham: "Deeds that *ought not to be done* have you done to me!" Note the passive tense of the verb. Why ought they not to be done? Well, just because. Because God commanded and is watching? No, just because that's the way *things are done*.

When temptation came Abimelech's way, he was defenseless against it. He saw Abraham's "sister," he wanted her, and so he snatched her.

In theft, as in the abuse of God's name, we see other people as resources to be plundered. Theft is the most impersonal of crimes. Unlike murder or adultery, where usually you care very much whom you're murdering or committing adultery with, in robbery you don't care whom you are robbing. It's better if you don't know.

Taking God's name in vain is also impersonal. God and his word become empty vessels to fill with anything you like, or don't like. Is it useful to you to use God or use the Bible for some secular purpose? Then go ahead. If a person or a culture is willing to treat God this way, why not treat people in a similarly cavalier fashion? You'd be right to worry about spending time in Gerar.

A few years ago when I was writing a book about Abraham and was visiting Israel to see some of the Abraham-related archaeological sites, my wife and I drove back and forth for hours on the road between Beersheba and Gaza, looking for where Gerar was supposed to be. It was on the map, but it was not on the road. Finally, we gave up. It occurred to me later that this was appropriate. Gerar once was in ancient Israel, on the Beersheba-Gaza road. But it no longer is.

It's right here and right now, all around us. The Gerarites are here. America is Gerar. They are us.

NINTH COMMANDMENT

PRIDE AND PREJUDICE

You shall not bear false witness against your fellow.
(Exodus 12:13)

The town of Wenatchee, on the other side of the Cascade Mountains, three hours from Seattle, is known for three things. It's the home each April of the Washington State Apple Blossom Festival. Its residents were at one point in the mid-1990s revealed to be the country's foremost consumers of Prozac. And it was the location of the most outrageous example of mass false-witness bearing since the Salem witch trials.

The Prozac habit makes sense because about the same time, merely to live in Wenatchee put a person at grave risk of being accused of and arrested for bizarre acts of child sexual molestation. In a situation like that, who wouldn't be depressed?

In 1994 and 1995, sixty adults here were arrested, charged with 29,726 acts of sex abuse inflicted on forty-three children. This was supposed to have taken place at twenty-three separate sites around town, all identified to police detective Bob Perez by his star witness, an eleven-year-old girl who was also his foster daughter. Based on coerced evidence from child witnesses, lives were destroyed, families torn apart. As *Wall Street Journal* writer Dorothy Rabinowitz vividly reported, one of the stars among the accused was a local pastor, Robert Robertson of the Pentecostal Church of God House of Prayer:

> One child claimed he was so tired from having to engage in
> sexual acts with all the adults at the church on weekends that the
> pastor would write a note to school to get him excused. Another
> told of inflatable sex toys kept under the altar, of the pastor lying
> on stage crying "Hallelujah!" while attacking young victims
> during services, of mass child rape (at the church and elsewhere)
> by men all in black wearing sunglasses and by ladies wielding
> colored pencils and carrots, and of crowds of adults so organized
> that everyone got a turn with each of the children. . . . [Afterward]
> hot cocoa and cookies were served.

At one point, twenty-eight Wenatchee residents were in jail for crimes, it would later turn out, they didn't commit. Eighteen were convicted, but in every case the convictions were later voided.

The needless suffering of the Wenatchee sex-ring defendants was all administered by judges, courts, and police officers. You may think, therefore, based on a simple reading of the Decalogue, that if you never appear as a witness in court, as most of us probably will never have an occasion to do, you are in good shape as far as this commandment goes. In fact, we need to abandon any notion about the ninth commandment being a matter that only formal witnesses have to be concerned about.

This exchange did not take place before a court of law. It occurred on a bus, crossing Lake Washington on Seattle's Route 550, to be exact.

Q: Did you see the Asian girl he went out with? Do you think he
   paid for her? She was like not good-enough-looking to be a real
   call girl but too good-looking to be a regular prostitute.
A: I lost whatever respect for him that I had, and I didn't have
   much to begin with.

In Hebrew, the verb translated as "to testify" has a very broad application. It refers to all speech and other communication about your fellow human beings. As the classical medieval exegete Sforno explained,
the ninth commandment additionally covers the person who "goes
about as a tale-bearer or a slanderer." The two terms each mean something specific. Being a "talebearer" implies reporting hurtful *truths* if
there is no good reason for doing so. In Hebrew, the sin is called either
rechilut ("talebearing") or *lashon hara* ("evil speech"). The Bible forbids
this elsewhere, as well, saying, "You shall not go about as a tale-bearer
among your people" (Leviticus 19:16). The idea that saying mean-
spirited things that are true would constitute a grave moral offense may
be hard for many of us to wrap our minds around, but the Bible takes it
very seriously indeed: "He who maligns his friend in secret, I will destroy" (Psalms 101:5). In his compendium of biblical law, the Mishneh
Torah, the medieval sage Maimonides gave the following definition:
"One who speaks *lashon hara* is someone who sits and relates: 'This is
what so and so has done'; 'His parents were such and such'; 'This is what
I have heard about him,' telling uncomplimentary things. Concerning
this [sin] the verse [Psalms 12:4] states: 'May God cut off all guileful lips,
the tongues which speak proud things' " (Hilchot Deot 7:2).

Relating malicious *untruths*, or slandering (*motzi shem ra*), is, of
course, even more serious. For this offense, the prophet Jeremiah said,
the Jews were exiled from their land at the hand of the cruel Babylonians: "Their tongue is like a drawn arrow, speaking deceit; with his
mouth one speaks peace with his fellow, but inside of him he lays his
ambush. Shall I not punish for these [things]?—the word of the

Lord . . . I shall make Jerusalem heaps of rubble, a serpent's lair; the cities of Judah I shall make a wasteland, without inhabitant . . . I shall scatter them among nations that neither they nor their fathers have known" (Jeremiah 9:7–8, 10, 15).

Clearly, it's worth understanding what spiritual and psychological dynamics underlie the habit of talebearing and slandering.

Even politicians seem to realize the gravity of the problem, and its ubiquity in American life. During the 2004 presidential election season, ex-President Bill Clinton delivered a blistering sermon at a liberal Manhattan church against what he thought was a propensity by the GOP to trample on the ninth commandment: "It's wrong to demonize and cartoonize one another, and to ignore evidence, and to make false charges and to bear false witness," said Clinton. "Sometimes I think our friends on the other side have become the people of the Nine Commandments." He had in mind attempts by zealous conservatives to undercut Democratic presidential candidate John Kerry's status as a Vietnam war hero, as well as to tar him as an adulterer. The latter charge, initially spread by Internet gossip Matt Drudge, centered on rumors that Kerry had a two-year affair with an intern, a claim that was almost certainly unfounded.

But neither party has a monopoly on unsupportable slander. An exgirlfriend of Clinton, Gennifer Flowers, swung back at him in the context of his denying, in his memoir *My Life*, that he'd had a twelve-year affair with her: "Bill Clinton pretends to be contrite, but he continues to bear false witness against his neighbor. He is a national disgrace." One of the most notorious political slanders of recent years was directed at Republican president George W. Bush by a CBS *60 Minutes* report, based on a forged letter, that Bush had blown off his Texas Air National Guard service. When the forgery was revealed, CBS offered a self-defense that amounted to the claim that the letter was "fake but true"—it was a false document, but the idea it contained was nevertheless true.

There are two frequently heard explanations for the ubiquity of slander in our culture. One cites the influence of the Internet and points out how often gossip arises there—for instance, the rumor of John Kerry's intern lover. Outside the political realm, the anonymity of writing on a Web site has also contributed to much private pain. A 2001 story in the *Los Angeles Times* documented the popularity of Web sites run by high schools students and devoted to airing the meanest possible rumors and innuendos about fellow students. One Web site, www.schoolrumors.com, received 67,000 hits in just a couple of weeks and concentrated on sexual insults, naming girls who were thought to be "tramps," "sluts," and "whores," and boys who might be "gay"—or might not. A disclaimer on the site noted that "the rumors can be true or false." Thanks for the warning.

There is another reason, having to do with the American legal system, why we are seeing more free and flagrant abuses of other people's good names in the media. That is because it has become increasingly difficult to sue for libel, especially since a 1964 Supreme Court ruling, *New York Times v. Sullivan*. If you're a public figure, winning a libel case is nearly impossible. The chief justice of today's Supreme Court, John Roberts, once wrote that *Sullivan* "crown[ed] the media with virtual absolute immunity for falsely assailing public officials."

This is why, nowadays, if you're a public figure and you feel you've been libeled, your only recourse is to sue in Great Britain, where the law places the burden of proof on the accused libeler. Only in Britain could Roman Polanski win a libel decision against *Vanity Fair,* as the filmmaker did in 2005, for falsely reporting that he crudely propositioned a Swedish model in 1969, days after his pregnant wife, Sharon Tate, was murdered by Charles Manson's gang. *Vanity Fair* had to pay $87,000 for running that juicy, but apparently false, bit of gossip.

But I want to bring out some of the insights about the predominance of false witness suggested by the Ten Commandments, insights that were valid before anyone ever heard of the Internet or of the *Sullivan* decision.

Belief forms behavior. In three words, that's the thesis of this book. God put the Decalogue on two tablets instead of one to show the direct correspondence between the commandments about the relationship of God to man (first tablet) and those about the relationship of man to man (second tablet). When we come to the ninth commandment, dealing with the sin of bearing false witness, the corresponding commandment on the first tablet is the fourth commandment, concerning Sabbath observance.

Understood this way, the Decalogue makes a prediction. If a culture neglects the fourth commandment, it will also neglect the ninth. We've already seen what a tatters the observance of a Sabbath rest has been reduced to in our secularized American culture. So if the theory of the Ten Commandments as a cultural diagnostic tool holds up, we should also expect to find evidence of rampant acts of bearing false witness. That's exactly what we do find.

Am I saying that Americans commit the sin of bearing false witness because they neglect the Sabbath? Am I saying the converse also—namely, that if we were more careful about the Sabbath, we would see fewer people bearing false witness in our culture? In point of fact, biblical tradition makes even more radical claims about the benefits of keeping the Sabbath. Based on an interpretation of two cryptic verses in Isaiah—"Thus says the Lord concerning the eunuchs that keep my Sabbaths . . . Them I will bring to My holy mountain" (56:4,7)—the Talmud promises that if the Jews were to properly observe two Sabbaths in a row, the ultimate redemption would immediately ensue and the Messiah would come (Shabbat 118b). But I'm really saying something more modest, which is that the diagnostic theory of the Decalogue offers insights. It helps us understand the cultural genesis of bad behavior patterns. It illuminates the failings and misunderstandings that lie behind those patterns. It doesn't necessarily say anything as stark as the above-mentioned Talmudic teaching that two Sabbaths in succession would bring the Messiah.

In the instance at hand, that of the ninth commandment, there are three lessons of the Sabbath that, if appreciated, tend to lessen the impulse to commit false witness. If those same lessons are unappreciated,

bearing false witness is likely to be a common offense. In America today, it is depressingly common.

The *wrong kind of community.* The first lesson of the Sabbath that
concerns us here has to do with the sort of community that the
holy day of rest is intended to generate. When the Sabbath is not ven-
erated, this sense of community will suffer and observance of the ninth
commandment will fall into disrepair.

The Sabbath is about relationships. Traditionally among Christians,
and among religiously observant Jews to this day, Sunday or Saturday
has been a day not only to stop work but to limit travel—not in order
to burrow in your room and meditate silently but, rather, to join friends
and family members for meals, and church and synagogue services, and
the like. In Judaism, this is especially marked because, according to Jewish law, one may not ride in a car on the Sabbath. Also, there are traditional meals on Friday night and Saturday afternoon that aren't
optional, but, rather, are obligatory and surrounded with ritual. This is
apart from spending time in synagogue Friday night and Saturday
morning. The result is that on the Jewish Sabbath, you are constantly
around other people, talking with them, cementing relationships.

You may thus speak of a Sabbath community—one that is built and
nurtured by the Sabbath. When this kind of community is lacking, the
result will be gossip and backbiting, which invariably continue the
work of tearing down sociable feelings among a group of people. Nothing poisons relationships—whether in a circle of social friends, in an office, or in a school—more effectively than gossip. As psychologist
Jeremy Robinson noted in the *Christian Science Monitor* (September 5,
2001), "One of the core competencies of emotional intelligence involves self-awareness and the capacity to empathize with other human
beings. A gossipy, mean-spirited world is not a world where people are
empathizing with each other. . . . The corollary is that if everybody gets
gossiped about or thought unfairly about, then it's every man or woman

for themselves. There's no community, no bonds, no trust, nothing that goes deep."

This explains why, popularly, the vice is associated with women. When men or women gossip, they are doing something feminine.

Women, as life experience shows, are the builders of communities and of relationships. As men get older, many stop making new close friendships. Women never stop making new friends. This is why, among married couples, you will often notice that the husband relies on his wife to round up friends for dinner parties and the like. She makes the friendships with other women who become, along with their husbands, the new "couple friends" of the marriage. A lot of men, once they reach their late thirties and forties, would be effectively friendless were it not for their wives.

This might seem to lead to the conclusion that gossiping is the opposite of feminine. After all, if women are experts at building relationships, then ruining relationships should be, if we must choose to blacken once sex or the other, a male vice, not a female one. But it's not—because passing along rumors is done, most often, by people who are seeking a cheap way to get close to others, to feel bonded and included. In other words, if the Sabbath is about building a community the right way, then a culture that has lost that art will likely also lose the art of building relationships more generally. It will seek shortcuts to cementing friendships, shortcuts like gossip.

This idea, that gossip is a cheapened or warped expression of a feminine art, explains the perception that women gossip more than men.

Certainly there has been more recognition lately of how central a role gossip plays in the lives of women—and girls. In her book *Queen Bees & Wannabes: Helping Your Daughter Survive Cliques, Gossip, Boyfriends & Other Realities of Adolescence* (2002), Rosalind Wiseman devotes a chapter to the heartbreak teenage girls cause one another by passing around hurtful rumors. "Gossip is like money. We exchange it, sell it, and lend it out. It's what we have of value," sixteen-year-old Jane told Ms. Wiseman.

Wiseman's book joined a growing shelf of other books about social aggression by girls in the form of mean behind-the-back whispers—books like Leora Tanenbaum's *Slut! Growing Up Female with a Bad Reputation* (1999), Emily White's *Fast Girls: Teenage Girls and the Myth of the Slut* (2002), and Rachel Simmons's *Odd Girl Out: The Hidden Culture of Aggression in Girls* (2002).

As Rachel Simmons admits of herself in her book, illustrating the appeal of bearing false witness to cement relationships, "I have gossiped. I have relished the ruse of inclusion at the expense of an odd girl out. Have you?"

Thus it has come to the attention of marketers that books about cattiness, by women and about women, sell. Which explains the rise of "gossip lit"—best-selling books by insiders that are tell-alls. The genre includes like *The Nanny Diaries* (2002), by Emma McLaughlin and Nicola Kraus, two former nannies who made a bundle by dishing about their former employers; *The Devil Wears Prada* (2003), by Lauren Weisberger, who served as an assistant to Anna Wintour, *Vogue* magazine's editor in chief, who wrote a thinly disguised exposé of the experience; *Bergdorf Blondes* (2004), by Plum Sykes, a *Vogue* contributor, who writes about her own contemporaries; and *The Right Address* (2004), by Carrie Karasyov and Jill Kargman, which, according to the dust jacket, "sears through the upper crust of New York's glittering Park Avenue scene to dish the dirt on the ladies who lunch, the men who club, and the desperate climbers who will stop at nothing to join the back-stabbing, champagne-sipping, socialite-eat-socialite stratosphere."

The Bible confirms the connection between effeminacy and false witness, revealing the curious taste on the part of Joseph, son of the patriarch Jacob, for certain feminine grooming habits. According to biblical tradition, as a young man he would dress his hair and adorn his eyes to appear beautiful (Genesis Rabbah 84:7). His father, Jacob, noted in him a tendency to vanity and encouraged it, bestowing on him a splendid coat of many colors. Joseph was also a gossip, and this had disastrous results. As a seventeen-year-old, he was a shepherd with his brothers, and, as Genesis puts it, he "would bring evil reports about them to their father" (37:2). Basically, he would report unfavorable gossip about them.

The brothers became so annoyed with him that, at first, they contemplated killing him. However, they settled for abandoning him to be sold into slavery in Egypt. In the land of the Nile, Joseph rose to a prominent position as the household slave of Potiphar, a courtier of Pharaoh. But Joseph couldn't resist indulging his habit of primping, for he "was handsome of form and handsome of appearance" (Genesis 39:6). Unfortunately, this attracted the attention of Potiphar's wife, who set about to seduce Joseph. When he rejected her advances, she claimed he had tried to rape her—a false charge, but it served him right.

During several years in prison for the alleged attempted rape of Potiphar's wife, Joseph established a friendship with another prisoner, whose later recommendation of him to Pharaoh would result in Joseph's being appointed as the Egyptian king's viceroy. This, in turn, led to his brothers' emigrating from Canaan and joining him in Egypt to escape the consequences of a famine. And *that* resulted in their children—the children of Israel—living for generations as oppressed and miserable slaves of the Egyptians. All this flowed from the initial offense of Joseph's gossiping about his brothers' supposed misdeeds to their father.

Those descendants were freed from servitude by Moses, who acted as God's messenger to Pharaoh. They hiked to Mount Sinai, where they received the Torah, which recounts Joseph's story, with its lessons about the disastrous consequences of tale bearing, and which, in the form of the Ten Commandments, links Sabbath desecration with the sin of the false witness.

Joseph's life may shed further illumination on that link. That's because his tattling on his brothers didn't happen in a vacuum. There was an atmosphere in the patriarch Jacob's home, where Joseph grew up, that proved conducive to the young man's cattiness toward his brothers. In the verse immediately prior to the one that refers to the "evil reports" Joseph conveyed to his father, the Bible notes that "Jacob settled in the land of his sojournings, in the land of Canaan." In traditional exegesis, when Scripture tells us seemingly irrelevant (who cares that Jacob "settled"?) and immediately follows it up with something apparently unrelated (the "evil reports"), then a hidden connection or explanation is being hinted at by the ever-cryptic text. The evil reports and all the tragedy they produced resulted directly from Jacob's settling.

Which means what? Rabbi Matis Weinberg, a modern writer, cites the commentary of Rashi to the effect that Jacob wished to "settle in tranquility" and it was *this* offense that led to the alienation of Joseph from his brothers. What's wrong with seeking tranquillity? Rabbi Weinberg argues that Jacob sought to retire from the hustle and bustle of family life. He wanted to regain the life of solitary scholarship he knew before he was married, back when he was a "simple man, abiding in tents" (Genesis 25:27), when he could lock the door of his study and not be bothered with interruptions from other people. But early retirement, especially from social interaction, is not what God wants from us.

That again is one of the messages of the Sabbath, with its enforced sociability. When the Sabbath is completed on Saturday night, the hope is that its atmosphere of fellowship will pervade the coming of the workweek, too. In biblical religion, life is about other people.

Jacob seemingly forgot this, and it poisoned the air in his home. It poisoned his sons against one another. Because he neglected this aspect of Sabbath observance, the fourth commandment, Joseph broke the ninth commandment, as well.

How this illuminates America's addiction to gossip and talebearing is made clear by remembering how things were, briefly, after the attacks of September 11. For all the pain of that day, it led to a salutary, if short-lived, revival of certain civic virtues. There was a sudden outbreak of admiration for frankly expressed masculinity, even machismo. Remember how everyone loved firemen, police officers, and soldiers? There was something else about the immediate aftermath of that day. Suddenly, gossip was out. "Gossip Holds Its Tongue," the *New York Times* reported on September 23, 2001:

New Yorkers, jaded by celebrity, seem thoroughly tired of it now. They are also shrugging off the industry that both sustains celebrity and feeds off it: gossip, as natural a part of New York as designer martinis and trophy wives. In the days immediately after the attack, the city's professional tattletales fell appropriately silent. The *New York Post's* most popular column, Page Six, by Richard Johnson, failed to appear for the first time in 25 years. And in a chastened statement, the eminent Liz Smith, whose syndicated column also appears in the *Post* and about 70 other newspapers, complained to readers of the trivial nature of her work at such a time. "I want to go somewhere and volunteer," she wrote. "To hell with gossip and entertainment."

For those weeks when a feeling of fellowship ruled and masculinity was admired, talebearing faded. The normal condition in our culture is the reverse. Fellowship of the kind the Sabbath nurtures is rare, and genuine masculinity is, too.

American men are more and more like certain American women, with the result that when they seek a shortcut to community, they often engage in catty, bitchy, back-stabbing gossip.

P*ride and prejudice.* There's a second lesson to be gained from the Sabbath that, if a person or a culture fails to learn it, also encourages neglect of the ninth commandment. It has to do with hubris.

In his fine memoir *The Search for God at Harvard*, Orthodox Jew and former *New York Times* reporter Ari Goldman recounts how when he was young and somewhat foolish, swept up by his "vocation" as a newspaper journalist for the country's most prestigious newspaper, with "a moral responsibility to report the news," he rationalized working on the Sabbath. It was necessary, he figured, because his work was so critically important. It is exactly this kind of hubris that the Sabbath is meant to guard against.

For if that holy day's only purpose were to give us a rest and help build community, it could be observed any day of the week. The Bible set the Sabbath on the seventh day, Saturday, because that was when God finished the work of creation. One moral message is that just as God could afford to rest from His creative activity, so can we. Indeed, the world goes on quite nicely without our participation in any of the thirty-nine categories of creative work—from building fires and transporting goods and other objects to sewing, writing, and cooking—specified by biblical tradition and clarified in the Talmud. Many of us, like the young reporter Ari Goldman, suffer from the prideful delusion that what we do for a living the rest of the week simply can't be neglected for a day, perhaps not even for an hour. We have a "moral responsibility" to work!

This mistake has been greatly reinforced with the introduction in recent years of portable wireless communication devices—cell phones, and especially BlackBerrys—that allow people to do their work on the road, on the train, at home, on vacation. The impression we convey to ourselves is that our work is so terribly important that it simply cannot wait until we can reach a landline telephone or a desktop computer. The moral message of the BlackBerry is: God may have been able to take a break from His work, but not me! My contribution is too critical to allow that! At all times, I am indispensable!

The Sabbath delivers a sound beating to this kind of obnoxious pride in oneself and one's "vocation."

What has this got to do with the ninth commandment? Rare is the person who says in his heart, Okay, now I'm going to bear false witness against my neighbor. It's far more common for the talebearer to believe himself to be perfectly truthful. That's because gossip and slander almost always involve an estimation of one's own ability to ferret out the truth that is almost God-like.

Or more than God-like. Immediately after Adam and Eve sinned by eating from the Tree of the Knowledge of Good and Evil, against God's directions, He sought them out in the Garden of Eden to ask for their version of what had happened: "They heard the sound of the Lord God manifesting itself in the Garden toward evening; and the man and his wife hid from the Lord God among the trees of the Garden. The Lord God called out to the man and said to him, 'Where are you?' " (Genesis 3:8–9). In asking this, God didn't mean that He did not know where the first man and woman literally and physically were located. Of course He knew. Rather, He was seeking to open a dialogue with Adam, to give the man a chance to formulate a reply, and to repent.

God followed the same course when Cain killed his brother, Abel: "Then He said, 'What have you done? The voice of your brother's blood cries out to Me from the ground!' " (Genesis 4:10).

Again, God knew what Cain had done, but He sought to model for us a humility when confronted with the challenge of understanding the motivations that lie behind other people's mischief. If even all-knowing God took the time to inquire and investigate, this must mean that comprehending a human is a task within the reach only of the Deity and certainly beyond your reach or mine. To accept this, the difficulty of truly understanding another person and penetrating the clouds that surround him takes humility.

In this way, gossip has at its root the temptation to view yourself as God-like in your power to pierce the layers of obscurity that guard the human heart. Almost invariably, the really interesting piece of gossip doesn't report merely about facts but also about motivations and feelings. It seeks to report not just about the *what* but about the *why*. It recounts what another person did and purports to explain what that meant. Alternatively, it takes a fragment of fact and spins that fragment into a rich and complex narrative web that seeks to explain the action and the motives behind that action. However, these are things—reasons, motives, feelings—we often can't know even under the most favorable circumstances, where we've had a chance to interview the subject of our story at length.

It's for these reasons that the best rumor or gossip is almost invariably not only morally wrong but factually inaccurate. When the commentator Sforno lumped false witness together with apparently "truthful" gossip, he was right to do so, because the two are so often one and the same.

The Internet seems almost tailor-made to encourage the hubris that feeds gossip. The perspective on the world it gives may easily be confused, by the prideful, with God's perspective. One may know, seemingly, everything about everyone merely by following a few hyperlinks.

Much of that information would fall into the category of what Jewish law calls "evil speech"—which, of course, needn't be conveyed in spoken words. The feeling of being in the know, whether about celebrities and their sexual peccadilloes or about your next-door neighbor, whose fenced backyard you just scoped out on Google Earth, can be intoxicating, arousing.

Some of this purported information may be true, but nevertheless, it's not something we needed to know. Much is flat-out wrong. Either way, the Internet feeds the rest of the media and in this way shapes the ethos of journalism as a whole in the direction of a greater and greater tolerance and appetite for talebearing. Talk radio, for example, a medium I value and enjoy, is fed to an extraordinary degree by the Web—not least the Drudge Report, with its ten million hits per day, which packages Internet rumors from around the globe, including from the extraordinarily unreliable European media.

When Matt Drudge had to retract a rumor he was circulating about how Clinton presidential adviser Sidney Blumenthal abused his wife, Drudge's lawyer, in the face of a thirty-million-dollar defamation suit, insisted that his client was "reporting accurately on a rumor."

We now live in a culture where getting the content of the tale that you're bearing right—regardless of whether that content has anything to do with reality—may be regarded as a valid defense.

S*ense and sensibility.* The Sabbath is, finally, a major source and root of meaning in life for those who practice it. It's possible, of course, to take a day off on Saturday or Sunday and have it mean absolutely nothing to you other than addressing your need for rest. But the Sabbath is much more than that.

In biblical religion, meaning is conveyed in narrative. That is why the Bible takes the form of a story—beginning with the creation of the world and concluding with the expiration of prophecy after the Second Temple was built in Jerusalem. Scripture does not take the form of a code of laws, though of course it contains many laws. Instead, the norms and rules are all embedded in a story, a narrative.

The Sabbath has as one of its chief purposes to remind us of two stories: the creation of the world, and the exodus of the Jewish slaves from Egypt. While the version of the fourth commandment given in the Book of Exodus notes the link with creation, the parallel version in Deuteronomy emphasizes the link between Sabbath and exodus: "And you shall remember that you were a slave in the land of Egypt, and the Lord, your God, has taken you out from there with a strong hand and an outstretched arm; therefore the Lord, your God, has commanded you to make the Sabbath day" (5:15). In Jewish practice, at the inauguration of the Sabbath on Friday night at the family meal, a sanctification (Kiddush) is said over a cup of wine. The text of the Kiddush is worth reproducing. After an introductory reading of a scriptural passage about how God finished the work of creation and then rested on the seventh day, followed by blessing the Lord for creating the "fruit of the vine," he who recites the Kiddush on behalf of the others gathered around the table says:

> Blessed are You, the Lord, our God, King of the universe, Who
> has sanctified us with His commandments, took pleasure in us,
> and with love and favor gave us His holy Sabbath as a heritage, a
> remembrance of Creation. For that day is the prologue to the holy
> convocations, a memorial of the Exodus from Egypt. For us did
> You choose and us did You sanctify from all the nations. And
> Your holy Sabbath, with love and favor did You give us as a
> heritage. Blessed are You, Lord, Who sanctifies the Sabbath.

Both the creation and the exodus bear witness to God's mastery of nature and of history. God created nature, after which He rested on the first Sabbath, and He manipulates men and nations as He sees fit, as the miraculous liberation of the Israelites from Egyptian slavery demonstrates. When reciting Kiddush, many Jews have the custom of standing because, in a religious court governed by Jewish law, witnesses stand to give their testimony. Those who observe the Sabbath become God's witnesses, as He told the people of Israel through Isaiah's prophecy: "I, only I, am the Lord, and there is no savior aside from Me. . . . *You are my witness*—the word of the Lord—and My servant whom I have chosen, so that you will know and believe in Me, and understand that I am He; before Me nothing was created by a god nor will there be after Me!" (43:11–12, emphasis added).

At the simplest level, the relationship between neglecting the Sabbath and bearing false witness is apparent: If a person or a community fails to see the importance of testifying truthfully about God, then testifying falsely about your fellowman should be a snap. The Talmud, indeed, sees the two—breaking the fourth commandment and breaking the ninth—as basically interchangeable: "Rabbi Levi taught: God declared, 'If you dare testify false concerning your fellow, I will view it as a testimony that I did not create heaven and earth'" (Jerusalem Talmud, Berachot 1:5). One classical rabbinic understanding of the ninth commandment even goes so far as to say that the "fellow" or "friend" (depending on your translation) against whom we're commanded not to bear false witness is none other than God Himself. This is the understanding of the medieval Spanish sage Nachmanides. To deny that God is the world's creator and designer is, then, to fall afoul of the ninth commandment.

A key purpose of the Sabbath, again, is to remind us of the narrative that gives meaning to life. If we can't fit our lives into such a story line, that means no God stands behind history, or at least no God we can know about. In such a universe, any values we may attach to our lives—indeed the value of life itself—are arbitrary human inventions.

In such a universe, as conceived by the alternative human value system called secularism, there is still a need to give meaning to life. Meaninglessness creates a void that must be filled with something. That something is almost always a narrative. We must have narratives to frame our lives. In the absence of religious stories to give meaning to life, people predictably invent stories, secular stories, that they hope will serve the same purpose.

Life is full of anomalies that need to be made sense of. A religious culture may call upon a religious narrative to weave those anomalies into a somewhat coherent story. A secular culture like ours is more likely to call upon secular narratives—we call them ideologies—often demonstrably false ones, with the result that innocent people are slandered and hurt, much as Joseph was. In a secular culture, these ideologies more or less take the place of religion.

It was an ideology of racial grievance, for example, that resulted in a notorious case of false witness that began to unfold in 1987 in Poughkeepsie, New York. That year, a fifteen-year-old black girl, Tawana Brawley, made her famous accusation that a gang of white men had raped and sodomized her and smeared her body with feces. A grand jury later determined that she was lying, but this didn't stop a trio of her advisers, led by black activist Al Sharpton, from spectacularly slandering Steven Pagones, a local assistant district attorney who was Caucasian and therefore suspect as one of the alleged "rapists."

A decade later, when Pagones's $170 million defamation suit against Sharpton and his colleagues (Alton Maddox, Jr., C. Vernon Mason, and Brawley herself) came to trial, Sharpton offered the defense that, after all, he was black and blacks are oppressed, so therefore it was reasonable to assume that Pagones, a white man, would lie, while Brawley, a black girl, would tell the truth. That was Sharpton's narrative, and it produced the slander that made havoc of Steven Pagones's life.

Sharpton explained: "If you come from my world, where people get plungers stuck up their rectums in precincts"—referring to a then-current case in which white police officers brutalized a black Haitian man—"why would I not believe Tawana Brawley?"

At least Pagones escaped a prison sentence. Not so the victims of another, even more shocking instance of false witness—or rather, really more a phenomenon than a mere instance. I have in mind the men and women accused, during the witch-hunts of the 1980s and 1990s, of sexually molesting young children—accusations based on the most dubious kind of witness there is, young children. The children in question were coaxed and coached, and thereby produced extraordinarily wild charges against such people as the Amirault family, proprietors of the Fells Acres day-care facility in Malden, Massachusetts; a big slice of the adult population of Wenatchee; physician Patrick Griffin; marina owner John Carroll of Troy, New York; and North Miami policeman Grant Snowden.

In her reporting and in a 2003 book, *No Crueler Tyrannies*, Dorothy Rabinowitz showed how here again the cases of false witness were spun out of a modern political ideology, a narrative that centered upon the notion of the widespread victimization of women and children. In this ideological understanding, wrote Rabinowitz, "arguing for due process on behalf of a person charged with child sex abuse violated the politically progressive views held" by many liberals:

> In the late 1980s, as today, there was a school of advanced
> political opinion of the view that to take up for those false
> accused of sex abuse charges was to undermine the battle against
> child abuse; it was to betray children and all other victims of
> sexual predators. To succeed in reversing convictions in such
> cases was to send a discouraging message to the victims and to
> encourage the predators.
>
> Where advanced reasoning of this sort prevailed, the facts
> of the case were simply irrelevant. What mattered was the
> message—that such crimes were uniquely abhorrent and must be
> punished accordingly.

The Wenatchee defendants and the rest were victims of what biblical tradition refers to as *motzi shem ra,* or slandering. Between this and the more common and seemingly benign vice of mere gossip, or *lashon hara,* in which nuggets of interesting and also true news are passed around among friends about other friends, many of us may feel there exists a gaping Grand Canyon. Surely the two are not remotely comparable!

Am I guilty of needlessly extending the reach of the ninth commandment? In applying the full force of the ninth commandment to, let's say, ordinary scuttlebutt around the office, am I overreacting to a mild fault, a trivial indulgence? As Emrys Westacott, a philosophy professor at Alfred University, wrote in 2000 in a scholarly meditation on gossip in the *International Journal of Applied Philosophy,* "All things being equal, we should be grateful for the opportunities for pleasure that life offers us, not have a bad conscience about them. Talking to people about people is one of these. To refrain from it for fear of moral corruption is a form of moral neurosis." It is certainly a common activity. Anthropologists reckon that people around the world, in ordinary conversation, devote between one-fifth and two-thirds of the time they spend chatting to gossiping about others.

So if the scuttlebutt is true, if the party being gossiped about never finds out and suffers no harm, what's the basis for my coming down so hard on gossips?

The harm that's suffered may not be by the gossiped-about party but, instead, by us, the gossips and by those who listen to gossip. The Bible, indeed, makes listening to *lashon hara* a sin no less serious than speaking it: "Do not accept a false report, do not extend your hand with the wicked to be a venal witness" (Leviticus 23:1), which the Talmud understands as a warning against accepting as true *any* negative rumor or gossip. First of all because rumors are, if not always false, then a species of truth as damaged in transit as many a postal parcel delivered through the U.S. mail. Sometimes you can appreciate it for just this quality: gossip so naïvely, patently fictional as to be almost touching.

But second of all, gossip really is as bad as I'm making it out to be, because the reality is that it is almost always motivated by unashamed malice, or at best by the guilty pleasure of savoring someone else's discomfort. By listening, we both encourage these unworthy feelings in others and fuel them in ourselves. For men, it's even more despicable— feminine, catty, swishy, unmasculine, and unmanly.

Yet Americans, in being addicted to gossip of both the true and false varieties, are hardly different from those in other nations and cultures. And for a country with a history of venerating the Ten Commandments in a way other cultures don't, that may be the worst condemnation of all.

JEALOUS AGAIN

*You shall not covet your fellow's house. You shall not covet
your fellow's wife, his manservant, his maidservant, his ox,
his donkey, nor anything that belongs to your fellow.*
(Exodus 12:14)

Stuck in traffic on the Evergreen Point Floating Bridge that crosses Lake Washington, there's little to do but gaze out the window at the gold coast of Seattle's fanciest suburb, Medina. One can just make out Bill Gates's Pacific lodge–style mansion, valued at $135 million. This residence, belonging to Microsoft's $56 billion man and America's wealthiest individual, is one of the most expensive in the world. There is an irony here. Gates, who has no one to covet and whose philanthropic gifts amount to billions of dollars given away to fight disease and other ills, innocently creates an occasion for coveting on the grandest scale.

In a more painful irony, however, covetous sentiment is stimulated to an even greater degree by another Seattleite: Gates's own father.

The nationally influential lawyer William H. Gates, Sr., who helps direct the Gates family's charitable efforts through a $33 billion foundation, has made it a personal crusade to give moral credibility to the inheritance tax. Also known as the death tax, it is levied against a dead person's property before his heirs can inherit it. Gates's own grand-children stand to inherit his son's estate. Thus the elder Gates, extend-ing personal generosity beyond its appropriate limits, calls for the seizure of other, much lesser persons' estates when they die. Testifying before the U. S. Senate Committee on Finance in 2001, Gates insisted that "it is not in the interest of this country to have large fortunes passed from generation to generation forming ever larger pools of money and accre-tion of power." One appreciates this gentleman's sincerity, but his ad-vocacy unintentionally encourages others to regard the fruit of their fellow citizens' labor as somehow not properly belonging to them.

In American life, there is a hard core of the envious. How large a group is this? The popularity of the inheritance tax sheds light on the question. Spite, resentment of someone else's good fortune even in the context of his personal grief at the loss of a parent, is transpar-ent here. The wealth of the parent who passes on was, after all, taxed already when it was originally earned. According to a 2005 *New York Times* study, 17 percent of Americans favor the death tax. That fig-ure, it seems, represents the most die-hard element of envious Ameri-cans.

How basic coveting is to human nature, stamped into us very early in life, is something that only parents may fully appreciate. Whenever I hear our three-year-old daughter, Naomi, screeching in outrage, I can be fairly sure it is because she covets something that her brother, Ezra, age four, has in his possession and that Ezra isn't willing to give up. She only decides that she wants whatever it is—a Lego police station or a fire truck, for example—when she sees Ezra playing with it. She won't be satisfied with another but identical toy. In fact, unlike Ezra, she is not sincerely interested in law enforcement or fire-fighting equipment at all. She simply wants to take *his* police station or fire truck away from *him*.

I have before me a pile of newspaper articles all bemoaning, with a dash of irony, the sin of coveting as it's practiced in various localities across the country. For example, if you believe the *Los Angeles Times*, in that city people covet one another's high-end entertainment equipment: "The Screen-Eyed Monster: Coveting thy neighbor's oversized television? You're not alone" (July 14, 2002). We learn that "experts call screen envy a genuine social phenomenon that is on the rise from New Jersey to the far side of the Pacific." Feel the pathos:

> "I had a 25-inch TV for a while, and then my buddy got a 32-inch TV, and that was it. It's been a competition from there," says Mike Surbrug, a stockbroker in Roselle Park, N.J. "Right after that, my TV broke, and I got a 35-inch. . . . I thought, 'I have the biggest TV.' " Until another buddy bought a 36-inch weeks later. Overnight, Surbrug's inadequate diagonal count became the butt of jokes. Then, within another few weeks, Surbrug's roommate trumped everybody by getting a $3,000, 57-inch behemoth.

In suburban New York, it is kitchen envy that's giving grief. This is according to the *New York Times* ("My Sub-Zero Is Bigger Than Your Sub-Zero," March 20, 2005), which recounts the sorrows of Eve Marx, a writer who lives in Katonah, New York:

> "I go to other people's houses and come home and gnash my teeth," Ms. Marx said. "I remember one kitchen that had three sinks and each one had a different function, one was for vegetables, one was for dishes, one was for pots and pans. I thought it was some kind of new kosher thing."

In such cases, the assumption is that coveting or envy involves seeing something that your friend has that you don't, wanting it, and going out and buying it, if you can afford to do so. Is there really anything sinful about this?

Before seeking an answer, we need to know that in reality, coveting, jealousy, and envy are all different things and that the Ten Commandments has something specific in mind by the Hebrew word it uses in the tenth commandment, "You shall not covet . . ."—the noun form of which is *chemdah* ("covetous desire"). Curiously, in the Book of Deuteronomy, when Moses recounts for a second time the narrative of the giving of the Decalogue, he repeats the tenth commandment with a twist. Instead of merely forbidding us to "covet," Deuteronomy's version adds another verb, *desire*: "And you shall not covet your fellow's wife, you shall not *desire* your fellow's house, his field," and so on (5:18). The Hebrew noun form there is *taivah*, which might also be translated as "lust," though not necessarily in a sexual sense—unless you sexually desire real estate ("your fellow's house"). In English, these words seem like mere "elegant variation": A clumsy writer wants to spice up his prose by using synonyms that add no additional meaning. As I remember learning in high school, that's bad writing. In biblical Hebrew, far more care is paid to the gradations of meaning in different words.

Clearly, we're going to need a more precise definition of the words *covetous desire* than we'll get from our preconceived notions or from a foggy understanding of ambiguous English words.

Since you have got this far in my book, you won't be surprised to learn that I believe biblical tradition, taught by the rabbis since antiquity, has concrete, objective, and scripturally based definitions for all these words corresponding to variations on the idea of covetousness. Without this tradition, it is hard to discern what exactly the tenth commandment intends to warn us against.

From the Bible's text, it certainly seems that "to covet" means something more sinister than to see a luxury car advertised in a slick magazine and then to feel a surging desire to purchase such an automobile yourself. That would be for amateurs. Real coveting involves at the very least a desire to take such a car, or whatever the object happens to be, *away from someone else*—and not by stealing, which would be covered by a separate commandment, the seventh.

Thus when the Torah promises the Jews security when they leave their homes to go on pilgrimage to Jerusalem at the time of the yearly Jewish festivals, it says, "No man will covet your land when you go up to appear before the Lord, your God" (Exodus 34:24). When Moses commands the people not to acquire the paraphernalia of Canaanite idolatry, he says, "The carved images of their gods you shall burn in the fire; you shall not covet and take for yourself the silver and gold that is on them, lest you be ensnared by it, for it is an abomination of the Lord, your God" (Deuteronomy 7:25). In both of these verses, there is something more than just wanting what doesn't yet belong to you involved. Otherwise, what would be the great kindness in God's promising that no one will merely hanker after the unoccupied Jewish homes, if the hankering isn't likely to amount to anything more than that? Wishing to seize belongings from another is definitely part of the deal. Acting upon the wish evidently is, too.

Technically, biblical tradition therefore defines coveting (*chemdah*) as scheming to obtain your neighbor's goods, not by force (which would be outright theft) but by applying some form of pressure that remains, from a superficial perspective, within the bounds of the law. In other words, if I seduce my neighbor's wife *not* by asking her to engage in an adulterous affair with me but, rather, by asking her to leave her husband, divorce him according to all required legal procedures, and then marry me—that is coveting.

It sounds like a somewhat unusual offense, and not as serious in its social ramifications as we've come to expect from the Decalogue—that is, until you contemplate the other key word in the phrasing of the tenth commandment as it appears in Deuteronomy: "And you shall not covet your fellow's wife, you shall not *desire* your fellow's house, his field," etc. As tradition clarifies, to "desire" in this context is the emotion that precedes my carrying out the sort of covetous scheme outlined in the previous paragraph. It is a special sort of "desire," one that isn't content with acquiring a good or possession like yours. When gripped by such desire, I want what you have in particular. Indeed, I would not be satisfied with even the most perfect replica of your wife, your house, your stuff. What really excites me, fills me with malicious joy, is not so much the acquiring for myself but the *taking away from you*. And this is a different matter, far from rare, and very serious in its malignity.

W e are all familiar with the destruction and fear this emotion may call forth, not least in other parts of the world. When we observe terrorists issuing from the global Islamic community, threatening to burn down our cities, and it's obvious that what motivates them in large part is envy of the success and comfort of Western lives as compared to the futility and misery of so much of existence in the Arabic cultures, then we know that coveting is at work.

It's said that terror is violence employed without a constructive political goal—as distinct from conventional warfare, which, whether just or not, generally has a concrete purpose. Rather, so goes this line of analysis, terror's only goal is *terror*. But the tenth commandment suggests otherwise. Much of regular warfare over the ages has been directed at stealing other people's land so that the aggressor state can enjoy it instead. The desire called *taivah* would be more interested in *destroying* that other nation's land or cities so that *no one* can enjoy them. Terrorism has a goal other than terror: it is to satisfy *taivah*.

In our own culture, a temptation to commit terrorism isn't the issue—although nonterrorists, too, may find satisfaction, and release from envy, in the spectacle of mass murder. The novelist Kathryn Chetkovich wrote an affecting and brutally frank autobiographical piece, entitled "Envy," in a 2003 issue of the literary journal *Granta*. It recounted a relationship she had with a man who was a more successful writer than she is. The relationship was sagging under the weight of her jealousy of him. Then a week after a novel he had written was published to general acclaim, the events of September 11 happened. As the calamitous news diverted attention from all else—including, not incidentally for Chetkovich, her boyfriend's brilliant new novel—she felt an unseemly pleasure: "Because for one day, at least, for the first time in what felt like months, he and his work had been eclipsed—and I was relieved." She then admitted, "That was the place envy had delivered me to." Obscenely, the death of thousands of people, because it assuaged her ego, seemed almost—well, worth it.

The envious striving of writers aside, we Americans have our own addiction to the destructive urge to take from others so they can't have what they currently enjoy. Some call it "class warfare," and it is invoked every election year in the hope that a majority of the electorate will be so electrified by the prospect that it will vote the class warriors into the highest office. Evidently, campaign pollsters have found the hope to be realistic, because every election cycle has its call to make jihad on the "haves" on behalf of the "have nots." Usually the class-war party loses, which would suggest that less than half of American voters feel energized by the theme.

There was, for example, A1 Gore in 2000, when he declared himself to be the presidential candidate "for the people, not the powerful." Gore emphasized that George W. Bush "favor[ed] the rich," that reprehensible "wealthiest 1 percent of taxpayers." In 2004, Democratic vice presidential candidate John Edwards said of Bush, "By the time he's done, the only people who pay taxes in America will be the millions of middle class and poor Americans who do all the work." As matter of fact, at the time Americans in the lower 50 percent of the income range paid about 4 percent of all income taxes collected. But the facts didn't bother John Edwards, who invoked the notion of the "two Americas":

> One America that does the work, another America that reaps the
> reward. One America that pays the taxes, another America that
> gets the tax breaks. One America that will do anything to leave
> its children a better life, another America that never has to do a
> thing because its children are already set for life. One America—
> middle-class America—whose needs Washington has long
> forgotten, another America—narrow-interest America—whose
> every wish is Washington's command. One America that is

struggling to get by, another America that can buy anything it wants, even a Congress and a president.

While Gore assailed the "wealthiest 1 percent of taxpayers," Edwards and his presidential running mate, John Kerry, laid siege to the top 2 percent, meaning anyone making more than $200,000 a year—hardly the wealthy. It didn't matter that Kerry and Edwards possessed personal wealth in the range, respectively, of a billion and dozens of millions of dollars. The point, in fact, was to ride the tenth commandment—or rather, the voiding of that commandment—to the White House.

In 2004, the Kerry-Edwards team appealed to the envious. The strategy wasn't impaired, either, by the fact that a portion of the electorate was consumed with hate for George W. Bush. Because it was so personal in nature, the hate cannot have arisen only from political disagreement; it was driven by something else, too, something deeper. That something was resentment at the bond between Bush and his father, former President George H. W. Bush. Try probing, as I have, a genuine Bush hater about why he *hates*, instead of merely opposes, Bush. Eventually, after some time conversing and patiently questioning, a particular sentiment almost always comes out. There is a perception that the younger Bush benefited from nepotism, that he was "handed" the presidency, was "given" it, that he "inherited" it. We see how deeply entwined resentment of others' good fortune is with resentment of the privileges entailed by the parent-child bond. Which is interesting.

For I think you will find that, in striking at the parent-child bond, the resentment of inheritance is important for understanding the tenth commandment in an additional respect. It recalls the relationship between the tenth commandment and the commandment directly opposite it on the first tablet of the Decalogue, which is the fifth: "Honor your father and mother." Why a culture that fails to respect parents is also a culture likely to be prone to coveting is the question that will occupy us for the rest of this chapter.

The Bible's most extensive treatment of envy is the story of Naboth's vineyard in 1 Kings, chapter 21. The story takes place during the reign of the wicked king Ahab, whose antagonist was the prophet Elijah. Next door to Ahab's palace, a man named Naboth had a vineyard, on which Ahab set his covetous eyes. Said Ahab, "Give me your vineyard, so that I may have it as an herb garden, for it is close by my house; in its place I will give you a better vineyard, or, if you prefer, I will give you its price in money." While Ahab didn't say so directly, it's evident from the writings of the other prophets active in this general time period (see Isaiah 1:29, 66:17) that his garden was intended for something more sinister than growing dill and parsley. Ahab planned to set up an idol in the garden and worship it there, as was the custom among Jews then with a secret fetish for strange, foreign worship.

This explains the sharpness of Naboth's reply. It wasn't just an herb garden at stake but, in Naboth's opinion, also the inheritance he had received from his father: "Far be it from me before the Lord that I should give you my ancestors' heritage!" For it was not merely his heritage of real estate but his moral heritage that he would be relinquishing if he sold to Ahab and thus indirectly participated in an idolatrous scheme.

After this, Ahab sulked gloomily. Again, it wasn't his being denied the herb garden that angered him so much as it was Naboth's rebuke, wherein he refused to "give you my ancestors' heritage." By which, as the rabbinic commentator Malbim (1809–1879) explained, Naboth meant to imply, "To me, the inheritance of my forefather is dear. Not so to you, who have abandoned the inheritance of your forefathers, the Torah and worship of God, to worship Baal and other pagan deities."

Ahab fumed, refusing to get out of bed or even to eat, until his wife, Jezebel, even a nastier piece of work than he, suggested a plot of revenge involving a false accusation that Naboth had cursed the king and blasphemed God. After the innocent Naboth had been executed,

Jezebel celebrated, telling her husband, "Arise and inherit the vineyard of Naboth the Jezreelite, which he had refused to give you for money; for Naboth is not alive, for he is dead." Note the linking of *inheritance* with the results of Ahab's coveting.

It was for this deed that God subsequently instructed Elijah to rebuke Ahab in gruesome terms: "In the place where the dogs licked up the blood of Naboth, the dogs will lick up your blood as well . . . Behold! I am bringing evil upon you, and I shall annihilate after you, and I shall eliminate [every] male offspring from Ahab and all property, whether hidden or public, in Israel." Whereas Ahab's sin of coveting involved pressuring Naboth to despise his own inheritance, Ahab's punishment, which fit the crime admirably, involved annihilating any inheritance Ahab hoped to pass on to his successors. For he would have no surviving offspring to inherit from him.

The causal link between the fifth and tenth commandments is thus clearly alluded to. Ahab despised his moral inheritance, so he coveted Naboth's inheritance of real estate.

To really understand what drives the covetous inclination, however, we need to be more specific about the nature of the relationship between it and the failure to honor parents. How exactly does the latter lead to the former? I can suggest three possible answers, three truths about parents and children that, if a culture fails to grasp them, create fertile ground for the seeds of covetous desire. They are:

We don't choose our parents or our life circumstances. God does.

Parents, and everyone else close to us, deserve our care and honor more than do exotic peoples and other strangers.

Nepotism inoculates against envy.

W*e don't choose our parents or our life circumstances. God does.* The first and simplest observation about parents is that we never get a chance to choose them for ourselves. They are assigned to us by fate, by Providence, by what in traditional Jewish terms is called *mazal*—as in the exclamation, known to Jews and others, "*Mazal tov!*"—literally "Good *mazal!*" Though it's often used as if it means "Congratulations!"—a cheerful way of recognizing that your friend has been dealt a desirable hand by Providence, which is to say, by God. Just as parents are assigned by *mazal*, so, too, are most of the circumstances of our lives. "Everything is in the hands of Heaven except the fear of Heaven," as the Talmud puts it (Berachot 33a). Another rabbinic book, the Mishnah, asks, "Who is wealthy? He who is satisfied with his lot" (Avot 4:1). If Americans thought more in terms of *mazal*, there would be a lot less envy.

One of the first ways we question the happiness of our lot is by doubting we have gotten the parents we deserve. This occurs in childhood—in my case, at age eight, when I thought the best mother in the world to have would be my Cub Scout den mother, Mrs. Komodoi. Nothing my own mom did could measure up to Mrs. Komodoi, or so I thought at the time. The failure to appreciate parents is typically the original mold in which our capacity to envy is formed.

There is also a flip side to the concept of *mazal* that illuminates another avenue by which abandoning the fifth commandment results in abandoning the tenth. It has to do with failing to appreciate parents not as your lot, but, rather, as your responsibility. The second truth secular cultures forget is:

Parents, and everyone else close to us, deserve our care and honor more than do exotic peoples and other strangers. What's this got to do with coveting? Complementary to *mazal* is a notion found in the Bible, as it is in cultures around the world: the evil eye, or *ayin ha'ra*. The evil eye is a spiritual force fed by envy and dissatisfaction with your lot in life. "One overeager for wealth has an *evil eye*; he does not know that want may befall him" (Proverbs 28:22). It is certainly unhealthy to the envious person to be possessed by the evil eye: "The evil eye, the evil inclination, and hatred of other people take a man out of the world" (Avot 2:11)—that is, they shorten his life in this world and, after death, deprive him of a reward in the next. Or again, "Jealousy, covetous desire [*taivah*], and [seeking] honor take a man out of the world" (Avot 4:21)—a sentiment echoed, by the way, in Buddhism, with its doctrine tracing all personal suffering to *tanha* (desire), a more or less straightforward translation of *taivah*.

Just as the evil eye is deadly to the envious person who experiences it, it is held by tradition—not only in biblical religion but in cultures everywhere—to be dangerous to the person who arouses the envy, who is its object. In the Bible, this is illustrated in the story of Sarah, the patriarch Abraham's wife, and Hagar, his concubine.

As the book of Genesis tells it, Abraham and Sarah had been married for some years but were having difficulty conceiving a child. So Sarah suggested that her husband take a concubine and have a child with her, a child that would be credited to Sarah, as if Sarah had given birth to it herself, in line with ancient Near Eastern custom. When Hagar conceived a child by Abraham, however, the concubine became haughty toward her mistress, taunted her, while Sarah grew increasingly resentful, and jealous. According to tradition, Sarah cast an evil eye on Hagar, who consequently miscarried. So the Bible implicitly suggests when it records Hagar as conceiving once (Genesis 16:4), with no birth resulting from this, and then conceiving again (16:11). From the latter pregnancy, which succeeded in coming to term, there was born Abraham's son, Ishmael.

From the idea of the evil eye, there long ago developed, quite naturally and almost universally, a fear of envy, an archaic terror of this evil eye. Those on whom fortune, or God or *mazal*, has smiled are wary of displaying their blessings too openly, for fear of arousing envy. This is no less true in primitive cultures than it is, with some modifications relative to time and place, of our own culture. This explains some taboos that we so take for granted that we may never even wonder where they come from—for example, the taboo about revealing your salary.

In a fascinating study, *Envy: A Theory of Social Behavior* (1966), the psychologist and philosopher Helmut Schoeck traced to its origins in the fear of envy the phenomenon that we call "liberal guilt" or "limousine liberalism." This guilt, he observes, is directly related to personal privilege. The more privileged you are, the more you have to fear from envy and thus the greater interest you have in appeasing the envious. Do you really care about the underprivileged? Not really, but you do care about your luxurious life and the danger that it could be taken from you by arousing the evil eye. What's the solution? To give up your privilege? Of course not. But how about buying off those who might cast their envious eyes on your lucky lot?

When a culture is overly intimidated by envy, by the evil eye, it seeks to protect itself by capitulating to the perceived desires of the envious. This is understandable but lamentable. Of course the capitulation only stokes the fire of covetousness.

Thousands of years ago, the Bible cautioned against the temptation to suck up to the underprivileged, to glorify them—which, unlike actually helping the poor, comes cheap, while also carrying with it the thrilling buzz of moral superiority: "Do not glorify a destitute person in his grievance" (Exodus 23:3); "You shall not commit a perversion of justice; you shall not favor the poor and you shall not honor the great; with righteousness shall you judge your fellow" (Leviticus 19:5).

Yet of this warning, guilt-inspired liberalism knows nothing. On the contrary, it has generated one of the more widespread, and sillier, myths of our time.

That myth holds that whatever is most exotic should automatically be held most highly in our esteem. Americans live in an affluent society. Glorifying the destitute must, then, mean flattering them to the extent they are distant from us according to any measure by which societies are evaluated—that is, in culture, lifestyle, geography. This shows up as the attitude that denigrates anything American in favor of anything foreign. It sees modern Europe, never our own country, as the grand arbiter of political morality. It sees Native Americans anachronistically as always embodying ideals of civilization, ecofriendliness, and gentle wisdom, while it dismisses America's European heritage as pure savagery and racism. It sees the homeless not as bums but as so many wandering philosophers and saints in disguise.

Which brings us back to our relationship to parents.

In contrast to this patronizing attitude toward the exotic, there is an older view, one that gives greatest honor to whatever is closest to us. Biblical tradition, for example, brings this out in the way it creates a hierarchy for charitable giving. First, one supports one's own family members, with parents first on the list; then needy individuals in one's own city; then the needy in a neighboring city; then, and only then, the needy in other countries. For those who want to see how the hierarchy is expressed in detail, the great medieval rabbinic sage Maimonides offered a crisp summary in his Mishneh Torah, based on a verse in Deuteronomy (15:11). It is in the section devoted to "Laws of Gifts to the Poor" (7:13), and it begins this way: "A poor person who is your relative comes before every other person."

The problem of envy, in other words, sets up a tension between two opposing worldviews. One seeks to appease the envious by glorifying the exotic. The other recognizes the role of a divine order to things (mazal), encourages satisfaction with one's lot, and is content to risk the resentment of envious strangers in order to attend first of all to the needs of the least exotic of all other people—namely, those to whom one is most closely related, especially family members.

The practical application of the fifth commandment involves very humble tasks performed for our parents' benefit, tasks especially relevant when parents are elderly: feeding, clothing, and cleaning them. To honor parents means, above all else, to care for their needs when they are at their most vulnerable. The Ten Commandments makes this a priority distinctly more urgent than caring for the needs of strangers. To honor somebody else's father and mother is not a commandment in the Decalogue.

Helmut Schoeck is simply putting this in clinical terms when he writes:

The stereotyped *love for those who are distant*, today a favorite practice, may in some cases be a failure to love one's neighbor, as a certain amount of personal testimony goes to show. A number of leading figures have, on occasion, explained their abstract social idealism and their struggle for social justice and radical reform movements as a result of their inability to establish uncomplicated, natural and relaxed contact with their neighbor. This poverty or lack of contact—a legitimate problem in psychotherapy—probably leads to "distant" and generalized human love in many intellectuals.

A culture that makes the choice to deemphasize honoring parents (fifth commandment) is more likely to seek to appease envy by honoring exotics (tenth commandment). By contrast, a culture that honors parents has inoculated itself against the temptation to appease and thereby encourage envy. The degree of idealizing the exotic that one sees all around today is evidence of the choice we have made.

The third way the parent-child bond, if it's strong, impedes the spread of envy may seem paradoxical. Whereas the second way relates to what we can do for parents, this one emphasizes what they do for us. It centers on inheritance, and the failure to appreciate the legitimacy of it. A secular culture like ours tends to forget the following truth:

Nepotism inoculates against envy. Go back to the example of George W. Bush. He is hated in no small part because of a perception that he inherited his office. The fact that this bothers many people is explainable as a function of the present popular belief in meritocracy, the notion that we should enjoy only those privileges that we have personally striven for and earned. Meritocracy in its most extreme form can tolerate no inheritance at all. They are, in a sense, opposites.

Let's consider inheritance in its purest expression, where every single privilege is inherited from parents or otherwise determined by family membership. A biblical society, we should know, would be one based on a *limited* system of nepotism. As Maimonides wrote in his law code, the Mishneh Torah (Hilchot Melachim 1:7—based on Deuteronomy 17:20), not only the king but all appointed officials in Israel could receive their respective positions from their fathers, who held these positions previously—providing that the sons were of a good moral character. In a society governed *entirely* by inheritance, if the society's culture also includes a belief in divine Providence, seemingly there can be no envy.

That is because your parents are simply conduits for God's bestowing blessings, whether deserved or undeserved, according to His own frequently inscrutable wisdom. The members of a society like this—a society that exists only as a hypothesis, a theory, not as a reality—would see their circumstances in life, however desirable or undesirable, as just and appropriate, designed for their benefit, if not for their comfort. This happens to be the way biblical tradition wants us to see our place in the world: "Everything is in the hands of Heaven except the fear of Heaven."

In a purely meritocratic society, on the other hand, every benefit or comfort is allotted by our having fought for it. Nothing is designated for us by divine Providence. You might think that this, too, is a sure antidote against envy. After all, can't we all simply accept the results of a fair competition, whether those results are favorable to us or not? But it doesn't work that way, because even when the competition truly is unfettered by nepotism or favoritism, the outcome will never be "fair" in everyone's eyes. Few people who don't rise to the top will be able to look on themselves and on their failure to do so and say, "Well, I guess the better person won—and it wasn't me!"

An example from contemporary life will illustrate this. In a smart little book called *Envy*, part of a series on the Seven Deadly Sins, the essayist Joseph Epstein reflects on the class of individuals in our own culture that is more prone to jealous resentment than any other—namely, professors. Writes Epstein:

How little it takes to make one academic sick with envy over
the pathetically small advantages won by another: the better
office, the slightly lighter teaching load, the fickle admiration of
students. For years in universities, if a scholar wrote well and
commanded a wider than merely scholarly audience because of
the accessibility of his prose, he was put down as a "popularizer."
Pure envy talking, of course.

Epstein is right. I have never heard a group of people more prone to
cut down colleagues in the nastiest-possible terms—behind their backs,
usually, but not always—than men and women involved in professional
scholarship. Not only that, but what class of people is more likely than
any other to express utter contempt for fellow citizens outside their profession, especially if those fellow citizens have achieved a bit of success
in business, the loathsome, dreaded "middle class"? Again, professors.

How come? Epstein speculates that the problem for professional
scholars is that they were probably the smartest in their respective
classes when they were growing up. Yet the material rewards bestowed
on their profession, the results of their meritocratic striving, tend to be
paltry by comparison with the rewards for striving in other, less intellectually exalted fields. Feel the pathos:

One's students refuse to demonstrate a passion for the life of
the mind worthy of one's own. The leisure that teaching allows
is as advertised, but the pay really isn't quite adequate; certainly
it doesn't allow one to live up to one's own high state of
cultivation. . . .
    And so envy mixes with snobbery, with impotence added, all
mounted against a background of cosmic injustice, to put a large
class of persons into a permanent condition of *ressentiment*.

To repeat: A divine plan acting through the agency of inheritance
is the social organizing principle least likely to produce envy or covet-

ing, while meritocracy is the most likely. The medieval Bible commentator Ibn Ezra expressed this idea in a parable. He gave the example of
a rustic peasant who lays eyes on a king's beautiful daughter. If the peasant is of "sound opinion," he wouldn't dream of coveting her for himself. That's because he knows that his inherited position in society—his
relationship to his parents, who are peasants, just like he is—as well as
the princess's relation to her own father, the king, makes winning the
princess simply impossible. In fact, he would no more aspire to bring
the princess to his bed than he would desire to grow wings and fly like
a bird. Without the aspiration to acquire her, there will be no coveting.

Similarly, said Ibn Ezra, any wise person knows that his lot in life is
won not through striving but through "*mazal*," the working out of the
divine plan:

> And once a person understands that the Lord has forbidden his
> neighbor's wife to him, even more so than the king's daughter is
> off limits to the rustic peasant, he will rejoice accordingly with his
> portion and not set his heart to coveting and desiring anything
> that does not pertain to him. For he knows that the Lord does
> not wish to give it to him and he cannot take it through force or
> cleverness or schemes. Thus he will trust in his Creator to provide
> for him and will do what is good in [God's] eyes.

In this view, coveting represents a failure to grasp how rewards in
life are allocated. In the end, they come to us ultimately not from striving but from *mazal*, of which inheritance is an example.

I have concentrated up till now on the relationship between the commandments on the first tablet of the Ten Commandments with
those on the second tablet. I hope it is apparent that the Decalogue, by
the mere fact of its being arranged on two tablets rather than just one,
means to tell us something simple but crucially important. That is: How

a culture thinks about God will go a long way toward determining how it thinks about other people—whether it encourages respect for others, for their belongings and for their lives, or not. The process of societal secularization is thus necessarily a process of interpersonal degradation. Moses knew that more than three thousand years ago. Americans are forgetting it today, to our own peril.

If you doubt that we are forgetting it, if you think our performance of some or all of the Ten Commandments is better than I have portrayed it, then the tenth commandment stands ready to refute you. For the arrangement of the Decalogue is significant in another way, as well. The tenth commandment is not only opposite the fifth; it functions as the culmination of the previous nine, and as an introduction to all in the Bible that follows it.

A nineteenth-century German commentator on the Torah's text, Rabbi Samson Raphael Hirsch, noted the way the commandments progress from the simple affirmation of God's existence (the first commandment, "I am the Lord your God . . ."), a commitment that a person makes in his heart and mind, to a succession of practical, outwardly observable applications of this affirmation (the second through ninth commandments). By contrast with these middle eight commandments, the tenth commandment's forbidding of covetous desire (*taivah*) is, like the first commandment, once again a matter purely of the mind. Hirsch sensitively pointed out that the Bible is not satisfied with intellectual assent to God's rule, nor with the "control of deeds and words"; rather, it demands "control of spirit and feeling," as exemplified by the commandment not to covet.

There is something like a moral-spiritual feedback loop going on here. Without the first commandment, a culture's observance of the second through ninth commandments is in doubt. That's because the premise of the Bible, with its system of commandments, is that God commands us on the basis of His standing as the transcendent basis of existence. On what basis other than God should a person, if he can get away with doing wrong, feel obliged to choose what's right? Philosophers have tussled with this question for thousands of years, but they have never supplied a satisfactory alternative to morality expressed as divine revelation.

But without the tenth commandment, any supposed commitment we may make to the preceding nine commandments is hollow. That is because the commandment against coveting is really a test of how much reality we invest in the commandments that come before it. Ibn Ezra communicated this idea, too, with his story of the peasant and the princess. If the peasant doesn't covet the princess, that is because he sees the social distance between himself and her as an objective reality. He knows he is not assenting merely to a projection of some other person's preferences for him. To labor to seduce the king's daughter would, for a peasant, be to deny reality.

When we articulate with our mouths that God stands behind the first nine commandments, do we really believe this? If, having said so, we still covet in our hearts what does not pertain to us, then we are like a peasant who pines for a princess, the fellow who doesn't believe there is a reality behind his role as a peasant or hers as a princess, who in the deepest part of his mind thinks the whole social relationship between peasant and princess is an illusion, a projection.

Do we as a culture embrace the first nine commandments as an objective reality, or as a subjective construct, a useful fiction? To the extent the tenth commandment lies derelict, and we have seen that in large part it does, then the rest of the Decalogue seems liable to crumble when tested, if it has not crumbled already.

THE WAYWARD CITY

HERE THE HELL ARE YOU? WHAT THE HELL IS GOING ON?" A lunatic homeless person is screaming into the afternoon gloominess outside the Everett, Washington, police station as I drive past.

A similar question is on my mind. With heavy, low clouds dripping in the sky and smudging my windshield, I'm trying to locate an honorable survivor of the recent wave of anti–Ten Commandments iconoclasm that swept the country and resulted in the removal of dozens upon dozens of public representations of the Decalogue. Like a demented parody of the iconoclastic crazes that periodically swept Christian Europe from the eighth century to the sixteenth, resulting in countless artistic depictions of human figures being hacked apart because it was felt they violated the second commandment, America's drive to be rid of all reminders of the Decalogue overlooked or failed to get rid of some examples of the offending art form. One of these is the six-foot granite monument donated by the Fraternal Order of Eagles that has stood outside Everett's city hall (lately converted to the police station) since 1959. A twenty-year-old agnostic, backed by lawyers from Americans United for Separation of Church and State, sued to have it removed, costing the city $130,000 in legal expenses. In 2005, the case was turned aside by a U.S. district judge here in Seattle, of all places, thirty miles south.

Of course the agnostic and the lawyers promptly vowed to appeal the decision, on the grounds that it's not covered by the pair of ambiguous Supreme Court rulings of that year that allowed some but not all depictions of the Ten Commandments on public property.

The Everett monument is said to be directly outside the police station, but I miss it entirely because it is partially concealed by shrubbery, as if hiding from the iconoclasts. Driving back on Wetmore Avenue the way I came, then getting out of the car, I finally manage to locate the elusive survivor. It is impressive but forlorn, bearing a brief version of the King James text, surmounted by an American eagle with a flag in its talons and an all-seeing eye in a triangle like that on the back of a dollar bill.

Though the Everett police station does a good job of maintaining a monument just a few feet away (dedicated to local residents who died fighting in recent wars), the Ten Commandments are being overtaken by foliage. They are still standing, but a lot harder to discern than in 1959.

So it goes, in the Seattle area as in America. The Decalogue has fallen on hard times.

Secularists argue that the sort of morality that everyone agrees is necessary for the maintenance of an orderly society—the morality embodied in the laws of relationships between people, crystallized in the commandments on the second tablet—can easily be detached from beliefs about supernatural beings, beliefs embodied in the commandments of the first tablet. The Decalogue itself argues to the contrary, insisting on the need for a religious belief in maintaining a moral culture.

It poses a radical challenge to our secular culture, arguing, as Deuteronomy does elsewhere, that we must "Beware for yourselves, lest your heart be seduced and you will turn astray and you will serve other gods and prostrate yourselves to them" (11:16). One who turns astray from God's authority has, by definition, turned to idolatry, with all the cultural depravity that must, in the end, inevitably entail.

The Bible takes this seriously. It even has a special category for a city that turns, with a majority of its citizens, toward the worship of alien sources of moral authority. It is called the "wayward city": "If, in one of your cities that the Lord, your God, gives you in which to dwell, you hear, saying 'Lawless men have emerged from your midst, and they have caused the dwellers of their city to go astray, saying, 'Let us go and worship the gods of others, that you have not known'—you shall seek out and investigate, and inquire well, and behold! It is true, the word is correct, this abomination was committed in your midst. You shall surely smite the inhabitants of that city with the edge of the sword; lay it waste and everything that is in it, and its animals, with the edge of the sword" (Deuteronomy 13:13–16). As I pointed out in chapter 7, "gods" here is really a mistranslation. That expression in Hebrew refers more generally to other sources of *marut*, or authority. The wayward city is to be left a ruin forever, as a warning to others.

It sounds cruel, but the law, we know, was never carried out in practice. Not because God didn't mean it. One provision was that before it could be executed, the court would send two delegates, religious teachers, to beg and warn the residents of the city to change their ways. However, the significance of the law of the wayward city is moral, rather than juridical. The purpose, I think, is to inform us that a culture can reach a point of no return, past which the turn to false and alien sources of moral authority can no longer be halted or reversed. According to the details of the law, the point is reached if more than half the residents of the city have, in this manner, turned astray.

In the introduction, I said that the church-affiliation rate in the region where I live, the Pacific Northwest, has sunk to about 30 percent.

Perhaps that would make Seattle a "wayward city" by the biblical definition of the concept. According to the respected Glenmary Research Center (2000), from whose data the preceding figure is drawn, the percentage of Christian church adherents in the country as a whole has now slipped below half, to 47.4 percent. If you add the percent who claim to be Jews (a claim of dubious significance), that's another 2.2 percent, for a total 49.6 percent—in other words, just under half of Americans—who would claim a formal affiliation with a religious body that affirms the validity of the Ten Commandments as a source of moral authority. We are, or are fast on our way to becoming, a wayward nation. Have we reached the point of no return? It is in the forlorn hope that we have not that I have written this book.

ACKNOWLEDGMENTS

In writing this book, as always, I have relied continuously on the assistance, support, thoughts, criticisms, and general encouragement of friends, colleagues, and family members.

Adam Bellow, my editor, stands out as an intellectual guide and benefactor who has seen value in my thoughts ever since we first met, when I was an assistant editor at *National Review*, barely out of college. I hope I can live up to his confidence in me. A few years later, I met Milly Marmur, my literary agent, who has never wavered in seeking my best interests.

This book was written under the sponsorship of the Discovery Institute's program in Religion, Liberty and Public Life. My colleagues at Discovery have provided warm friendship, reading earlier drafts of this book, feeling free to argue with me on many points. Their courage in fighting for causes that aren't popular in academia or parts of the media has inspired me to write frankly about the issues that matter to me. Of course my views are not necessarily theirs, and any errors should be attributed to me alone. We share the eighth floor of a building in Seattle. My colleagues may not feel about Third and Pike as I do.

Thank you to my family's amazing community of loving and ceaselessly giving friends on Mercer Island and at Congregation Shevet Achim, friends who might as well be family members, including but certainly not limited to Diane and Michael Medved, Susan and Rabbi Daniel Lapin, Devorah and Rabbi Yechezkel Kornfeld, Tami and Marty

Rabin, Shelly and Michael Brown, Robin and Yoel Lessing, and Michele and Paul Isherwood.

I'm grateful for the encouragement of editors who have published articles of mine that turned out to be early renditions of ideas I later incorporated here: J. J. Goldberg and Oren Rawls at the *Forward*, Kathryn Lopez at *National Review*, Susan Brenneman at the *Los Angeles Times*, Zelda Shluker at *Hadassah*, Alice Chasan and her colleagues at *Beliefnet*, Rebecca Frankel and Jennie Rothenberg at *Moment*, and Rob Eshman at the *Los Angeles Jewish Journal*. Thank you to Daniel Feder and Rudy Faust at Doubleday; and to Rabbi Nosson Scherman, creator of Artscroll, whose books have been such an immeasurable help to Jews like me.

I started work on this book just as the new Seattle Central Library opened its beautiful new facility, where I've been fortunate to find refuge in the Eulalie and Carlo Scandiuzzi Writers' Room. During this time, I not only did my own research but benefited from the teaching of those much wiser and better than I am—notably, Rabbi David Lapin. His recorded lectures on the Ten Commandments (available at his Web site, www.iawaken.org) set a standard of lucidity, brilliance, and insight.

My wife, Nika, and I are blessed with wonderful, generous, and loving parents: Arlene and Paul Kaye, Nina Erastov, and Harriet Waring.

Finally and above all, thank God for my endlessly patient, forgiving, and loving wife, Nika, whom I don't deserve. I love you.

Seattle, Washington
January 3, 2007

INDEX

ABOUT THE AUTHOR

David Klinghoffer is a senior fellow at the Discovery Institute in Seattle, a columnist for the *Forward*, and the author of *Why the Jews Rejected Jesus: The Turning Point in Western History* (2005), *The Discovery of God: Abraham and the Birth of Monotheism* (2003), and the spiritual memoir *The Lord Will Gather Me In* (1998), which was a National Jewish Book Award finalist. His articles and reviews have appeared in the *New York Times, Washington Post, Wall Street Journal, Los Angeles Times, Seattle Times,* and other publications. A former literary editor of *National Review* magazine, he is the 2006 First Place winner of the Rockower Award for journalism excellence. He lives on Mercer Island, Washington, with his wife and children.